MEN WHO DARED
THE SEA

Books about the sea
by Gardner Soule

THE OCEAN ADVENTURE
SEA RESCUE
UNDERSEA FRONTIERS
UNDER THE SEA
WIDE OCEAN
THE GREATEST DEPTHS
NEW DISCOVERIES IN OCEANOGRAPHY
REMARKABLE CREATURES OF THE SEA

MEN
WHO DARED
THE SEA

The Ocean Adventures
of the Ancient Mariners

Gardner Soule

THOMAS Y. CROWELL COMPANY
Established 1834   New York

For Cynthia Smith Vartan and her family

Designed by Ingrid Beckman
Manufactured in the United States of America

Library of Congress Cataloging in Publication Data

Soule, Gardner.
    Men who dared the sea.

    Bibliography: p.
    Includes index.
    1. Seafaring life—History. 2. Navigation—History. 3. Oceanography—History. I. Title.
G540.S66   910'.45   75-34451
ISBN 0-690-01095-8

1   2   3   4   5   6   7   8   9   10

Contents

27. The Mediterranean, 200s B.C.:
    Travelers on the Sea   163

28. Alexandria, 200s B.C.:
    A Man Measures the Earth   169

29. 222–51 B.C.:
    Incredible Rowboats, Unknown Continents   175

30. Sea of Sardinia, 100 B.C.:
    How Deep Is the Ocean?   179

31. Roman Empire, 63 B.C.–21 A.D.:
    A Man of Christ's Time   184

32. First Century A.D.:
    Roman Ships and Sailors   192

33. Italy, 79 A.D. A Man Watches a Volcano   199

34. Late First Century A.D.: A Voyage to India   205

35. Alexandria, 150 A.D.:
    Ptolemy and His Geography   209

36. 150–500 A.D.:
    As Rome Fades, Men Sail On—and On   215

37. Postscript: What Came After   223

Notes   236

Bibliography   245

Index   251

Illustrations follow pages 58 and 138

Foreword

Back to the Very
First Beginning

THERE ARE today more men in more ships exploring and studying the ocean than ever before, even more than during the golden age of exploration of Columbus, Magellan, and Drake in the fifteenth and sixteenth centuries. Today, men from hundreds of businesses and universities and from over fifty nations in over a hundred highly-equipped vessels sail all of the surface—and that is seven-tenths of the globe—and investigate everything on the surface and in the air above it and in the depths below it. They seek to learn about winds, weather, currents, fish and shellfish, minerals, metals, oil. The knowledge they bring back to port benefits all men today; all men may need it desperately in the future.

When and where did it begin? I set out to find out, to track down the very first beginning of oceanography. I found I had to go back farther and farther—to the first sailors. Who were they? A prehistoric man paddling a large log boat and diving after shellfish for food. A man on a papyrus raft, maybe using wind in a very simple sail to cross an entire ocean. A man on the deck of a Red Sea ship of an Egyptian pharaoh. An ancient Greek tuna fisherman telling of his catch, and of the habits of fish, telling it all to Aristotle. A man pulling an oar on a Phoenician galley—and maybe rowing his vessel all the way around Africa. About 300 years before Christ, a man on a Greek ship reaching as far as a sea of ice floes, and exploring the Arctic. A man of the same time, living in the city of Tyre, practicing marine chemistry—mixing products of three ocean animals to make a beautiful and costly dye. A sailor, of the same time, carrying the first tourists—a brand-new idea and a brand-new business—to gaze at the pyramids. A man a hundred years before Christ lowering a line overboard and for the first time finding a place in the sea over a mile deep—a feat not accomplished again for 2,100 years, or until the 1800s. A man on a Roman grain ship.

The sailors, these unknown men who left few records and almost never are mentioned in books of history unless they commanded a fleet in battle, found for other men all of their world; in the process, they improved the living for all man and womankind; and in the process, they began the study of the sea, they began to establish a science that is burgeoning only in the last years of the twentieth century, oceanography.

My story is the story of these men who started on the voyages that led to oceanography, the earliest sailors, of the Stone Age, of the Bronze Age, in the ships of the Egyptians, Babylonians, Greeks, Phoenicians, Romans, northern Europeans, Asians. Why did they go to sea? How did they do it? How did they navigate? When and how did they begin the study of the sea? What were their ships like? Who helped them? How far from home could they go and with what results?

The more I learned about the first men on the sea, the more important their story seemed to me to be. It is a large part of history itself, and much of it is as unknown as the sailor himself.

We are in a certain sense amphibious, not exclusively connected with the land, but with the sea as well.

—STRABO,
a Greek geographer in the Roman
Empire at the time of Christ

1

Somewhere, Some Time: A Man on a Log

You CAN SEE him now. A prehistoric man, a man built pretty much like us, maybe slightly smaller. A man from a cave or the jungle, shakily standing on a log or straddling it and drifting down a river with the current, the first man to be carried on the water.

Somewhere, some time it happened. Perhaps tens of thousands of years ago, perhaps hundreds of thousands, maybe millions. A man, perhaps one of a small band of men out hunting, left behind him the solid bank, the land, the earth to which he was accustomed. He took a risk and scrambled onto the log and floated downstream. This was a man, a land animal, taking a step into or onto a new environment, the water.

The man was a hunter. He had to feed his woman, his child, and himself. To do so, prehistoric man had to leave his home—his cave or jungle clearing—and hunt for animals or nuts and berries. It is hard work to feed a family on animals one can catch and on wild plants one can gather; to do it a man must cover many square miles of territory. This man, the hunter, had to put in dawn-to-dusk physical toil and effort to keep his family alive. He also had to take risks, as he was doing when first he stepped onto the water. He constantly had to move out, to go into the unknown. He had to look everlastingly for a new hunting ground.

A man lacks the weapons built into the bodies of other hunters. He is without the teeth of the killer whale, teeth that tear apart porpoises, seals, squid, and penguins. He lacks the large claws of the lobster, claws that capture crabs, starfish, sea urchins, and mussels. Instead, a man has a brain, and hands that can clutch or hold. He has stereoscopic eyes that (a vital fact whenever a man is on the water) can judge distance. With his brain, his hands, and his eyes a man obtains or makes and uses tools or weapons to catch his food.

And a man has something else: a voice. With his voice he can pass on what he learns and knows to his family or tribe or race. He can tell other men how to make and use tools and weapons.

For a long time now there has been somewhere on this earth a man or manlike creature hunting with tools or weapons—an ax, a spear, or maybe a bow and arrow—that he obtained with his own hands, his brain, and his eyes. It was done 12 million years ago in Africa, to judge from fragments of the skull of an antelope, now extinct, and the nearby fragments of the hammer that killed the antelope. It was done four million years ago in southern Ethiopia with crude stone tools that have been found, and also in northeastern Ethiopia. There, in 1964, manlike bones estimated to be four million years old—the oldest yet found—were dug up, three jawbones complete with teeth. According to Dr. Carl Johanson of Case Western Reserve University, who uncovered the fossils, "The small size of the teeth in these jawbones leads us to hypothesize that the genus *Homo* was eating meat and probably using tools, perhaps bones, to kill animals three to

four million years ago." [1] He thought his fossil men had
"some sort of communication system, and that they might
have come from Arabia across the Red Sea, over a land bridge
that once joined them.

A fossil hyena was found nearby.

Men hunted 2.8 or 2.6 million years ago near Lake Rudolf
in Kenya and in Africa's Great Rift Valley. Here a team of
scientists led by Richard E. Leakey in 1969 found crude stone
tools whose age was established by laboratory tests at 2.6
million years, more or less. Manlike skulls were nearby.

East of 18-mile-long Lake Rudolf in 1972, Leakey found
hundreds of fragments that formed a manlike skull, about 2.5
million years old. He calls the skull, assembled by his wife,
Meave, "almost certainly the oldest complete skull of early
man." Leakey, whose work is sponsored by the National
Geographic Society, says the skull is "different from all other
known forms of early man." The brain was much larger than
that of any others, and the shape of the brain case "is
remarkably suggestive of modern man."

The skull may be 2.8 million years old and may be that of a
woman. Found nearby were the teeth and cranial pieces of a
skull apparently of a child about six years old, as well as the
leg bones of a remarkably advanced man. Almost three
million years ago, he could have been a man who, to feed his
woman and child, went out hunting and stepped off the
riverbank to sail on a log.

Relics of other men from the long past before written
history have been found together with the tools or weapons
with which they struggled to feed their families. Richard
Leakey's parents, Mary D. and the late Louis Seymour
Bazett Leakey, found in the Olduvai Gorge, Tanzania,
Africa, the remains of a manlike creature, 2-million-year-old
Homo habilis, who had cutting tools. In 1950 they found,
from 1,750,000 years ago, two teeth and bits of a skull of

another manlike creature, *Zinjanthropus,* also known as *Australopithecus boisei.* In 1975 in Tanzania, Mary Leakey came upon the jaws and teeth of at least eleven creatures that, instead of being manlike beings, appear to have been true men. The fossils are almost 3.75 million years old—by far the oldest remains of true men, men very similar to today's.

Knives, stilettos, saws, clubs (big baboon bones), and picks of bone and stone exist from South Africa of a million years ago. These and manlike remains were found by Professor Raymond A. Dart. And in France, by about 750,000 years ago, man apparently had acquired a new and different tool that would help him become supreme over all animals: fire. A hearth estimated to be that old has been discovered. In Africa, man has used fire at least about 70,000 years. When he began to use it to keep his family warm and to cook his food, he was doing something enormously significant: he was tapping the energy in nature to supplement his own efforts. It was one of his giant leaps.

It may have been his greatest leap of all, because when he began to draw on the unlimited energy in nature to help him, he no longer was dependent only on his own muscles.

With some energy from nature at his beck and call, man could be infinitely more powerful than an animal, even an animal with teeth, claws, or tusks; man would become something different from all other living things, past or present.

Water was vital to man for drinking, cooking, and washing, long before he sailed its surface. In the Olduvai Gorge, in 1972, Mary Leakey discovered a complex system of pits and channels dug apparently to carry and hold rain water, a complex perhaps 500,000 years old. Nearby were traces of finger marks and the print of a left foot that seems to be that of a child. These, says D.V. Tobias, an expert in the anatomy of prehistoric man, are the oldest evidence of the soft anatomy of early man that we have discovered so far.

The man who stepped upon or straddled the log, man the hunter, had everything against him except maybe the flame in his fire and a dog at his side. He lived in a frightfully dangerous world. He was naked—or almost—to the elements and to his enemies. He had no protective shell, no thick hide, no coat of fur, no insulation of blubber. When he was away from his fire or his dog, the wild animals, unafraid of him, could maul and kill him. In 1967, near Lake Rudolf, the lower end of a manlike upper-arm bone was discovered among bones of "extinct species of rodents, sabertooth cats, hyenas, elephants and mastodons, rhinos, pigs, hippos, giraffes, antelopes, turtles, crocodiles and fishes." [2]

For man the hunter the underbrush or even the rough ground could trip him. A rock or even a pebble could cause him to stumble and fall. A pothole could snap his leg. Because he lived by hunting, he ate irregularly, sometimes only occasionally, and he was weaker and less well nourished than a man today. He lived a total of 18 years, or 20 or 25 if he was lucky.

He was struggling, but, with his brain, hands, eyes, voice, and tools, he was also capable. In the world he lived in, he had to be to survive and to keep his wife and children alive. He needed all the help he could get.

He needed a better and safer way to travel. And a better way—besides his back and shoulders—to carry any animals he might kill. He had noticed logs floating down the river, and one day he climbed onto one. Or he might have been walking on a log fallen across a stream. The log might have fallen in with him. Or he might have been a boy playing.

It probably happened hundreds of times, on all the continents of the globe. However it happened, and wherever, some time a man was waterborne.

He probably would have felt surprised, uncertain, and alone in a strange place, on a moving thing he did not understand.

He could not have known it then, but we can look back on him now and know it: this man was the first sailor.

In northwest Australia in the twentieth century, you can still see a native inhabitant moving downstream on a log of lightweight wood. The log may be pointed at each end, but it has not been hollowed out, and there is no other improvement.

There is no more to the scene than that: a man on a log.

There is no way to tell how many times a log carrying a man may have rolled over. The ability to swim seems to be born into many animals, but it is not born into the gorillas, chimpanzees, orangutans—or man.

He would have helplessly drowned, or a crocodile might have gotten to him. It was as easy as falling off a log.

The man on the log again was tapping the energy of nature—this time the current taking him downstream, perhaps his second use of the power in nature, after fire.

Up to the moment when he scrambled onto the log, he had only his aching feet and weary legs to travel on. Now he had an additional method of transportation, something to take him from place to place without exertion and physical exhaustion on his part. The log, his first vehicle of any kind, would change his entire future.

Struggling but capable, this prehistoric man quickly would have learned to guide and propel the log by his hands. Soon he would have picked up something to use as a paddle—a wide piece of wood, perhaps. He would learn to push against the river bottom with a tree branch to move the log. And the log eventually would be hollowed out to become a boat or canoe, or many logs lashed together to form a raft, and eventually man would have boats and ships.

When a man first rode on a log he made a breakthrough, another giant leap, as when he first used fire. For on the water man would find more food for his family. He would travel farther and from the places he reached he would obtain more goods of all kinds. Eventually he would reach all the seas and all the lands on the globe.

On the water man would find his world.

2

Far Away, Long Ago: Man, the Sun, and the Stars

SOMEWHERE, SOME TIME the man who was carried down the river on a log began to use something else besides fire and a current to help him. He began to use the stars.

One can imagine him, this man, this hunter, roaming far from home, into unknown territory and getting lost, and then, lying flat on his back on the ground at night, and gazing upward with those splendid binocular eyes of his. And one can almost hear him make sounds that meant something like, "Those stars move, I swear they do."

This man who had to chase game animals a far distance needed a sign to show him the way to go home. Much of man's story has been a search for signs; he is always looking, always wondering, as he must have wondered, flat on his back, in an unknown place, after a day's hunting: Where am I? Which way should I go?

He learned to ask the questions of the stars, of the stars by night and of the sun by day.

If he could see them. If his view was not blocked by rain, clouds, snow, or fog.

As he kept his eyes turned upward toward the sky, he would have seen very early that the sun traveled a regular course each day. And from this path he could have conceived the idea of east and west. Either side of that course would have become north and south. Thus, from the sun, he could have grasped the idea of four directions.

By the time when man was using weapons and tools of stone, he knew the phases of the moon; he had scratched them onto reindeer horn.

Stone Age man would have observed movements of many of the stars. He perhaps learned fairly early that the North Star stays in position with only relatively slight movement around a tiny bit of sky over the North Pole.

A steady star. A fixed point to depend upon. A star to steer by.

The Greeks had some thoughtful ideas about this world, the sun, and the stars that were largely speculative but partly knowledge.[1] One early Greek notion was that the earth was a stationary center of a fairly small universe. The universe consisted of the earth and the visible objects in the sky.

If a man went far enough north, the Greeks eventually believed, he would be right under the constellation we call the Great Bear or the Big Dipper. The Greeks called the Great Bear "Arktos." From this Greek name, the northern-most area of the earth came to be called the Arctic.

The earth appeared to be flat. But movements of the sun, the moon, and the stars could have made ancient man begin to wonder—and the Greeks did begin to wonder—if the earth were not spherical.

In time, men learned that movements of sun and stars foretold the seasons. Just as one example, when the bright dog star Sirius rose with the sun, it was time for Egypt's Nile River to flood. Logically enough, men thought that the stars might predict all the future. Astrology was born. Millions believed in it, millions still do.

Slowly, as man's eyes searched the skies over thousands of years, astrology was replaced by astronomy. Astronomy probably was the first science man had, even before agriculture. The sun and stars would help answer the two questions of the lost hunter, or of any man who had wandered away from familiar landmarks: Where am I? Which way should I go?

In time man grasped enough so that the sun and stars provided him a sort of map or chart that led him safely home again. Later the sun and stars guided his caravans and flocks of sheep across the desert. Still later, after the man riding a log had developed into a sailor in a boat, astronomy would guide him over the trackless ocean. It still does.

3

Europe 10,000 Years Back:
Men Go Fishing

A MAN RIDING a log downstream with the current of a river is likely eventually to reach the sea. Whether that is how a man first reached the seashore, or whether he always lived along the ocean, he had become a fisherman long before he put down in writing any of his story.

Thousands of years ago he was fishing off the western, or Atlantic Ocean, shores of Europe. This is more than the pure guessing we must make about the first man stepping onto a log or gazing upward at the stars. We have some evidence. We have unearthed, from Scandinavia to Spain, prehistoric fishhooks so large that they are suitable only to catch big deep-sea fish. These fishhooks, of flint, make one wonder how man, possibly not long after the Ice Age, could have gotten out onto the deep sea, and on the North Atlantic, one of the world's roughest oceans.

Very early, we speculate, prehistoric man in the Atlantic must have found herring, which he took in nets, and cod, which he took either with trawls or hooks and lines. Both herring and cod, we believe, were abundant. And both were suitable for salting and drying and therefore could fill a desperate need for the man who caught them: they could be preserved for his family over the winter.

In Portugal, nine or ten thousand years ago, men were depending on seafood for much of their diet. Near Lisbon, near where the Tagus River meets the ocean and where Europe sticks farthest west out into the Atlantic, archeologists in 1880–85 dug up the bones of about 120 people. The archeologists also dug up their middens, their kitchen waste. The middens included bones of sheep, deer, and pigs, as well as piles of shells, the remains of crustaceans, and huge piles of fish bones.

The people along the Tagus had tools with which to obtain their seafood: nets, lines, scrapers, and their most common tool, a pick, apparently to pry shellfish off rocks and open them.

In the Americas, at the time of the Tagus River people, and long before, men already were depending on the sea. Near Puebla, Mexico, scrapers and spear points have been found along with remains of Ice Age creatures, including the mastodon and mammoth, and fossil shells. These tools, dated as 40,000 years old, are evidence of the earliest known man in the Americas.[1]

In Alaska, by 25,000 to 12,000 B.C., there were men who seem to have been the forefathers of American Indians. They may have come from Asia by sea, or by a land bridge that may have existed between Siberia and Alaska, or across a frozen sea.

In a cave in the Sandia Mountains of New Mexico, the flint lance points of 12,000-year-old Folsom men were found among bones of extinct animals: giant sloths, bison, Taylor's camels, mammoths, and sabertooth tigers.

The Folsom people are believed to have been a coastal

seafood-eating people and to have come from Asia across land
or ice where Bering Strait is now, and then to have gone
south along the eastern slope of the Rocky Mountains,
pursuing big game. This is an indication of how far hunters
had to travel to feed their families, and how much they
needed ships. On Santa Rosa Island, off Santa Barbara,
California, the skeletons of a people who ate seafood have
been found.[2] They dived for red abalone and took sea lions,
whales, and seals—big game at sea—even as prehistoric men
were killing big game on land. Prehistoric men such as the
Santa Rosans, who had to dive for food, must have learned to
swim, and may have learned by watching the large sea
animals.

By 8500 b.c., according to one anthropologist, there were
tool-using men along the coast of Peru.[3]

Thousands of stones and pieces of wood that had been
worked by their tools have been found. Their dwelling sites
were near the sea—their plants nourished by fogs coming in
from the ocean. Their tools were mainly hunters' tools—
scrapers, knife blades, and projectile points for hunting
lizards, deer, guanacos, and burrowing owls—and tools for
gathering wild grasses and wild potatoes, such as stone flakes
that may have been crude sickles.

And by 6700 b.c., men had reached the cold southernmost
tip of South America, Patagonia, and there, at Cape Horn, in
Tierra del Fuego, or Land of Fire (for the fires they always
kept lit), men had to feed themselves largely from the sea.

All of these men once might have migrated from Europe,
especially from Siberia via Alaska, or they could have
originated in America and could have migrated the other
way. At least some of them traveled by water, along coasts,
and many of them knew the seashore.

Once men had reached the ocean, they would have begun
to explore it with all their five senses. "Man could see the

ocean stretching beyond the horizon, he could smell it, he
could hear its surf pounding the beach, he could feel its
coldness and wetness, and he could taste its salt. This
prehistoric man can be considered the world's first oceanographer." [4]

The world's first marine fishermen that we know of—the
northern Europeans with their big fishhooks and the people
near the Tagus River—had to watch marine animals, fish,
and shellfish, to learn how and when they were to be caught,
and when they were to be eaten. They had to watch birds
that could show them the way to land. They had to observe
weather, winds and waves, clouds and lightning, tides and
currents. Thus driven by necessity, looking about him, did
man the land animal begin to learn something about the sea.

4

North Europe, Stone Age: Men on the Sea in Hollow Logs

A MAN WITH A FIRE and a log took the next step forward. With the fire, he hollowed out the inside of the log. Then he had a boat. Men with scrapers, such as the Tagus River fishermen, nine or ten thousand years ago, may have done, and probably did, the same thing. Or a prehistoric man might have started with a log whose inside already had rotted out. In any case, very ancient men did sail in hollowed logs. Such dugouts have been excavated in Germany, Sweden, Norway, Scotland, and England.

Several log boats were excavated in 1720 in marshes of the river Medway, near Maidstone, England—one so well preserved it once again was used as a canoe. A log boat seven feet long was found in 1736 near a Scottish swamp, with a paddle nearby. Another was 8 feet 3 inches long. Near North Stoke, Sussex, in 1834, there was unearthed a large dugout, 35 feet 4 inches long, 4 feet 6 inches wide, that appears to have been hollowed out with sharp instruments.

In May 1866, at Brigg, Lincolnshire, England, a dugout was found that we call the "Brigg boat." There is not a trace of metal in it, so it is believed to be from the Stone Age, an age that is not exactly defined by dates, but that lasted till men began to make things out of copper, and included the time of the Tagus River shore dwellers. There are no dates for the Brigg boat, but it may be 3,500 to 2,500 years old. Its excellent quality, the skill and knowledge that went into it, suggest that prehistoric man had been making such craft for a long time.

The Brigg boat is 48 feet long (about the length of a bus). It is 4 feet 6 inches wide (about the width of a car seat). It appears to have been too large for a single family, unless you count the whole tribe or clan. Because there were no signs of oarlocks, it is believed to have been paddled.

When man learned to use some kind of paddle either on a floating log or to move a dugout, he learned something new: once he could paddle and more or less steer, he could turn into the bank at will. And he could do something even more surprising: he could move his craft upstream, against mild currents, at least.

It was another big step forward.

The Brigg boat was paddled by about 15 men on each side, so men were learning teamwork and were organizing themselves into crews. Another big step.

Because there are no signs of branches extending from the trunk of the oak that was hollowed out to make the Brigg boat, except at the bow, it appears that the tree must have had its lowest branches 50 feet above the ground. Its trunk must have been 18 feet around.

How Stone Age men, with only stone axes, could have cut down such a gigantic oak escapes us today. But as archeologists uncover more remains of prehistoric man, more and more does prehistoric man compel our admiration. Stone Age man did things we cannot imagine him doing.

There was another early means of water transportation,

another of man's useful tools, near the Brigg boat. A large
wooden raft, 40 feet long by 9 feet wide in the middle. These
two things, dugout canoes and rafts, were, so far as we know,
the first two conveyances that struggling but capable prehistoric man ever built for use upon the water to carry his
family, himself, his friends, his fish and game animals and
other food—that is, the first loads of freight.

About 7000 B.C., or about the time of the Tagus River
fishermen, it is thought that men in Denmark sailed on the
ocean. A pair of oars, found in an excavation, appears to be
that old.[1] Oars are an advanced invention and indicate men
had been working with boats for a long time. So far as is
known, oars did not appear in the Mediterranean Sea till
about 3500 B.C., or three and a half thousand years later than
those found in Denmark.

With or without oars, even with paddles alone, the boats of
Stone Age man were excellent enough to have been used
between Scandinavia and Britain, or across the Baltic Sea, or
between Norway and the Lofoten Islands, or Denmark and
Scotland, or Germany and Britain—they were vehicles
capable of carrying men across at least narrow seas. The fact
that the dugouts have been unearthed both on the continent
of Europe and in the British Isles suggests the same thing.

Stone Age man, who could cut down a huge oak and
fashion a fine boat from it, appears to have been, as a result,
able to make long voyages. He was not simply a cave man
limited to moving a few miles from his cave entrance. Stone
Age man was a traveler upon the water. He was going places.

5

After Seeds Are Planted: Men Ship Their Food Crops

SOMEWHERE, SOME TIME—perhaps toward the end of the Stone Age—someone planted a seed in the ground.

Many believe it was a woman. She was in need of security. She had to stay home, in the cave or grass hut, when she was giving birth, when her babies were helpless, or when her children were being raised. The woman was the logical one to plant a seed and cultivate a garden.

Man, who had begun to formulate his first science, astronomy, a science that would lead him across the unmarked oceans, now began to formulate his second science, agriculture. Agriculture also would have a profound effect on man on the sea.

Around the eastern end of the Mediterranean, man has had agriculture at least as long as we can trace his past in some detail—and that, very approximately, is back to somewhere around the time of the Tagus River fishermen, nine or ten thousand years ago. Elsewhere we have found other evidence of man the farmer: grains of wheat have been found in prehistoric lake dwellings in Switzerland and in 6,000-year-old ruins in Turkey.

Once he had agriculture, man no longer was limited to hunting, fishing, and gathering nuts, berries, and fruits to obtain food. He became a farmer. He and his family were fed partly at least by homegrown crops.

About the same time, he learned to domesticate and raise animals. No one is positive what was the first animal man ever domesticated. It may well have been a member of the dog family, since canines apparently have been walking faithfully at man's side ever since he was a hunter in prehistoric times. The fossil jaws and teeth of a domesticated canine were dated as 14,000 years old at the British Museum (Natural History) in 1975—the oldest known bones of a tamed wild animal, in this case the wolf. The jaws and teeth had been found at Kirkuk, Iraq, twenty years earlier by Dr. Bruce Howe of the University of Chicago and Harvard University on an expedition led by Dr. Bruce W. Braidwood. It is believed that tame animals' bones evolve slowly, so presumably the Kirkuk dog followed thousands of years of canines already tamed. Stone tools found nearby suggested his owner was still a hunter and gatherer. Another domesticated dog, 10,500 years old, previously had been found in Idaho. The bones of domesticated dogs have been discovered as well among the kitchen middens of a seashore people in Denmark who had crude boats and who lived about the same time as the Tagus River fishermen.[1] Also unearthed have been the remains of sheep and goats between 10,000 and 10,500 years old, and pigs 9,500 years old—about as old as the earliest known domesticated plants and cereals. Thus the dog, apparently preceding all these, may have been the first wild animal to become the friend of man. Indeed, some people believe that the dog, as much as fire, helped man become dominant on the earth.

Other possibilities as the first animals to be domesticated are the honeybee and the goat. In any case, man had all the domesticated animals—sheep, goats, cattle, horses, camels, bees, and the others—at least as far back as the New Stone Age, the end of the Stone Age.

In ancient Egypt men even domesticated and used in their religion one animal that today is no longer cultivated: the dung beetle, or scarab. The dung beetle rolls a bit of camel dung uphill and the female may lay an egg in her ball of dung. The Egyptians, noting larvae or grubs in balls of dung, mistakenly believed that the male produced his own young without help from the female. The scarab therefore became a symbol of the soul of man and of immortal life.

Domesticated animals, of course, meant home-grown meat. And both domesticated animals and cultivated crops meant, for the first time, home-grown clothes.

Tame animals and farm crops came, along with sophisticated boats, during the last of the Stone Age—after more than 99 percent of the time man has existed on the earth. The time since then—say, ten thousand years or so—is one percent or even less, maybe far less, of the time man has been on the globe.

All man's recorded history is in this last one percent. Therefore, most of all the progress of man that we know about has been made during this time—the time, so far as we know, of the sailor.

The sailor did not cause all of man's progress, but he caused a lot of it, much more than is usually realized, as I hope to show.

Once he began agriculture, man was extending something he was doing when he rode a log down the current of a river: he was working with nature, not against it.

When man hunts or simply gathers food, or when he hunts wild animals for their skins or furs, he takes only what is already there, and he reduces the total supply. When he grows his own, he multiplies the supply. In time there may be something left over beyond his needs.

He then can trade what he has for what he wants but doesn't have. A result of agriculture was—and is—trade routes, to obtain more goods for a man's family and for his neighbors. In the late Stone Age and thereafter this meant a need for bigger and bigger boats to carry larger amounts of food.

So even the planting of seeds resulted in more and larger ships. And more sailors. And more attention paid to ships, the sea, and the skies above the sea, than ever before.

6

Ancient Europe and Egypt: Wind in the Sails

MAYBE A MAN, when he stood up to paddle a dugout such as England's Brigg boat or the raft found near it, noticed that the wind against his body pushed him along. Or he might have hung up a shield in a smaller boat and noticed the effect of the wind upon it. In Egypt he might have raised up a palm leaf. In time, he might have erected a small sail—an animal hide perhaps—for the wind to blow against. Gradually, slowly, the sail came into use.

Boats like the Brigg boat, found all around the North Sea, might have acquired masts and sails. They often were strengthened with ribs. In them, prehistoric Europeans might have paddled, rowed, or sailed to each other's lands. With a sail, Stone Age man could have made long voyages over the sea.

The men of ancient Egypt, at about the time of the Tagus River people, paddled and towed their boats along the banks of the river Nile by means of their aching arms, legs, and backs, but also had sails to help. A boat that could have been paddled and towed, and had a sail up at the same time, we can imagine because of a toy-size model boat of clay found in a province of Egypt, the Fayum, on the Nile south of Cairo. The Egyptian model may have been intended to go into a tomb to provide transportation for the deceased in the next world. It is ten thousand, maybe twelve thousand years old. It looks as though it once had a mast.

If a boat like that had a mast, it probably also had a sail, and the sail could have been made of matting from a rush, or water reed, known as papyrus, that grows in Egypt. It would have been small and near the bow, catching a little wind but in the wrong location to do much good. It would have been a single sail, for that was what ships carried for thousands of years. Not till Roman days, after Christ, was a second sail often added. A single sail, but highly significant in the story of man.

The Egyptian boat also has a cabin, something that probably would have been added to boats only after men had been using them for some time, after they had learned something of the weather along stretches of river or sea coast, and wanted something to protect themselves from storm, rain, or sun.

An Egyptian jar, or amphora, from 6000 B.C.,[1] now in the British Museum, shows the earliest known form of sailing vessel, not unlike the model boat turned up in the Fayum sands. The boat on the jar has a mast and a square sail of matting, with men paddling at the same time. She is a crescent-shaped boat, with a high bow and stern, and cabins forward and aft.

She looks as though she might have influenced Chinese junks. She could have, for wind in the sails was the breakthrough that made possible long voyages. The ancient Egyptians could have traded with China, sailing along the coast all the way. She looks as if she influenced later Greek and Phoenician ships, too. She has a figurehead on her bow—a forerunner of the eyes later painted on Phoenician ships and Portuguese fishing boats and the figureheads of American sailing ships.

As the artwork on the jar indicates, the Egyptians long ago were operating many boats on the Nile. In Egyptian hieroglyphics, a ship with a sail came to mean a ship sailing with the wind behind her up the Nile. A ship without a sail meant a ship drifting downstream with the current.

For struggling but capable ancient man, the ship was a blessing. He probably did not have to use his brain—at least not very much—to see what a ship does. That is so obvious that it is taken for granted and its importance often is overlooked.

A ship in ancient times was, and still is today, the only vehicle man ever has had that runs on a ready-made roadway, the ocean. This roadway can carry a cargo of any weight without deteriorating. It never needs repairs. It covers seven-tenths of the globe and therefore can take men and their freight almost anywhere on the earth. The sea is a ready-made long-distance highway girdling the world.

A ship does not have to use power to climb hills; the sea remains level. Neither does a ship have to use fuel to keep herself afloat (as does a plane to keep airborne). With all these advantages, the ship from her early days could carry large cargoes to those living around the Mediterranean Sea.

Ever since then, the ship probably has kept more people from hunger than any of man's inventions except the plow and improved grains. And the ship put man on the track of something he never had had, something he could not have obtained without the distribution of food provided by the ship, something that was to benefit him beyond estimate: regular meals.

The wind in the sails of his ship would put man on the way

to something else. A source of energy from something other than muscles and the current of a river was as great a breakthrough in human affairs as it was when a man first learned how to use fire or when he first became waterborne on a log. The first man with a sail did not know it, but the sail, a way to tap nature's energy, would be the tool that would take man across all the seas of the globe. Wind in the sails would enable men to find their world.

7

The Mideast, 6000 B.C.:
Ships Carry Copper

SOME TIME, SOMEWHERE, man first found copper, probably by noticing its greenish color in the rocks. It was, except possibly for gold, his first metal. He could mine copper right on the surface of the ground. He could harden it, by beating, into sharp tools and weapons that would replace those of stone. Gold he could not harden, so he used gold for ornaments, necklaces, and bracelets.

Copper, like farm crops, increased the need for ships. Man discovered it in many places—Asia Minor, central Asia, Europe, and eventually in Egypt, on some of the Greek islands and on a Mediterranean island named for copper, Cyprus—and it had to be moved around.

By 6000 B.C., man was using copper, and a metal era was beginning, succeeding the Stone Age. Some things made of hammered copper have been found in the Fayum of Egypt, where the small boat in the sand was turned up.

By 4000 B.C., ships had replaced camels (capacity: 500-pound loads) as carriers of copper. A carving on stone of about that date shows a trading boat on a river in the Middle

Eastern land of Mesopotamia. By that time, the Mesopota-
mians, and others around them, certainly had many ships.
They also had canals, to provide irrigation for agricultural
crops, and also waterways for ships. Babylonia (located where
Iraq is today) eventually became a grid of canals and ditches
that made her otherwise barren land lush with wheat. Some
of present-day Iraq's canals follow the routes of ancient ones.

By 4000 B.C., copper—as well as the domesticated animals
that were being raised by agricultural man—led to another
vehicle. Some capable ancient men trained oxen or asses to
haul, others invented the wheel and axle, and with that
invention came carts. There exists today an impression of
wheels from a four-wheeled cart of 2,500 years ago from
Kish, Mesopotamia (or the land between the rivers, the
Tigris and the Euphrates, where was traditionally located the
Garden of Eden).[1]

Where did man get the idea for the wheel? Perhaps from
the very same thing that first carried him on the water, a log.
He may have noticed—probably many men noticed many
times—a log rolling. In time, he might have used a log as a
roller on which to move heavy objects.

The wheel may not have lasted everywhere it was
discovered; in roadless, deep-sand deserts of the Middle East,
men may have had to give up on wheels and revert to camels.

At least as long ago as between copper (6000 B.C.) and the
wheel (around 4000 B.C.), man had begun another journey—
his voyage beneath the sea. Already he was a diver. This we
know from Mesopotamian ornaments dating to 4500 B.C. that
use mother-of-pearl.[2] That cannot be obtained in any amount
except by repeated dives. Mideast pottery exists from 4000
B.C. that shows men swimming or diving.[3] Seashore people,
such as those on Tagus River, may have been doing some
diving for shellfish.

All were giant leaps for men: obtaining fire, becoming
waterborne, astronomy, agriculture, capturing the energy of
wind in sails, the change to copper from stone, acquiring the
wheel, and learning to dive.

8

The Mediterranean, 3500 B.C.:
Men Sail Along the Coast

THE EARLY SEAGOING SHIPS in the Mediterranean were from Egypt, from the Minoans of Crete, from Greece, or from a part of Egypt that won independence, Phoenicia. They were paddled or sailed or sometimes paddled with sail hoisted, along the coast. Their officers navigated by what they could see on the land—a hill, a cape, a tree. Or the silhouette or skyline of a coast. Or a house or a temple. The Greeks built temples—in some cases high towers—atop capes or promontories as help to their mariners, who, all too often, continued to get lost.

Rugged, ragged, rocky coasts, such as Greece's, provided more and better natural landmarks than Egypt's flat coast. Sailors, when there was a choice, might follow a rugged coast, though in foul weather ships often foundered off rugged coasts. Off shores of Greece today is one of the world's busy areas for modern undersea archeologists diving to uncover ancient wrecks.

Because they were paddled, early ships needed a lot of men aboard. But they were not large enough to carry food for many men, so the ships had to be drawn up on the beach every night where food, fresh water, and wood for cooking might be obtained. Sailors also ran their ships onto the beach whenever a storm approached.

By 3500 B.C., both the wheel and the ship were being improved. The Babylonians were using wheeled carts as war chariots. And not long afterward, capable Mediterranean men added a new device to ships that for thousands of years had had sails for at least some of their propulsion. The new device was oars. (In Denmark, men may have had oars as far back as 7000 B.C.)

Oars brought the principle of the lever to propelling a ship; they replaced and were more efficient than paddles. Oars had another great advantage: better control over the then-unwieldy and hard-to-steer vessels. For the short periods, from a few minutes up to 2 hours, that the oarsmen could labor before becoming too tired, oars provided more dependable power than did the fickle wind. Accordingly, rowers were used to bring a ship into, or take her out of, a harbor.

The use of rowers was about as revolutionary as the substitution of steam for sail in the late 1800s.

By 3500 or 3400 B.C., single-sail ships were widely used in Eridu, Mesopotamia. This is suggested by a clay boat, perhaps the model of a fishing skiff, dating from this period, that was found by modern excavators. Near the bow, the model has a socket, as though for a mast.[1] Within the next 500 years, or by around 3000 B.C., Mesopotamia (the land of Ur of the Chaldees) also had wheeled vehicles, irrigation for agriculture, pictorial writing on clay tablets, and trade around the Persian Gulf. Her mathematicians gave men the division of the circle into 360 degrees and the hour into 60 minutes.

Shortly before 2900 B.C., according to modern dating, in southern Egypt hundreds of pictures of boats were drawn both on pottery and on outcroppings of rock. A number of the drawings show boats each equipped with a single broad sail, square across the hull, on a single mast. They are the first drawings we know of that show sails.[2]

Some time after 3000 B.C., the Minoans on Crete are believed to have had ships narrow in beam, rowed by men—long ships that developed into warships; and larger sailing ships, round ships, broader in beam—the sort that became trading ships, cargo ships, which over the next five thousand years would have swelled into today's giant tankers and bulk carriers.

Man, lacking the killing teeth or tearing claws of a beast of prey, by 3000 B.C. had come a long way. His food came not only from hunting and gathering but largely from farming. Man, the tool-making animal, was using copper and the wheel to transport food. At sea, with his eyes on the landmarks of his coasts, and up his rivers and canals, the sailor was using the ship to carry food. And along that ready-made highway, the sea, a sailor's eyes watched the sky for sun or stars and guided the ship. With a sail hoisted, the wind did much of the propelling of a ship. A bigger ship was possible, and so also was it possible for sailors to move more food—huge amounts instead of camelback loads and the tiny loads of the first crude carts.

When it comes to feeding people or transporting petroleum and other things that help man to live with a bit of comfort, nothing else, in ancient times or today, has ever done what the ship routinely does.

The ship has been and is one of man's most useful tools.

9

Place and Date Unknown:
The First Out
of Sight of Land

MEN SAILING along the coast, making improved ships, obtaining startling new mechanical devices such as oars would inevitably feel more and more capable. They were still struggling, men always are; but they slowly, probably painfully felt more and more capable of longer voyages. And looking out to sea toward the horizon, they could not help but wonder: What is out there?

From what they had discovered close to shore, and from what their imagination told them, they developed some ideas. Storms. Waves that could capsize a ship or pitchpole her (turn her end over end). Hidden rocks and shoals. Jagged reefs they could not see and were shipwrecked on and probably drowned. Shores that, if they did reach them, were inhabited by hostile people. Not to mention an assortment of strange people, some giants. At sea, too, there were grotesque and enormous monsters, such as sea serpents, that could gobble a man. And many other horrors.

Ancient man also imagined something else, that he might

reach what he called the "fortunate isles," or Isles of the Blessed, a land where all was milk and honey and roses (or the equivalent at the time). Many an ancient people had its tale of Isles of the Blessed; if any myth runs back into the most misty time of man's history, this one does. Man always has looked for Utopia.

The result of man's imaginations about what might lie beyond the horizon was that, just about as soon as he could, he set out to answer the question that has beset exploring man ever since: What is out there?

Somewhere, some time, somebody—a small group of men in a ship or a fleet—got ready, said prayers, and went to sea. They sailed out of sight of land—intentionally. They left behind the life-giving, sustaining, safe land, man's natural environment, the only haven he has. They kept going till their snug harbor vanished behind them.

They were the first men alone on the wide ocean.

They were entirely out of touch with their fellowmen. There was no communication of any kind back to the shore they no longer could see. Probably they didn't even have lifeboats.

But they did have some help. One thing, in particular, made their trip possible. This was astronomy, man's first science, which he improved constantly. At an early date, man's knowledge of the stars was detailed. In the Middle East, on open deserts or plains, on clear nights filled with stars, man learned fast.

The Egyptians learned to tell time by the stars and did it so well that thousands of years before telescopes, they invented a calendar 365¼ days long. It led to the calendar we use today.

Babylonians, Sumerians, Egyptians, Chinese, Greeks, Arabs, Minoans, Phoenicians watched the skies. So did northern Europeans—including the Stone Age people who built the circle of large upright stones at Stonehenge, England. They brought the heavy (some weigh 26 tons) stones to Stonehenge, it is believed, by boat or ship.

The ancient astronomers were so far along that some of them already knew how to predict eclipses. They were far along, too, in describing courses of the sun and the moon and telling something about the movements of the stars. So using the map in the sky—navigating by sun or stars—made voyages possible out of sight of land.

This is not to suggest that the early sailor ever became expert about the sun or stars. He did not. He mainly navigated by measuring the sun's height against the mast, or steered by Polaris, the North Star. From these he picked up clues that helped him answer those always-present questions for a man on the trackless sea: Where am I? Which way should I go?

Almost as often, the sailor got no answers at all and was completely lost.

He sailed ahead—or many sailors did—into the fearsome unknown, full of storms and monsters and cannibals.

The first moment beyond the horizon, out of sight of land, was as significant as the first step taken on 20 July 1969 by Neil Armstrong when he became the first man to set foot on the moon. Armstrong called his step "One small step for a man, one giant leap for mankind."

With Armstrong's arrival on the moon, man no longer was confined to a single planet. At that moment man ceased to be only an earth creature.

At the moment when the first sailors passed beyond the horizon from the land, man ceased to be confined only to the land, which makes up only 29.9 percent of the globe's surface. He entered a vast new area: the wide ocean that covers 70.1 percent of the globe. And, centuries later, a Greek geographer named Strabo, who lived at the time of

Jesus, could write words that would be true in the last decades of the twentieth century:

"We are in a certain sense amphibious, not exclusively connected with the land, but with the sea as well."

Who the first voluntary sailors were out of sight of land is not known. The sea is full of mysteries, and so is the story of man on the sea.

There are many possibilities. The leading candidates according to many scholars are the Phoenicians. This may change when there is more evidence about other ancient mariners.

The Old Testament book of Ezekiel, Chapter 27, waxes enthusiastic about the Phoenicians as sailors: "Their borders are in the midst of the seas. . . . They have made all their ship boards of fir trees; they have taken cedars of Lebanon to make masts. . . . Of the oaks of Bashan have they made . . . oars. . . . Fine linen with broidered work from Egypt was that which [they] spreaded forth to be . . . sail."

Between 3000 and 2000 B.C., or between four and five thousand years ago, the Phoenicians lived in cities, including Sarepta, Sidon (a name that means "fish") and Tyre, in a coastal strip only 200 miles long and extending to no more than 35 miles inland, a part of Egypt where Lebanon, Israel, and Syria are today. They called their land Canaan and themselves Canaanites. The Greeks called them Phoenicians, after a word for palm trees, or *Phonikes*, meaning "red men"—perhaps for a red-to-purple dye and cloth the Phoenicians eventually sold all around the Mediterranean.

This purple dye of the Phoenicians was invented or discovered by Hercules Phoenicius and had been "appropriated to Princes" as far back as the reign of Ham, the son of Noah.[1] Ham was called Porphyrion, or Moloch, "a king wearing purple." This same Phoenician Hercules was also said to have sailed through the Strait of Gibraltar and to a place where he built a temple, Gadira or Gades or Tartessus (near present-day Cadiz, Spain). Some 300 or more years before Christ, Hercules would come to be regarded as an ancestor of Alexander of Macedon—the mythological Hercules, that is, who may or may not have been one and the same as the Phoenician Hercules.

The son of Noah, Ham, the one who wore the purple, was consecrated by both the Phoenicians and the Egyptians and was worshiped as a god.[2] His name would be known in many versions: Hamon, Amon, Amoun, Hammon, and so on. Phoenicia itself was believed to be near where the earth was repeopled after Noah's ark survived the flood. That would be in the area of Lebanon. Today Lebanese assert Noah's ark came to rest in their land; they have, they say, Noah's tomb. They also claim, as does Iraq, that their land held the Garden of Eden.

The Lebanese also have the ruins and Roman temples of Baalbek, a city said to have been built originally by Cain, and there is a coastal town, Byblos, where archeologists have found ruins as old as 1200 B.C.

In their religion the early Phoenicians had a devotion to plants, "the food that grows out of the ground," wrote Philo Herennius of Byblus (Byblos). They had consecrated plants to the sun, moon, and stars, "and other parts of the universe," he wrote, "which are their only known Gods." [3]

Not quite their only gods; the winds were others. The Phoenicians, as later would the Greeks and Romans, regarded the winds as divine beings. In an early Phoenician cosmogony, the *Cosmogony of Taautus*, the principle of the universe was a dark and windy air, or a wind made of dark air.

The Phoenicians' narrow strip of land was an infertile, rocky soil, a desert and mountain country not good for agriculture, and they had to seek food and goods elsewhere, by land or sea. They established routes to far places across the desert, caravan routes, for perfumes, glass, gems, and probably some spices. Along the routes they erected inscribed stones, perhaps the earliest road signs in history, to answer for camel drivers the eternal questions: Where am I? Which way should I go?

The Phoenicians may have been fishermen who used reed or papyrus rafts. Phoenician folklore said that a Phoenician had been the first sailor. The folklore named several first sailors. One was Usous; he stripped a tree and made a boat of it. Usous, who must have been an innovator, was said also to have wrapped around his body the skins of wild animals—and thus to have invented clothes. Other candidates for the first sailors were Agreus and Haleus; they developed fishing. Another candidate for first sailor was Vulcan, who was said to have invented the fishing line, hook, and bait. Vulcan was called by the Phoenicians Machinator, "inventor" or "engineer." Later the Romans adopted Vulcan and, with the Bronze Age well under way, made him god of the forge and of fire.

The Phoenicians also claimed two men, Misor and Sidye, who learned the use of salt. A descendant of Sidye was supposedly the first shipbuilder. The Phoenicians claimed that one of their number, Taautus, "found out the writing of the first letters"—the alphabet, and that a Phoenician, Dagon, "found out bread, corn and the plow"—agriculture.[4] They had a concept—accepted today, but unheard of in their day—that the earth itself shone out, like a sun, moon, or star, and might be visible from far out in space.

The Phoenicians learned seamanship in the countless bays of Greece. They learned how to use a broad, shallow square sail, and how to use rocks as ballast in their ships to prevent them from capsizing. They learned how to navigate by sun or stars, and by 2000 B.C. they were sailing away from shore

out of sight of land. They were to cross and crisscross the
Mediterranean, which would be their highway to the world.
They called it the Great Sea.

If the Phoenicians were not the first out of sight of land,
who was? There are many sailors who could have led the
way.

They could have been ancient Minoans or Philistines or
prehistoric folk migrating to the island of Crete from the
Middle East mainland. That passage could have been made
only by sea. Greek civilization began on Crete, in the Bronze
Age (which followed the Copper Age), long before it
traveled to mainland Greece.

In the second millennium before Christ, engraved seals
from Crete showed large ships moved by both sails and oars.

Even in the third millennium before Christ, Crete was
trading busily with Egypt. Minoan sailors, overlapping the
New Stone Age and the Bronze Age, on this route would
have had to sail beyond the horizon. The trip required, either
for oarsmen or early sailing ships, five or six days—most of
the time out of sight of land. Their ships carried pottery,
vases, statuettes, silver bowls, weapons, jewels, textiles, and
beautifully worked bronze. All these products went to Egypt,
Greece, Cyprus, Syria, and to the Greek islands, the
Cyclades. In shallow-draft freighters the Minoans exported to
Egypt cypress wood, wine, resins, and perhaps honey, and
olives and olive oil. For it was on Crete, about the time man
invented the wheel, that the wild olive, with its spreading
foliage and crooked trunk, was domesticated. It was turned
from an unproductive evergreen (belonging to the lilac,
jasmine, ash, and forsythia family) into a tree that produced
fruit for men. The fruit was used not only as food, but also in
medicine, cosmetics, soap, and oil. As a result, on Crete and

elsewhere the olive branch became the symbol of growth, prosperity, and peace.

The Minoan ships and others brought back to Crete metal, elephant ivory from Tyre, and shellfish from which the Minoans and the Tyrians (Phoenicians) both made a purple dye. They brought back papyrus, gold beads, stone bowls. They brought copper from Cyprus and they may have brought back back tin from as far as Spain to be used with copper to make bronze. The Minoans, says Viljhalmur Steffanson, became dominant on the Mediterranean, all the way to the Atlantic Ocean, before the Phoenicians did.[5]

By 1500 B.C. Minoan artists were painting on vases the first pictures of octopuses. Into other designs they worked cockles and nautiluses. One of their artists added something else to sea lore: a drawing on a Minoan seal of about 1600 B.C. shows a sailor battling an unidentified sea monster—the earliest depiction of such a creature that we have.[6]

The first out of sight of land could have been Greeks.

About 2700 or 2200 B.C., in the early Bronze Age, a ship sank near the small Greek island of Dhokos, one of the Cyclades Islands, at the entrance to a today-forgotten harbor. It was among the Cyclades that those ancient Greeks who were the first known voyagers in the eastern Mediterranean sailed. The ship was located in 1975 and is the oldest shipwreck ever found.

In the early Bronze Age, the very ancient Greeks were beginning to make artistic pottery and statuary which the Cyclades islanders exported. Fragments of large storage jars have been found at the wreck, as well as many jugs of all sizes and shapes, used for drinking and eating, and suggesting a large crew of a trading ship. Ballast stones have also been found, and on shore nearby, a previously unknown New Stone (Neolithic) Age and Bronze Age settlement.

Northern European as well as Mediterranean sailors traveled far: Bronze Age Irish gold ornaments have been dug up in France, Scotland, and Denmark. The ornaments certainly indicate long trade voyages by sea.

The first men out of sight of land could have been a people from the Rhineland, who had copper weapons and beaker-like drinking cups and are called the "beaker people." North of Scotland, the beaker people reached Mainland, the largest of the Orkney Islands, and put up two great circles of huge standing stones, the Ring of Brogar (Temple of the Moon) and the Standing Stones of Stenness (Temple of the Sun). There are other examples of the standing stones at Unst and Fetler on the Shetland Islands, northeast of Scotland. On most of the Orkneys there is a large stone standing alone. We do not know what it was for. Over a thousand years ago, or around 800 A.D., the Norsemen, or Vikings, arrived in these islands. They found the stones but did not know their purpose. The best the Norse could do was to call one of the great solitary stones the "stone of giants."

The first men out of sight of land could have been other northern Europeans, from the Alpine regions, Belgium, France. From the third millennium B.C. these folk migrated in wave after wave to the Orkney Islands, the Shetlands, the Hebrides, and the coast of Scotland. On Mainland by 2300 B.C., a mile from the beaker people's Temple of the Sun and Temple of the Moon, they built a temple, Maes Howe, of stone slabs up to 18½ feet long and three tons in weight. They fit the stones so accurately that in many places a knife blade cannot be slipped between them. These people knew the sun: on the shortest day of the year, the winter sun sends its last rays through a passageway at Maes Howe. On the longest day of the year, the sun rises spectacularly over a monolith about a mile to the southwest.

Sailors of King Hammurabi of Babylon could have sailed beyond the horizon. At least we know that about 2200 B.C. Hammurabi was trying to help his shipping trade. "I dug the canal of Sippara," says a record he left us, "to Sippara, and supported it with a wall of safety."

About the time the Temple of the Sun and the Temple of the Moon were constructed, the North Star changed. About 2300 B.C., the star nearest the North Pole was a faint one, Alpha Draconis. Then the polestar became one of the brightest in the sky, Polaris, or Alpha of the constellation Ursa Minor, the Little Bear. Polaris' light power is 47 times as great as the sun's.[7] But Polaris looks small because it is so far away from earth: 25 million times as far away from our solar system as is the sun from the earth.

Polaris is the star at the end of the tail of the Little Bear, or at the end of the handle of the Little Dipper. Today Polaris is less than one degree from the north celestial pole. Within 200 years it will be only 28 minutes away. It is therefore overhead of a man at the pole; if he looks straight up at it, it appears to stand still, while all the other stars in the sky move around it. If a man anywhere in the northern hemisphere (a sailor taking a sight, for example) looks at the North Star, it appears to stand still. Actually it travels in a small circle in the center of all the other stars. If a man as far south as the equator looks at Polaris, it is so low on the horizon that it is hard to take a sight on it; early sailors to the equator gave up on it and figured their positions from the noonday sun. Below the equator a man cannot see the North Star at all.

Polaris will not always be the North Star. In around 12,000 years Vega will take over its position.

More or less about the same time as the Phoenicians, the Minoans of Crete and the beaker people of the Rhineland, the first men out of sight of land might have been the Egyptians, sailing to Crete. Two model boats taken from tombs in Rifeh, Egypt, and brought to England by Professor Flinders Petrie, after a 1907–08 expedition, are of ships with oars instead of paddles. Each shows a mast, yards for a square sail, a cabin, and a broad oar for steering hung over the stern.

In Egypt about 2500 B.C., an artist recorded the building of a ship in wall paintings and reliefs in the tomb near Serapeum of a landowner and courtier named Ti.[8] The tools—the adze, hand ram, and paring chisel—and the shipbuilding itself are so far advanced that they suggest long experience at sea. Men must have been building ships for centuries before the art work at Serapeum was done.

The Greeks, who went to sea after tunny (tuna) among rocky Aegean islands (where the tunny weigh as much as 400 pounds apiece) also could have been the first. Here under good conditions the Greeks learned seamanship: tides were slight, winds moderate, currents mild, the sun shone. The islands are generally near each other, but some are far apart and out of sight.

Going farther back into history, it could have been sailors of an early pharaoh, Seneferu, or Snefru, or Snofru, about 2720 or 2650 B.C., who sent 40 or 60 large vessels, some 150 feet long, to Syria for cedarwood. The fleet's size suggests long experience at sailing the Mediterranean Sea. Today it is believed that Seneferu's sailors, who could have been Egyptians or Phoenicians, paddled, against contrary winds, northward up the coast of Syria. Coming back, loaded or towing logs in large floats, they would have had favorable winds. To get the fullest advantage of the winds, they might have sailed out of sight of land, then turned due south when their officers estimated they were off the mouth of the Nile.

The first out of sight of land could have been southern Europeans who reached northern Europe. Hundreds of

cromlechs and dolmens—burial chambers of large stones—
have been found in a line running from Sicily to Malta,
Spain, France, Guernsey and other Channel islands, to the
west coast of England and Scotland and on to the Orkney
and the Danish Faeroe Islands, remotely located in the ocean
between Denmark and Iceland.

These tombs often were built of four large stones placed in
the form of a box with a fifth large stone on the top. The
people who moved these big rocks could have been the same
as those who erected the 100-foot-diameter circle of great
stones at Stonehenge, on Salisbury Plain, perhaps as the New
Stone Age was ending in England.

On Guernsey, in the English Channel, the story has been
told over the centuries that fairies hid their treasure in the
cromlechs. But when people come seeking the treasure, it
turns into shells.

The sailors who around 2950 B.C. sailed in eight ships in
the first sea expedition of which we have definite knowledge
are further candidates. Sahure (or Sankhere), pharaoh of
Egypt, sent the vessels to Punt, or Pwnt, wherever that was.
It may have been in East Africa in today's Somaliland, or it
may have been past Africa's easternmost point, Cape
Guardafui (now called Ras Asir). The fleet sailed down the
Red Sea, and its people traded for panther skins, rhinoceros
horns, gold, ivory, gums, cinnamon, and plants useful in
embalming. Sahure's was one of the earliest botanical expeditions to collect plants and plant products. His ships could
either have hugged the coast or sailed out from it.

A plant still alive today began to grow about 2900 B.C. or
earlier, about when Sahure's ships sailed. A tree, a bristlecone
pine, began to grow in what today is the Wheeler Peak
region of eastern Nevada. It is still alive, around 4,900 years
old, shown by its tree rings to be the oldest living thing in the
world.

Or maybe it is not the oldest living thing: the bristlecone has competition. Apparently alive at the same time, maybe even longer ago, there were some slow-growing lichens still alive today. A lichen, a combination of fungus and algae, makes a slow, spreading growth—perhaps a centimeter in diameter increase in each century—on rocks or tree bark. A mountain species of lichen, *Rhizocarpon geographicum,* has no known limit to its life-span, which may run thousands of years. Some lichens alive today may have been living since before Sahure sent his vessels to Punt.

The first men out of sight of land could have been other northern Europeans. Perhaps as long ago as 2900 B.C. or earlier, the Stone Age people of Ireland, Wales, Scandinavia, Belgium, Holland, and Germany were paddling large seaworthy boats made of skins (perhaps walrus) stretched over a wooden or wicker framework. In Ireland such boats later were called "curraghs," in Wales, "carracks." The Babylonians also had circular skin boats with wicker frames that they used on rivers. The forefathers of the Vikings used these boats in deep waters off Norway to fish for cod, ling, and pollock—bones of these fish have been found at a Stone Age site near Stavanger, Norway. And, using the big fishhooks that have been found in prehistoric Norwegian sites, the Stone Age Vikings must have sailed 20 or 30 miles to sea. This would put them out of sight of the mainland, out of sight of any land except possibly some of the many islands off Norway.

Fragmentary ancient tales, vague, and perhaps myths and legends, suggest the possibility of men from India or China, sailing the entire Asian coast before 2000 B.C., and also knowing Japan and the East Indies, and maybe crossing the Pacific to Peru, then crossing South America and even reaching the West Indies.

Or, they could have been the people who settled in the Canary Islands, or the people who brought them. When the Portuguese reached and settled in the Canaries, in the 1300s and 1400s after Christ, they found there a people who did not know the use of boats. How this could be possible is one of the mysteries of the sea.

Either the people of the Canaries had been there so long they had forgotten boats, or they had been brought and left there by someone else. No one knows.

Or, they might have been the men who carried Valdivia pottery between Japan and Ecuador. Men may not have made many such trips, and they may even have been accidental, but the evidence that they were made comes from a kind of pottery, dated about 3000 B.C., that has been found in both Ecuador and Japan. In Ecuador, where it is called the "Valdivia pottery," it was discovered among the relics of gatherers of shellfish and wild plants. In southern Japan it was located among the relics of shellfish gatherers.

Both the Japanese and the Ecuadorean pottery are decorated with finger grooving, fingernail impressions, corrugation, shell stamping, and incisions. Both have finger-pressed rims and small feet.

Two archeologists of the Smithsonian Institution have reported that the similarities are striking and feel that "however radical it may seem to postulate a trans-Pacific contact as early as 3000 B.C., this is the only conclusion that adherence to the principles of comparative analysis will allow." [9] Large ships, known to exist at least before the first millennium B.C., Pacific typhoons, and currents to Ecuador from north, south, or west all could have helped bring the pottery and its makers across the world's widest ocean as long ago as 3000 B.C.

Meanwhile, in Peru and Bolivia other archeologists found linted cotton—possibly introduced from Asia about the same time. Hybridized with Peruvian cotton, it produces a distinctive cotton still cultivated and may be a further indication of trans-Pacific voyages in prehistoric times.[10]

Another nagging clue is that the sweet potato, discovered by Columbus in 1492, has been found by ocean explorers almost everywhere they have been: in Central and South America, and all across the Pacific—Easter Island, Hawaii, Polynesia, New Zealand, Indonesia, Malaysia, China, Japan. The sweet potato seeds might have been carried by the golden plover, a bird known to make long flights over the Pacific. Or they might have been carried by men in ships. The seeds certainly did not float across the sea, for they are killed by salt water.

The golden plover flies nonstop over the Pacific for incredible distances (2,050 miles from Alaska to Hawaii, then south 2,500 miles to the Marquesas, 500 to the Tuamotus) and could have led ancient dugout mariners to new islands. (In the Atlantic, the 11-inch-long American golden plover migrates from Nova Scotia to South America.)

The first open-sea voyagers could have been men from the Malay Peninsula or island dwellers of the South Pacific, men who lived near the vast open spaces of that ocean. Men certainly traveled hundreds of miles from island to Pacific island, often beyond the horizon, in outrigger dugout canoes.

These sailors, who may have started from the vicinity of today's Singapore, may have encountered assistance they could not have anticipated. The coconut could have fed them. Its milk could have provided them drink, its husk could have provided twine. The coconut is not killed by salt water and could have floated across the Pacific—many think it did. It was discovered on the Pacific shore of Mexico by the Spaniards in 1513 and later transplanted to the West Indies and South American countries.

Or perhaps Asians or Arabs traversing the Indian Ocean

and the Red Sea in early practical ships from which today's
dhows perhaps are descended may have been the first. They
may have run between India or Arabia and Africa. These
voyages can be made entirely along the coast, but, with
monsoon winds to help, they can be made out of sight of land
straight across the Indian Ocean.

The Egyptians could have been among the first, on rafts
made of papyrus, believed to have preceded even the oldest
ships in Egypt. The largest papyrus rafts could carry perhaps
three tons and, with a single sail, might cross an ocean. There
is evidence that they did, as rafts similar to those of ancient
Egypt are made today at Lake Titicaca in Bolivia. The
Norwegian Thor Heyerdahl, who studies the travels of man,
has twice in the 1970s crossed the Atlantic in rafts like those
of the Egyptians, so he has proved that the rafts can make the
voyage.

Or those first sailors might have been South Americans
crossing the Pacific. Many years earlier, Thor Heyerdahl
made a trip aboard the raft *Kon-tiki* from South America to
South Pacific islands to show that a raft trip was possible
westward across the Pacific.

The first out of sight of land might have been sailors who
lived at the same time as, or even before, the fishermen of the
Tagus River or the earliest Egyptians to devise a sail—10,000
B.C. or before. There is some evidence that a seafaring people
existed at that time. Shell mounds left by these people suggest
they ate shellfish as did the prehistoric Tagus River people.
Similar shell mounds have been found in many places in
Europe, Asia, and America—a distribution that suggests a
seagoing people capable of navigating long distances. Along
with the shell mounds have been found half a million skulls of
men whose measurements are similar around the world.
Shell-mound skulls from Alabama's Tennessee River bed
seem like others found in Spain, Japan, and other far-apart

places.[11] If these were indeed the same people, they probably made long-distance ocean journeys, perhaps even around the world.

There are two other possibilities. Archeologists from the University of Pennsylvania and Indiana University excavated a site in the Peloponnesus in Greece, where men lived: Franchti cave, on the southern part of the Bay of Argolis. Obsidian tools were found. It was determined that the obsidian dated from about 10,000 B.C. It appears to have come from either the island of Melos or the Cyclades, 120 kilometers away, or from the island of Giali, 280 kilometers off the coast of Turkey. The shortest distance in this area between islands—between landfalls—is 50 kilometers.

Finally, the ancestors of the Norsemen or Vikings are a possibility. Rock carvings from Stone Age northern Norway show boats as do other rock drawings along the Scandinavian coastlines. A professor at Oslo has pointed to the thousands of islands of Norway. "It must," he said, "be ten thousand years at least since the hunting tribes of Finmark, of the Helgoland-Fosna coast and of Ostfold journeyed along the coast and out upon the deep sea which furnished a great part of their livelihood." [12] Ocean fishermen as well as hunters supported man in preagricultural days in Scandinavia. Near Stavanger, Norway, in a Stone Age site, there were found the bones of Greenland seals and porpoises and deep-water fish (ling, pollock, and cod) as well as fishhooks for deep water and sinkers for use in up to 90-fathom depths. All this suggests that Stone Age Vikings fished well out in the windy, stormy, foggy North Atlantic, where the weather can change in a flash and a loaded fishing boat could have a problem getting to harbor.

Wherever it took place, and no matter how many times it occurred, when men for the first time sailed out of sight of

land (at least so far as they knew), they must have done it in
boats very low in the water, such as that hollowed-out log,
the Brigg boat. Such a boat could be swamped by any high
wave.

And men must have done it in wicker boats no better than
large baskets, susceptible to leaks and waves.

Or they did it on rafts, such as the log raft found near the
Brigg boat or the Egyptians' papyrus rafts. In either case the
sea would constantly have swept over the raft and up through
the raft's wide cracks.

However it was done, to venture away from shore took
courage.

Whoever they were, the Phoenicians or the beaker people
or any of the others, the first mariners ever to venture of their
own free will out onto open sea were among the greatest
pioneers man has produced. Their giant leap forward—a leap
that may have been made separately, a number of times, by a
number of these peoples—was equivalent to the leaps forward
made by the men who learned how to read the stars, to travel
on the water, to use fire and copper, to use the land through
agriculture, and who in the last third of the twentieth century
went to the moon.

Once man was free of the land, he never would be the
same again.

10

After 2000 B.C.:
On His Way

WHOEVER THEY WERE, the earliest sailors beyond the horizon, they sailed out of sight of land a long time ago. Perhaps it is a myth that the first sailors hugged the shore as some think. The perils of rocks and shoals and onshore winds were always great. Perhaps sailors in small ships always have had an ability to know where they were without observations or instruments. Today a Mexican fisherman in the Gulf of California (between Mexico and Baja California) ventures out of sight of land with no instruments, not even a watch, and gets home safely. Says one authority: "Nothing is more sure, by whatever means they achieved it, than that the sailors of all ages have navigated in deep waters." [1]

However they began, sailing the open sea men sailed ahead into the unknown. Often the unknown measured up to their fears. Beyond the horizon were the worst winds, fogs, waves, and storms that men had ever encountered. Men were drowned. Seasickness made them wish they were dead. They ran into calms with no wind at all, when wind was necessary for survival. They encountered tides and currents that were dangerous to their awkward ships. And as the first men to ride logs down jungle rivers were sometimes eaten by crocodiles, so men at sea sometimes were eaten by sharks.

With a sail, a man could for the first time go far. He no longer was dependent for transportation on his own muscles, those of animals, or a river's current. The sail changed the ship from a short-range vehicle into a long-range one.

On the ocean, his highway to everywhere, a man in a sailing ship could keep going for weeks, not just days. He became a far traveler. He sailed till he ran out of drinking water and perished of thirst, or till he ran low on proper food and his gums swelled from scurvy and he could no longer eat, and starved and died. If he reached land at all, he could be shipwrecked on a barren island, far from home and beyond any hope of rescue. If he reached a populated shore, the people at best would be strangers, and at worst would be armed foes or cannibals. Still man sailed ahead.

He might encounter disaster, as did the shipwrecked sailor, about 1700 B.C., who left a record for us: "Then the ship perished, and of them that were in it not one survived." Except for the lucky sailor who was talking. "And I was cast on to an island by a wave of the sea." On the island the sailor found "figs . . . vines . . . leeks, fruit and cucumbers . . . fish and fowl; everything was there." [2]

His ship, he recalled, had been 180 feet long by 60 feet wide—a large one, huge for her day. Her crew was 120 men. She was sailing the Red Sea when a storm struck her. The sailor was eventually rescued by a vessel belonging to a pharaoh of Egypt. His account is the first story by a shipwrecked man on record. We do not know his name.

The oceans sometimes were friendly. The Greeks called the Mediterranean *Ho Pontos*, "the road" or "passage." When they reached the Black Sea, they called it *Ho Pontos Euxinde*, "the sea kindly to guests."

There still are seas to explore. Below the South Sea islands there is an area of the Pacific so vast, with not so much as a rock breaking the surface, that it could cover all of Russia. Late in the 1970s men aboard oceanographic vessels are exploring this little-known ocean area.

One thing the sailor found in midocean, to his surprise, were birds. Far at sea, watching the flight of a migrating bird or a flock of birds, the sailor very early was aware that they crossed oceans. Stories grew up about them. On Guernsey Island, in the English Channel, there was a legend from times shadowy in history that the robin first brought fire to the island. Flying across the sea with a torch in his beak, he burned his breast red.[3]

So with ships, the product of their hands, brains, eyes, and experience, and with wind in their sails to move the ships, and with the sun and stars to steer by, struggling but capable men went to sea, then out of sight of land and beyond the horizon.

Their voyages never would cease.

11

About 1500 B.C.:
Voyage to an Unknown Shore

SENNEMUT.

Nihisi.

Thuti.

These are the earliest sailors in history—so far as I can learn from my research—whose names we know.

We know other details besides their names. They were Egyptians, sent by Queen Hatshepsut in a fleet of ships south down the Red Sea, then on a long journey to a country unknown to us. Unlike many a sailor in those days, they came home safely.

Their successful journey was such an awesome event that Hatshepsut had a carving made at Deir al-Bahri, Egypt, to tell people about it. Inscriptions with the relief provide more information.

Hatshepsut is one of the very few people from so far back in history—about 3,500 years ago—of whom it can be said that you can see her now. Her face is upon the head of a sphinx at New York City's Metropolitan Museum of Art. It is a serene face, with fine features. She was probably slight and slim, maybe 80 pounds in weight and about 5 feet tall. We have the measurements of her people, because we have located the mummies of many Egyptian kings and queens, though we have not found Hatshepsut's.

About 1500 B.C., one might have seen Hatshepsut lying prostrate, nose to the ground, arms outstretched, in a vast stone cavern, the Great Temple, its darkness broken by sparkling jewels and silver and gold. There would Hatshepsut pray to her god, the god of Egypt, Amon. There she probably asked him to help her in what she later thought was her greatest achievement: to send the fleet on its expedition overseas.

Long before her, King Metuhotep I of Egypt had sent an expedition to Punt; so had the pharaoh Sahure. She planned a similar voyage.

Hatshepsut collected five ships. Each, according to the carving at Deir al-Bahri, had both oars and sail. To take charge of the fleet, she assigned her loyal steward, Sennemut, as commander. His co-commanders were Nihisi and Thuty.

The ships look about 70 to 100 feet long, 17 to 25 feet in beam, possibly 3 feet 6 inches in draught, able to carry perhaps 80 tons of cargo. Earlier Egyptian ships had the mast near the bow; these each have a mast moved back amidships, a more efficient position.

Queen Hatshepsut and many of the citizens of Thebes were at the wharf to watch the ships leave. The barge of Amon, the god, was also there. A strong wind filled the sails of the ships. They moved up the Nile. Then the ships went through a waterway, or canal, that had perhaps been built by a pharaoh named Sesostris, and that then existed from the Nile to the Red Sea. Surprisingly, 3,500 years ago, ancient man had built a canal that allowed ships to travel to and from the Red Sea and the Mediterranean, his equivalent of the Suez Canal.

Down the Red Sea coast for 1,500 miles Hatshepsut's ships went. One way we can trace their route is by the sea animals shown beside ships in the carvings—Nile River animals or Red Sea animals or fish, for instance. They traveled slowly, by today's standards, at a knot or two. But in Hatshepsut's time, ships and chariots were the fastest vehicles.

After a voyage beyond the Red Sea of 400 miles or so, we believe Hatshepsut's capable sailors reached Punt. There Sennemut erected a statue of Hatshepsut, long since lost beneath the sand or soil somewhere on the East African coast. Or so we suppose, for as already stated, modern research has not yet positively identified Punt.

The relief at Deir al-Bahri shows Punt as a place of domed grass huts on stilts in a marshland, surrounded by trees— ebony, sycamore, palm, and myrrh—and longhorn and shorthorn cattle.

Sennemut traded necklaces, hatchets, and daggers for a cargo of goods that, when he brought them back, would have pleased any woman and did please Queen Hatshepsut: ebony, ivory, gold, eye cosmetics, apes, monkeys, dogs, a live lion and lion skins, small cattle, cinnamon wood, 31 live heavy myrrh trees in tubs, and myrrh.

The gum of a thorny East African shrub, myrrh was the rarest and most fragrant incense. Hatshepsut used it in lotions and perfumes and many medicines were made from it. Her sailors also brought back another aromatic resin, frankincense, and frankincense trees were established in her garden. Myrrh and frankincense would be brought by the wise men, 1,500 years later, as a gift for the infant Jesus. They grow two places: in Africa and across the Gulf of Aden in Arabia. Partly because of frankincense and myrrh, the Romans at the time of Christ would call the Arabians "the wealthiest race," and the southern part of their peninsula *Arabia Felix*, "Fortunate Arabia."

Of the rich cargo brought back to Hatshepsut, the text with the relief at Deir al-Bahri says: "Never did the like happen under any gods who were since the beginning." Hatshepsut gave her thanks to the god Amon.

According to at least one modern writer, she received something else from the trip: peacocks.

Since peacocks are not native to Africa as were all the other things the ships brought back but live far away, across the Indian Ocean, in India and Ceylon, how did Hatshepsut's commander, Sennemut, get them?

My guess is that the African coast already was trading with India or Ceylon. We know that there were very early trade routes between India and Africa; sea voyages could be made between them entirely along the coasts.

What Hatshepsut received could have been chickens instead of peacocks. We think chickens came from domesticating wild fowl in India, perhaps by 3200 B.C. and surely by 2000 B.C. Both chickens and peacocks are pheasants; indeed, the peacock has been called a glorified chicken. Immediately after Hatshepsut, the king of Egypt, Thothmes III, had a hen (which presumably came from India) that regularly provided him fresh eggs.

One of the pictures at Deir al-Bahri shows a man standing at the bow of a ship with a single sail and 15 oarsmen to a side. He is measuring the depth of the water by means of a long rod, or pole. It was used in shallow water, in harbor, for instance. So far as I know, this is the oldest picture we have that shows a tool of any kind used by a sailor—the earliest-known aid to navigation. To measure the depth of deeper water, in Hatshepsut's time, vines might have been tied together, weighted with a rock, and let down over the side.

The sailor was beginning to get for his own use some of

the tools that the capable hands of man always have made to help him do a job.

Another picture shows a monkey walking along a cable—exactly what a monkey does on board ship.

Hatshepsut's has been considered man's earliest effort to send a fleet of powerful ships far away from home. It may have been that. Hatshepsut's sailors ventured into unknown waters. But they did more: Sennemut, Nihisi, and Thuti appear to have brought most or all of their men home. With concern for their crews, not by sacrificing them, they completed the voyage.

Hatshepsut's ships were so weak that each one needed a cable stretched taut from stem to stern to prevent the hull from flexing.

"At about the same date [as Queen Hatshepsut's fleet]," writes Nicholas C. Flemming, "the Phoenicians devised a brilliant technique. They built a wooden frame of ribs and stringers onto which light planking could be fixed, thereby reducing the weight, increasing the rigidity, and improving the shape of their vessels." The framework made their ships stronger, better, more able to stand up to longer voyages and rougher seas. Man's tool, the ship, thus was vastly improved. "From that time," says Flemming, "the Phoenicians were destined to be the greatest sea power in the ancient world." [1]

Also about Hatshepsut's time an Egyptian citizen named Amenemhet produced the earliest timepiece known, a water clock. A water clock keeps time by measuring the water that escapes from one vessel into another. The sundial by day and the water clock by night would lead in Egypt to the division of the 24-hour day into two periods, a 12-hour day and a 12-hour night.

The very idea that time might be measured would be of utmost importance to sailors. Over the next few thousand

years, man slowly would develop timepieces—sand glasses of
the kind used by Columbus, watches, clocks, chronometers—
that would measure time more and more accurately. They
would be, like the pole to measure water depth, aids to
navigation.

They eventually would help a sailor have an idea how far
he had traveled and would shed some light on the questions:
Where am I? Which way should I go?

ABOVE The very first man to become a sailor was probably a struggling prehistoric hunter who floated down a river on a log. In time,
men covered wicker baskets with skins like these British coracles
about 2900 B.C. (From *The Pictorial History of England*, 1838)

BELOW Over 2000 years B.C., perhaps in ships with a single sail, a
people traveled from the Mediterranean all the way to Britain and
left tombs along the coasts like this one in Kent. (From *The Pictorial History of England*, 1838)

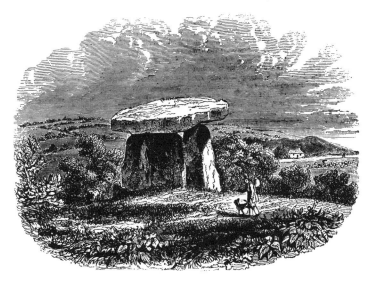

ABOVE A bas-relief from the Abusir Pyramids, near Cairo, from 2600 or 2950 B.C. This is one of the first known pictures of ships, and shows King Sahure's, which made the first known expedition. (The Science Museum, London)

BELOW A detail from the bas-relief. Lacking a keel to anchor a single mast, the Egyptians used a double mast that folded down. They at first used paddles, then added a single sail, then oars. Three paddles (right) are the rudder. (The Science Museum, London)

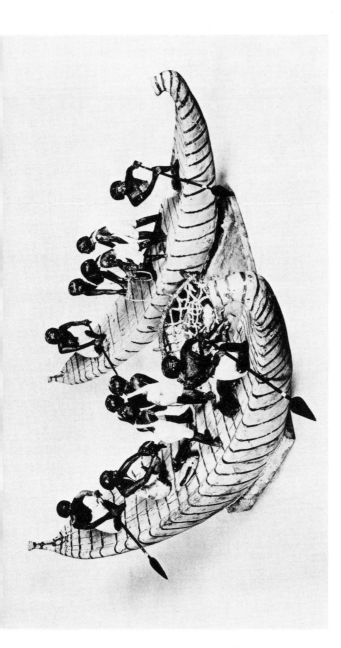

A model of Egyptian fishing canoes (2000 B.C.) made of papyrus, a reed growing in their marshes. (The Science Museum, London)

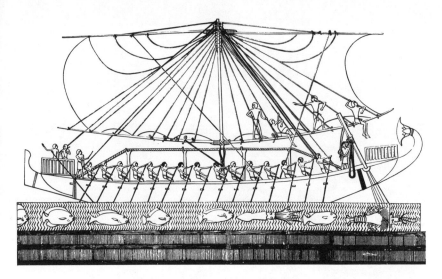

Two details of Egyptian ships of the Punt Expedition about 1600 or 1500 B.C., from a carving at Deir el-Bahari, Egypt. Above, at left, a man measures depth with a pole. This is the earliest known picture of an aid to navigation. (The Science Museum, London). Below, men are shown loading the ship with some of the rich cargo that was carried back to Queen Hatshepsut. (New York Public Library)

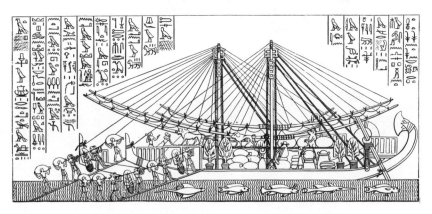

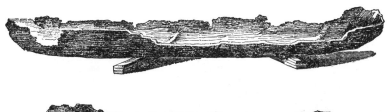

ABOVE By 1500 B.C., men using scrapers or fire were adept at hollowing out logs for small boats and then for ocean-going craft. In the eighteenth and nineteenth centuries, boats like these (in Sussex, England) were found in many places. (From *The Pictorial History of England*, 1838)

BELOW From the Minoan civilization on the island of Crete, which ended about 1480 B.C., is this fresco of a ship found in Thera, in 1973. It has a single sail ready for sea, double steering oars, and side weather cloths rigged. (Thomas Gillmer, Annapolis, Maryland)

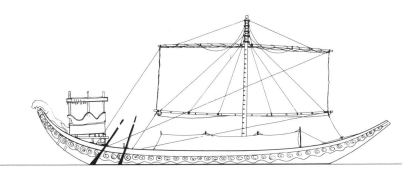

ABOVE About 800 or 900 B.C., men were beginning to be able to explore beneath the sea by breathing air from bags of skin, as shown in this bas-relief from Assyria. (New York Public Library)

BELOW A bas-relief, now in the Louvre, showing Assyrian ships transporting cedar logs from Phoenicia around 700 B.C. (New York Public Library)

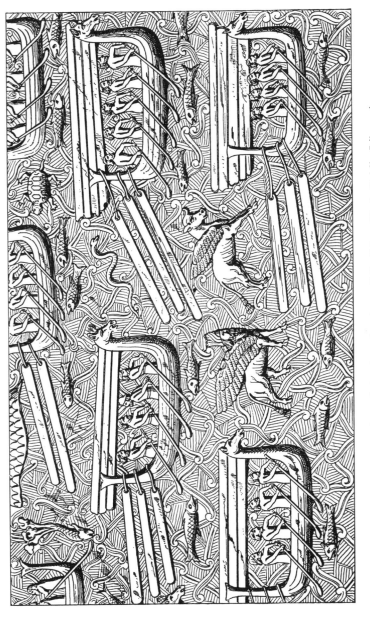

A drawing showing another section of the Assyrian bas-relief. (New York Public Library)

ABOVE A model of a Phoenician war galley from around 700 B.C. An advanced ship, it had a single sail with purple stripes and was assisted by oars. Two oars (left) were the rudder. Ram (right) could sink an enemy. (British Crown Copyright, The Science Museum, London)

BELOW An Assyrian ship from about 700 B.C. also shows ram (left) and two steering oars (right). Oars for propulsion are in two banks. Men on top deck are soldiers; their shields hang at their sides. The single sail is furled as oars move ship. (The Science Museum, London)

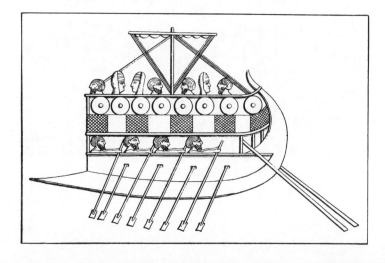

12

About 1500 B.C.:
Incidental Cargo

SAILORS CANNOT HELP but collect new information as they travel. Sailors visiting many ports cannot help but distribute the knowledge they collect.

Knowledge of geography, for instance. Hatshepsut's sailors brought back to Egypt information about Punt. In the Mediterranean Sea, the Phoenicians, sailing ever westward and searching for landmarks, located, for example, the volcanic mountain, 2,500 feet high, on the island of Pantelleria between Sicily and North Africa.

The Phoenicians sailed beyond the horizon—time and again to places where no one had been before. They took the information they collected to many ports. They crossed and crisscrossed the Mediterranean. In time, they had more ships on the Mediterranean than anyone else. Eventually, they went beyond the farthest horizon in the Mediterranean— through the Strait of Gibraltar, westward into the Atlantic, where they may have turned both north and south. But their voyages on the Atlantic are very shadowy to us today.

Far travelers for their time, the last two thousand years

before the Christian era began, the Phoenicians spread a kind of knowledge not usually credited to seafarers. Yet it is vital to us today.

To ports of Greece the Phoenicians brought an alphabet— the alphabet that became the Greek alphabet, then the basis of all Semitic and northern European alphabets. The word "alphabet" comes from names of the first two Greek letters, alpha and beta.

The Greeks owed it to the Phoenicians. The Phoenicians presumably had been influenced by such earlier writing as that of the Cretans, with 90 written signs, and that of the Babylonians and Egyptians, hieroglyphics, or picture writing, which had a separate symbol for every word—an incredibly awkward written language.

According to language teacher Charles Berlitz, the Phoenicians as they sailed along needed to keep a record of the days. They developed a sign for each day of the 28 days between the nights of the full moon. These eventually provided 28 letters, the number originally in many European languages. English, for example, has lost two of its letters from the Phoenicians' original symbols for days.

Another source of the Phoenician alphabet is said to be the signs they developed for use in bookkeeping records of their trade.

At any rate, the Phoenicians, who had put up man's first known road signs for their camel-caravan drivers, spread the alphabet around Europe, and thus brought an incidental cargo.

It was an alphabet that used the same symbol always to represent the same sound in any word—a system of letters. This system, Mr. Berlitz points out, invented consonants and vowels—the most practical base, he believes, on which to found a useful, flexible alphabet for spoken and written language.

In ancient times, as in primitive groups today, man's only source of knowledge was what he heard spoken by other men. The alphabet changed men's lives by making possible the written word. The written word would make it easier to pass along all kinds of information and knowledge.

From the name of one of the Phoenicians' principal towns, Byblos (now in Lebanon), the word "bible," meaning book, was derived. And from the name of a legendary Phoenician princess, Europa, the mother of Zeus of Minos, came the names of Europa Point and Great Europa Point at the tip of Gibraltar—and the name Europe for the continent above Gibraltar.

On the south coast of Lebanon in the summer of 1971, Dr. James B. Pritchard found a tiny scarab-shaped stone carved with the Phoenician letters "s r p t," standing for the name of the Phoenician city Sarepta. On a fragment of a storage jar, he found 6 letters scratched in alphabetical order. Looking backwards through thousands of years, Dr. Pritchard felt as though he were looking over the shoulder of a Phoenician schoolboy or girl, who, presumably, was learning the alphabet and scratched the letters there on the jar—one of the first pupils in history ever to learn the ABC's.[1]

In 1972 Dr. Pritchard was back at Sarepta. This time he dug up the first Phoenician temple yet found, a 12-by-24-foot limestone structure. It provided a hint that the Phoenicians were capable but struggling. Capable enough to devise an alphabet and to sail all the Great Sea (the Mediterranean) and beyond, they nevertheless used charms to help them along. Dr. Pritchard found figures of the Egyptian god Horus and of the god Thorth and other figurines of the Phoenician goddess of love and fertility, Astarte.

13

The Ancient World, 1500-930 B.C.: Some Surprising Achievements

By ABOUT 3,500 YEARS AGO, the achievements of ancient man were astonishing. To judge from rock carvings of ships about that old, found in Norway, he was putting to sea in vessels with sails or with as many as 50 oarsmen. We do not know what these ships were like in detail, but so many are shown in the rock carvings as to indicate a long and active seafaring history on the part of the people who made them.

By between 1400 B.C., or not long after, men in Asia were beginning to try to raise fish themselves instead of only fishing for them in the ocean. In Java, under Hindu influence, fish were raised in brackish water. In Asia, from then until today, men have raised their own carp, goldfish, and tilapias, mainly in fresh water. In the 1970s men are attempting to raise their own fish and finding it a difficult thing to learn.

About January 1343 B.C., the young King Tutankhamen of Egypt was dead. His magnificent tomb—uncovered in the twentieth century by Great Britain's Howard Carter and Lord Carnarvon—contained over two thousand objects, many of them treasures. One statuette shows a man in the act

of harpooning. A model of a ship, carved out of a single block
of wood, shows the high prow and stern characteristic of
Egyptian ships, and an oar on each side of the stern as a
rudder.

About 1200 B.C., the Philistines and their allies joined in a
group called "Peoples of the Sea." They invaded Egypt, and
in the Nile delta a naval battle took place. The battle is shown
in a relief in a temple at Medinet Habu, west of Thebes.

The Sea Peoples, with daggers and lances as weapons,
could fight only at close quarters. The Egyptians, on the
other hand, had what probably was the earliest mechanical
device man ever invented, the bow, which they had had
handed down to them by Paleolithic (Old Stone Age)
hunters. The bow stores up the energy gradually expended
by an archer's muscles and releases the energy in a single
burst; it was an early step toward today's era of machines.
During the battle, when the wind died, the Egyptians, with
their bows and arrows, could fight from a distance.

In the Medinet Habu relief, the ships of the Sea Peoples
have high prows and sterns; they have sails—but no rowers.
The Egyptian ships have oarsmen. The rowers sit at a level
with the bulwarks. When the wind died and after firing their
arrows, the Egyptians could row up to the fleet of the Peoples
of the Sea and capsize their boats. The Egyptians, under
Rameses III, won the battle.

Jagged, sawtooth cliffs rise from the bottom of the sea to
form the edges of an island off Cape Gelidonya, Turkey.
Today boats of sponge divers are likely to smash against the
rocks. Around 1200 B.C. a ship was wrecked there, a
Phoenician ship, five hundred years older than any other that
divers had previously located on the bottom.

The first diver to the ancient wreck, 90 feet down off Cape
Gelidonya, was a sponge diver who spied a bit of metal here

and there. When eventually George F. Bass and a team of undersea archeologists excavated the wreck, they found the ballast stones the Phoenicians had learned to use; these indicated a vessel about 35 feet long carrying perhaps a ton of cargo. The cargo was mostly copper ingots, the earliest ever found, many with handles, and among the ingots there was white powdery tin oxide. Copper ingots and tin oxide were the ingredients for making bronze. Bronze implements were found, many of them broken—knife blades, mirrors, bowls. At one spot the divers found what they thought were the captain's personal belongings: a crescent-blade razor, stone mace heads or hammers, a Syrian cylinder seal to stamp official documents, five scarabs, a merchant's balance-pan weights, whetstones for sharpening tools, and an oil lamp. There were sheep's knucklebones—perhaps used in a game like crap shooting. The scarabs, mace heads, and cylinder seal were found to date from about 1200 B.C. So was some pottery found nearby. There were traces of the last meal of almost 3,200 years ago: olive pits and what probably were the bones of fowl or fish. A study of Egyptian tomb paintings showed that copper ingots like those found were depicted on ships from Tyria—Phoenician ships. The bronze instruments appeared to come from Tyria rather than Greece. The scarabs also appeared to be Phoenician. Bass therefore concluded the ship was Phoenician. And the status of the bronze objects in it suggested that the Phoenicians of 1200 B.C. were much farther advanced into the Bronze Age than had been thought.[1]

After the destruction of Troy (date uncertain, but perhaps farther back than 1000 B.C., maybe as far back as 1200 B.C., the time of the sinking of the Phoenician ship), King Menelaus of Sparta may have made one of the striking voyages of man's history: westward through the Strait of

Gibraltar, southward down the African coast, then around Africa to its eastern coast, and, either along the coast or blown direct by monsoon winds, eastward to India. If Menelaus made this trip, it would be the first known voyage around Africa and to India.[2]

About the uncertain time of the siege of Troy, a captain named Jason may have taken a ship, the *Argo*, from the harbor of Iolcus (near modern Volos) in northeastern Greece. His crew went down in history, mythology, and poetry, as the sailors of the *Argo*, the Argonauts. The *Argo*, said to have had 50 oars, made (if she made it) the earliest trip of exploration on record. If she actually had the name *Argo*, she is also the earliest vessel to be named of which I can find any record.

She sailed, according to ancient tales, eastward across the Aegean Sea, then through the Dardanelles and Bosporus and into the Black Sea. In the Black Sea, Jason and his Greeks would at the time have been off the known map of the world, in unknown waters. His trip, which was regarded as fact by Homer and Pindar, was also regarded as an important step in opening the Black Sea to Greek ships.

Jason and the Argonauts sailed on east along the north coast of Asia Minor. Each night they pulled up on the beach unless the population was hostile; then they slept at their oars. They ended at a place they called Aea, a Greek word that meant simply "land." Later Greeks said Aea was Colchis, in the far eastern corner of the Black Sea. There the king's daughter, Medea, fell in love with Jason and ran away with him. Returning to Greece, Jason may have coasted along the north shore of the Black Sea—southern Russia. He told of wandering rocks, moving cliffs, which could have been ice floes off southern Russia—something that would have been entirely new to the sailors from the warmer Greece.[3]

Jason was said to have been seeking the golden fleece, but

what the golden fleece was is not positively known. It could have been the golden wool of a sheep of the eastern Black Sea area; it could have been gold itself, found in a river in the area; it could have been grain from the Crimea; it could even have been golden clouds that would end a drought in Greece. Whatever it may have been, and wherever the land of Aea may have been, and whatever Jason's routes going and coming, Jason—assuming he was real and not a fiction—was the earliest ocean explorer whose name we know.

About 930 B.C. under Pharaoh Sheshonk I, Solomon (the one with the biblical reputation for wisdom) employed a Phoenician, Hiram of Tyre, to provide shipwrights, pilots, and seamen for a Phoenician fleet on the Red Sea to sail to Ophir. Where was Ophir? It may have been as far away as the west coast of India, the Malabar coast. It may have been Yemen in southern Arabia or Zanzibar in Africa. It may have been Sofala, on the coast of East Africa, then ruled by the Ethiopian queen Sabea, or Sheba. The fleet could have sailed farther, and some men have asserted, because it was away three years, that it reached Peru and returned—something very difficult to believe. The fleet brought back to Solomon riches that appear to be African and Asian: ivory, silver, gold, precious stones, red sandalwood, spices, monkeys, and peacocks.

With other fleets, Solomon imported chariots from Egypt and horses from Asia Minor.

14

900 B.C.?
Sailors' Tales

AMONG THEIR OTHER ACHIEVEMENTS the Phoenicians began
Western literature. Having given man an alphabet, they
provided tales for him first to listen to, and later to read.

As the Phoenicians sailed the Mediterranean, they encountered competition from Cretan, Egyptian, and Greek sailors.
They didn't want to help the competition, so instead of
telling the world about the useful information they learned—
winds, currents, tides, depths, trade routes, snug harbors, and
landmarks—they kept quiet, and told instead horror stories,
about Scylla, a 6-headed, 12-footed monster which ate
seamen; or about Charybdis, which caused huge whirlpools;
or sirens who lured sailors to destruction (the sirens may have
grown over thousands of years of retelling into mermaids).

A (perhaps) blind Greek poet named Homer picked up
the Phoenicians' tales and put them into a long poem, the
Odyssey, which, along with his story of the Trojan war, the
Iliad, began Western literature. In the *Odyssey* Homer
describes the normal conditions for voyages of the time, as
recounted by the Phoenicians: storms, sea monsters, narrow

straits, shipwrecks, even Lamians—today's man-eating great white sharks of Australian waters and all oceans.

Homer's sailor, Odysseus in Greek, Ulysses in Latin, travels on a ship with a mast and a sail, uses an oar to steer by, and steers with his eye on the Great Bear, which "wheels round and round where it is and never takes a bath in the ocean." By Homer's time, the sailor was accustomed to venturing out of sight of land. On a Phoenician ship, Odysseus did: "No . . . land, nor anything but sky and water was to be seen."

On his 10-year wandering in the *Odyssey*, Odysseus often was trying to learn, to gain evidence and information. In particular, he tried to understand the sea and its mysteries and unfamiliar aspects. This seeking of knowledge was a frame of mind that over the centuries would prove vital to all sailors and all men.

Homer, who may have lived between 900 and 700 B.C., may have been a rhapsode, a public reciter who spoke his words out loud. Or, because the Greeks in Homer's time were taking over the Phoenician alphabet and adapting it to Greek, perhaps he wrote down some of his poetry. He called the ocean "deep-moving" and the Mediterranean "wine-dark." He called the tides "the ebb and flow of the sea."

Except for the Great Bear, which "keeps turning around in place," Homer said the stars followed the course of the sun. He mentioned many constellations, including the Pleiades and Orion; naming of stars in his day was obviously well advanced. As for the course of the sun, he thought that it rose out of the sea and sank into it; how the sun returned to its starting point each morning he does not say. He mentioned four winds, which came from north, south, east, and west—but did not mention the compass directions, the names of which apparently did not exist. Homer thought the world was flat and circular—the horizon, when a man stood on a high point, appeared circular—and was surrounded by Oceanus, a continually flowing current. The sky was a concave vault resting on the edge of the earth like a lid.

Basically this was the Greek idea of the small, limited universe that consisted of the visible earth, around the land, the visible sea, and the sun, moon, and stars and what a man could see in the dome-shaped sky above him.

Psalm 104:25, agreeing with Homer that the ocean was big, but appearing to drop Homer's idea that it was a land-encircling river, calls the ocean, "this great and wide sea." Today's astronauts, including Colonel Frank Borman on the first trip to orbit the moon, echo Homer and Psalm 104 and tell us that "this great and wide sea" makes the entire globe a blue planet.

Homer mentioned sticks of wood aboard ship, but no one knows what the wood was for. From the Phoenician vessel sunk off Gelidonya, Turkey, George Bass and his divers brought up pieces of wood and concluded they were a cushion, or shock absorber, used between the heavy cargo and the thin planks of the ship.

Homer's *Iliad* told of crews of 20, 50, and even 120 rowers. It told of divers seeking oysters, a step by men on their journey under the sea.

In the *Iliad*, Homer represented the Trojan hero Paris as "having sailed over the broad sea" to Phoenicia, where he bought Phoenician goods. The poem refers to Thebes in Egypt as wealthy. Obviously, therefore, Greece in Homer's day had contact with Egypt.

Homer knew Phoenicia and Egypt as civilized countries. But he mentions none of the other Middle Eastern countries, such as Assyria, Babylonia, Chaldea, Media, or Persia. He does mention pygmies in the interior of Africa, information that probably reached the Greeks from Egypt and which was finally proved true by European explorers in the 1800s.

He mentioned what he called the Islands of the Blessed: "By deep-eddying Ocean," where lived "happy heroes for whom the grain-giving fields bear rich honey-sweet fruit thrice in a year." This heaven on earth the Greeks eventually identified as the Canary Islands. For centuries after Homer, Greek sailors and others searched and searched for a Utopia beyond the seas.

15

900-600 B.C.:
Progress in Science

BETWEEN THE TIME of Homer and the lifetime of Christ, ancient man took some big steps forward in his journey over and under the sea. At the time of Homer or shortly after, off Assyria, divers, who could hold their breath for perhaps two minutes, were doing something surprisingly modern. Some of them were using underwater breathing apparatus. A relief shows the divers with a new tool: an inflated animal skin serving as an air tank. An inflated skin is belted to a diver's stomach and chest; an air tube runs to his mouth.

And a ninth-century B.C. picture shows Assyrian divers using animal bladders as water wings. They are crossing a stream and apparently know how to swim—in those days probably still a very uncommon ability.

Of all the achievements of ancient man, none perhaps is more astonishing than that the Phoenicians, probably after they were sailing the open sea, were well on their way to becoming marine scientists. From three sea snails, the Phoenicians of Tyre, or Tyrians (today the word has become

Syrians), obtained and made a dye in a process that was complicated chemistry. The Tyrians first lowered long ropes overboard along which were traps baited with mussels and frogs. These attracted and caught the mollusks: the 2- to 3-inch-long banded dye murex and spiny dye murex, and the smaller rock shell.

Each of these sea snails produced only one or two drops of dye, and 60,000 had to be gathered to produce one pound. The glands containing the dye were taken out of the two larger snails and thrown together. The entire smaller mollusks, the rock shells, were tossed in. Salt was added. This mishmash rotted under the sun 3 or 4 days. The resulting pulp was heated by steam from a distant boiler, impurities were skimmed off, and after 10 days, 8,000 pounds of pulp became 500 pounds of dye.

The dye, which became known as Tyrian purple, could produce either crimson or purple cloth. It was one of two or three dyes that would not run or fade, and it became—with the possible exception of rare metals and jewels—the most expensive item in the ancient world. A woman's scarf dyed with it would have cost the equivalent of $900 today. The rich purple became a symbol of privilege and excellence. The dye was used by wealthy Greeks and by Romans for stripes on the togas of magistrates and later of senators and emperors.

From about the 900s to the 700s B.C., because of the trade in the dye and in purple cloth, Tyre was the principal port on the Mediterranean Sea. The Tyrians established a number of colonies, including Palermo in Sicily; Tarshish, or Tartessus, past Gibraltar on the Atlantic coast of Spain, near today's Cadiz; and, near present-day Tunis and convenient to wheat fields, a town called New City, or Kart-hadshat, which would command the sea passage between the eastern and western Mediterranean. Other men would call it Carthage.

The Phoenicians peddled their Tyrian purple from a

thousand years before Christ to 800 years after—a very long time for any business to last. One might expect that the Phoenicians, capable enough to sail the entire Mediterranean, to build better ships, to use ballast, to advance the Bronze Age, to devise an alphabet, and to establish literature, would also be astute at advertising what they had to sell. They were. Their ships arrived in ports with their sails dyed Tyrian purple.

A wind that blows once a year was familiar to Greeks of Homer's time. Starting each May and lasting about four months, there blows across the eastern Mediterranean a strong wind, seldom at less than 10 knots. The Greeks dubbed this wind *Etesios*, "annual." The "Etesian winds" is the term today.

The Greeks spoke of a gentle west wind as though it were the breath of a god: a *zephyr*. And a strong wind from northeast or northwest, in the south-central Mediterranean, became *Graecus*, the "Greek wind." "Gregale" is today's name.

At least as far back as the time of Homer the women of northern Europe and today's British Isles had a word they used for stirring. It came to mean a "stirring of the skies." Spelled exactly as it is spelled today, it is sometimes the only word in an ancient manuscript that a modern reader can make out: *storm*.

Probably some time after Homer, a Greek, Hesiod, wrote some brief advice on mercantile navigation in a work called *Works and Days*. Echoing Homer, Hesiod mentions "lands beyond the sea," the Isles of the Blessed, which were located far away in the west, were extremely fertile, and were where the blessed among the dead—heroes and patriots—lived again in happiness. Pindar (about 520 B.C.) and Horace (65 B.C.–8

A.D.) also would talk of the Islands of the Blessed. Hesiod and
Pindar located the imaginary islands far out in the Atlantic
Ocean. This could have derived from ancient mariners who
had sailed west, intentionally or unintentionally, and seen
islands such as the Azores or even the coasts of North or
South America.

The original legends about the islands could have been
started by sailors in other seas who found idyllic islands
somewhere—for example, possibly Queen Hatshepsut of
Egypt's expedition to Punt. Even today tales of the South
Pacific tell of tropical paradises and owe something to
Hesiod.

Hesiod, a poet, was the first writer to put down some of
the fables that were to last in men's minds for a long time. He
told of men who lived far away and had the heads of dogs. He
told of men with heads of huge size, which may have been
Homer's pygmies. He mentioned griffins, who "guarded
gold"; a three-headed giant, Geryones, who lived on an island
across the stream of Oceanus; and men who lived beyond the
north wind, in what supposedly was a perfect climate.

Hesiod, like Homer, thought Oceanus was "the perfect
river," flowing in a great circular movement around the
earth. He knew of rivers that Homer did not, including the
Nile. He mentioned deep eddies in the sea. He vaguely
mentioned distant lands that may have meant Sicily or Italy.
He hinted that something unknown lay beyond Oceanus. He
thought that far to the west a strong man, Atlas, supported
the heavens with his head and hands, and that the Islands of
the Blessed produced beautiful golden apples. Just like Homer
not long before, Hesiod owed many of his stories to the
Phoenician sailors.

In the 700s B.C., in Corinth, Greece, a new ship was
invented—a trireme, with three banks of oars. Corinth could

well use triremes. She was building colonies at Syracuse and Corcyra. Other Greeks were establishing or had already established colonies around the Black Sea, in Italy, at Massilia (Marseilles, France), and one or two in Spain. There were also Greeks on the north shore of Africa, but not many, because Carthage and the Carthaginians and Phoenicians were already there.

Corinth was to be a busy port. Located on a narrow (four miles across) isthmus, across which ships had been hauled, Corinth had known many Phoenician vessels. The port would export her own goods, especially bronze and pottery, around the Mediterranean to Italy, Miletus, Phrygia, Cyprus, and Egypt.

Besides her triremes, Corinth tried something else new and different: she was the first to build a regular navy, as later Greeks would also. And in 664 B.C., according to Thucydides, there took place the first naval battle in history, between Corinth and her colony, Corcyra. Thucydides does not say how the battle came out.

About the 600s B.C., according to a much later writer, Herodotus, the Phocaean Greeks—from the town of Phocaea on the Gulf of Smyrna—set out on a sea voyage. The Phocaeans' home port, like other Mediterranean ports, had been given twin harbors so that, whatever the wind, their ships could enter one or the other. They sailed in long, narrow ships with 25 oarsmen on each side. Each ship carried a single woven cloth sail. Each ship had a deep keel to reduce drifting or being blown sideways. (The origin of the keel seems to be one of the mysteries of the story of man on the sea, but this may be one of the beginnings of the keel.) The small sails and the muscles of the rowers propelled the vessels west to Italy, both east and west coasts, farther west to Spain, and on through the Strait of Gibraltar to a city on the

Atlantic shore we have never been able to locate exactly: a lost, important seaport called Tarshish or Tartessus, established by the Phoenicians or Tyrians. It was near today's Cadiz, on the Guadalquivir River in Spain.

A ship from the Greek island of Samos, under a commander named Colaeus, also visited Tartessus about the same time—and returned with a valuable cargo. Ships from Samos already were carrying on trade in different parts of the Mediterranean, according to Herodotus. Thucydides said the Samians had got from a Corinthian named Aneinocles ships with three banks of oars, the triremes.

About 630 B.C., a Greek city or colony, Apollonia, was founded in today's Libya. Apollonia now is under water. A British expedition of divers found a piscina, or fish tank, that kept fish captive but allowed sea water to enter. Although rubble on the bottom made its exact depth unclear, the pool appeared to have been something over ten feet deep. It had steps from the shore down into it, and walls to separate species of fish. Such tanks appear to have been developed earlier, along the Nile, for cultivating freshwater fish.[1]

About 624 B.C., an infant, reputedly of Phoenician parents, was born who grew up to become known as Thales of Miletus. One famous story about him is that as an adult, as he was walking along, watching the stars, he fell into a ditch.

Perhaps from Egyptian records and Babylonian calculations, Thales accurately predicted to Greeks of Ionia an eclipse of the sun on 28 May 585 B.C. One of the terrors of ancient man, as he gazed at the skies, was the fear of a total solar eclipse. It would take time, but Thales had begun the process of ridding man of that unnecessary terror.

Thales was doing much more: he was turning astrology into the science of astronomy.

As other thinkers had before him, Thales puzzled over what all things are made of, and he concluded that there was a single permanent, imperishable, and eternal substance. He thought this substance was water. Other men would consider, before they were through, earth, air, fire, as well as water—and all four. They would even reach a consideration of the atom.

Thales discovered something else, that when he rubbed a substance we call "amber," the amber attracted other bodies. The Greek word for amber was *electron*. From Thales' original discovery there came, over thousands of years, our knowledge of electricity, the source of energy that man of the 1800s would harness, thousands of years after other men had harnessed the energy of wind in the sails.

A Babylonian map of 600 B.C.—one of the oldest in existence if not the oldest—shows the then-known world surrounded by ocean, as Homer had said it was. The map shows Babylon in the center, the Euphrates River, and several cities including Babel. One note about a distant place shown on the edge of the land says that here the sun is not seen. Dare we think that this indicates, 2,500 years ago, a knowledge of the Arctic? Probably yes—from overland trade routes to the Baltic and to Scandinavia that may have existed thousands of years earlier. At least one trade route to the North Sea and the Baltic, the Elbe River valley, was in use in prehistoric times. Trade routes along those natural highways, Europe's north- and south-flowing rivers, may have been used 20,000 to 40,000 years ago.

That Thales of Miletus could have experimented with amber is another clue. Amber is the fossil resin of cone-bearing, evergreen trees of great northern forests that once existed in Germany, Latvia, Lithuania, Siberia. Although amber also is found in Sicily and England, its main source in

Thales' day was the southern shores of the Baltic Sea. Cloudy or transparent, orange or yellow or brownish, it was used as beads, jewelry, and ornaments. Inside bits of amber even today scientists find pieces of wood, leaves, bubbles of air and insects—some of them previously unknown species.

Gazing up at the sky ancient man saw a universe that always was moving. The sun traveled around in a broad belt. The moon plus the five planets that his eyes could see also moved in this belt. He named the belt the "zodiac." The stars that showed upon the zodiac appeared to be in groups or clusters or constellations that took on shapes, and he named them accordingly. In Latin, they became Taurus (the bull), Cancer (the crab), Leo (the lion), Scorpio (the scorpion), Gemini (the twins), and so on. Names with the same meanings were found long afterward carved on tablets from 600 B.C. They apparently had been known to the Babylonians far longer ago than 600 B.C.

The Babylonians of the same time—2,600 years ago—also gave us the names of the days of the week.

This ancient period in astronomy has been labeled by scientists of today "farmer's or shepherd's astronomy." Men living in that period already knew that there were fixed stars that rose and set each night at the same place on the horizon. They knew the sun, moon, and planets did no such thing. They knew that stars along the zodiacal belt disappeared below the horizon, then reappeared each year. When the dog star Sirius reappeared, it was time for the annual Nile flood.

The Babylonians, in the last thousand years before Christ, began to apply mathematics to astronomy. It was no longer "farmer's or shepherd's astronomy." From then onward, it grew ever more scientific and sophisticated.

16

~~~~~~~~~~~~~~~~~

600 Years Before Christ:
All the Way Around Africa

In 600 B.C., or thereabouts, not long after Homer was reciting the *Odyssey*, an Egyptian pharaoh, Necho, or Neco, sent a Phoenician expedition in a number of ships to explore southwards down the Red Sea—and to make a voyage we know something about. The expedition deliberately sailed into unknown seas, in fact, set out intentionally to explore beyond one horizon and the next, and eventually returned home to Egypt.

Necho himself probably knew of Queen Hatshepsut's sponsorship, over a thousand years earlier, of the trip to Punt. He undoubtedly knew of other long trips that were being made around the Mediterranean during his reign. His expedition was from Tyre, the city of the purple dye, and may have included men from another Phoenician city, Sidon. The expedition's voyage was one of the most remarkable trips of all time.

The sailor of today starts out with a knowledge of geography, winds, and currents. The Tyrians must have had

to collect all their information as they went along. Through
and beyond the Red Sea, they went past the land of Punt,
wherever that was. From then on, Necho's people sailed into
the unknown—at least, so far as we today know. They
reached the Indian Ocean, went all the way to the southern
tip of Africa, and then changed course to west and sailed
around Africa's southernmost point, today's Cape Agulhas,
and the Cape of Good Hope. Then they traveled north up
Africa's Atlantic coast—the first known sailors on the South
Atlantic Ocean. After three years, the Tyrians passed
through the Strait of Gibraltar and into the Mediterranean. Twenty-six hundred years ago men circumnavigated
Africa.

The Phoenicians, close-mouthed as they were about their
voyages, probably left no written records of their trip. Their
trip was not known of, or was forgotten, by many mapmak-
ers after them, and Africa was shown on some maps as a land
that stretched all the way to the Antarctic.

Today it is believed there was a single sail on each ship.
The wind in their sails from Egypt down the Red Sea could
have been a fresh, northerly, favorable wind. The northeast
monsoon winds of the Indian Ocean—also favorable—would
have filled their sails to the Comoro Islands between today's
Malagasy Republic (Madagascar) and Mozambique.

Provided they missed storms as they went around the
southern end of Africa, winds could have continued helpful.
Once around the tip and running north along the western, or
Atlantic, coast of Africa, the Tyrians probably encountered a
favorable south wind, to push them along. Off the bulge of
Africa toward South America, however, the northeast trade
wind would have been unfavorable. We can imagine that the
sailors had to fight head winds all the way to Gibraltar and so
might have been forced out to sea and might have come upon
the Cape Verde Islands, the Canaries, or Madeira. They

might have thought any of these were the Fortunate Isles, the Islands of the Blessed. We have no record of their discovering any of these islands; it is only a possibility.

The Phoenicians nowhere would have found the wind impossible—for them. They had become the Mediterranean's finest sailors by handling unfavorable winds, as well as by navigating out to the open sea.

The Tyrians also were the earliest known mariners to experience the currents all around Africa. They learned that on the courses they sailed, the currents were mostly helpful. There was a helpful current flowing south from the start (there were fish to be caught, too). There was next the southward-flowing Mozambique Current, which flows around the Cape of Good Hope. Once around the Cape, they would have been pushed north by the Benguela Current. Off the bulge of Africa, the Guinea Current and the Canary Current would have been against them, along with the prevailing northeast trade wind. Things could have been difficult from here to the Strait of Gibraltar, and here is where the Tyrians might have been forced further out to sea and to have discovered the Canary Islands or others.

Upon their return, the Tyrians reported a fact unbelievable to men of their day. In sailing around southern Africa they had the sun on their right.

At least two modern authors say that the Tyrians made the trip by rowing. The early sails and ships of Necho's day were imperfect enough so this would be quite possible. Besides, the weak sailcoth in use then hardly would have lasted for such a trip. The Tyrians could have done it; the oarsmen of those ancient days were capable enough. If they did go all the way around Africa by muscle power, the 13,000 miles must have been the longest row ever made.

The single source of knowledge about this voyage is a later Greek historian and geographer, Herodotus. He mentions also a Persian attempt to sail around Africa which failed. Herodotus also says that in order to get food the Tyrians each year settled ashore, planted, grew, and harvested a crop.

Herodotus, although he told the story of Necho's Tyrians sailing around Africa, doubted that they had. He could not accept the idea of the sun on their right. Actually, as a German explorer, Alexander von Humboldt, pointed out around 1800, this was the most convincing proof that the Tyrians had made the trip. As they sailed west, far below the equator in the southern hemisphere, unknown to Mediterranean man, the sun would have been on their right.

There is a story that the Phoenicians on this trip actually sailed west till they landed at Paraíba, Brazil.[1] On a rock slab found by a plantation slave in 1872 at Paraíba, there is this inscription: "We are the sons of Canaan from Sidon, the city of the king. Commerce has cast us on this distant shore."

Says a modern commentator:

> This text chiseled in Phoenician script describes how the crew sailed with ten other ships from Ezon-Geber on the Gulf of Aqaba. This one ship was separated from the others by a South Atlantic storm. Upon arriving at Parahyba [Paraíba], the crew of twelve men and three women sacrificed one of their number to propitiate their gods.
>
> Furthermore, the peculiarities of the script suggest that the stone was carved by the characters used by Phoenicians about B.C. 600.[2]

This Phoenician ship could have been blown to the Canary Islands and, once there, could have been blown by trade winds across the ocean to Brazil. Later, after the Portuguese and Spanish had arrived there in 1500 A.D., sailing-ship skippers deliberately followed this route to reach Brazil.

According to Aristotle, several vessels from the Phoenician colony of Carthage reached the western hemisphere—possibly the West Indies, or Mexico, or Brazil—in 590 B.C.[3]

That the Phoenicians could have crossed the Atlantic about 2,100 years before the Portuguese and Spanish reached Brazil seems impossible, but it may have happened. Moreover, with the ability to navigate by sun or stars, the Phoenician sailor, starting from the Red Sea and probably relying more on sails and less on oarsmen, may have made three-year-long round trips to India and Ceylon on which he obtained peacocks. The close-mouthed Phoenician seaman left us nothing to go by, but it is believed that he may have gone on past India and Ceylon all the way to the East Indies, Indonesia. How many voyages of ancient man are not known to us at all?

17

Greece, 500s B.C.:
Eyes on the Stars, the Earth, and Man

A PUPIL OF THALES of Miletus, Anaximander, lived from 611 to 547 B.C., when the Greeks were establishing colonies. They had been the first Mediterranean Sea sailors to enter the Black Sea, and they named it the Euxine (friendly) Sea; Anaximander's city of Miletus, with a good harbor, sent colonists to the Black Sea.

With Greece expanding, it was natural that maps should begin to be made there, and the first one we know of was made by Anaximander. He based it on Homer's concept of the earth as flat and circular like a pancake. But on his map, which he probably made initially on a bronze tablet, he showed more of the world than any man had before—in fact, the first map of the entire known world.[1] This was one of mankind's steps forward—toward geography.

Anaximander is also believed to have introduced into Greece from Babylonia a primitive sun-dial, or gnomon. The gnomon for a long time was the only way the Greeks had to learn latitudes. He defined the wind as a flow of air, a description still accepted. He also suggested that man had evolved from a fishlike ancestor, an idea today regarded by some scientists as probable. He thought that there coexisted many different universes or worlds. And like Thales before him, he was puzzled about the universal substance from which all things are derived and to which they return. He came up with the idea that the beginning is the Infinite.

At a time when a man performed his astronomy with his bare eyes alone, Anaximander declared that the sun was at least as large as the earth. Today we know that the sun is "108 times the diameter of the earth; its volume is 1.3 million times that of the earth; its mass is 330,000 times the mass of the earth." [2]

Only 93 million miles from the earth, the sun, with a diameter of 864,000 miles, is tiny in the universe: a supergiant star can have a diameter 1,000 times as great. The sun, that is, is a dwarf star.

Along with Anaximander, 500 years before Christ, men were both gaining new knowledge and speculating about practically everything under the sun.

Not long after the Tyrians of the pharaoh Necho had sailed around Africa, or from 582 to about 507 B.C., there lived a Greek, Pythagoras. Born in Samos, he traveled in Egypt and the East. He learned something that is today taught to every high-school student of geometry: the square of the hypotenuse of a right-angle triangle is equal to the sum of the squares of the other two sides. This is one Pythagorean theorem.

Men watching the sun and stars move began to conclude that the earth was round. Pythagoras thought so. He may have reached his conclusion, however, for another reason: a belief that the sphere was the most perfect form. Followers of his concluded not only that the earth was round but that it was a globe freely poised in space.

The poet Homer had described a star that appeared at dawn, "proclaiming light on earth." He had described also an "evening star, that bringest back all that lightsome dawn has scattered."

Pythagoras is believed to have been the man who learned that both the stars are one—the morning star, the evening star, one of the brightest objects in the sky, the planet Venus.

Born about the same time as Pythagoras was Empedocles of Acragas (Agrigentum) in Sicily. Empedocles pondered about what today we call science. Over 500 years before Christ, he learned that air was not just empty space, but a real substance. He could see that things around him kept changing, and, like Thales of Miletus, he wondered if there was a permanent substance from which everything came. He decided that there were four such eternal substances: earth, air, fire, and water. These four elements, working on each other, he said, produced the changes men see in the material world. His view was accepted by many men for centuries.

Another Greek, Parmenides of Elea, born about 510 B.C., believed the earth was round. He also observed that the bright side of the moon always faces the sun. He divided the world into 5 zones—2 cold ones (at the poles), 2 with moderate climates, and a torrid zone (around the equator). Men could live, Parmenides thought, only in the moderate zones. His division of the globe into 5 zones would remain a popular idea for over a thousand years. His torrid and frigid zones would be among the fearsome problems that sailors had to worry about.

And not long before 500 B.C. in Babylonia, the astronomer Nabu-ri-mannu, observing the skies with naked eyes, figured that the length of the year was 365 days 6 hours 15 minutes 41 seconds. His figure was too long by 26 minutes and 55 seconds.

He was the first known man to calculate the year so accurately.

On a painted Greek vase from about 500 B.C., called the "Vulci vase," now in the British Museum, there is evidence that the Greeks were improving their ships. One picture shows a merchant ship, a sailing ship with no oars at all. The vase also shows a Greek warship, a bireme, with two banks of rowers, 24 men on each side. A long, narrow ship, she has also a mast and a sail, and a ram to crash into enemy ships.

And a warship with oars out of sight but with the ports for them under the gunwale clearly visible. From these ports there eventually developed gunports and the portholes on today's oceanliners.

There is also, on the Vulci vase, the picture of a man about to dive off a ship. He may have been after sponges, then already in common use in the Mediterranean area.

As long ago as 500 B.C., Anaxagoras was describing solar eclipses and believing that the earth moved around the sun. He was the first to say—correctly—that the moon is dark but lit by the sun. Or Anaxagoras may have lived a little later, in the 400s B.C. A contemporary, Diogenes of Apollonia, believed in the 4 elements, earth, air, fire, water. He thought air was the first cause of all.

About 500 B.C., Hecataeus of Miletus, who has been called the Father of Geography, traveled widely and wrote a book based on his travels with information he had collected on countries, their inhabitants, and animals; he included a map said to be the second (after Anaximander's) made in Greece.

Hecataeus, c. 549–486 B.C., on his map showed the known world, the Mediterranean and the land around it, but almost nothing else. Around the edge of the map the ocean flowed like a river; it was shown as a thin ribbon-like band. There was not an inkling of the vast expanse of the sea.

The Phoenicians having brought an alphabet to Greece, and Homer (possibly) and others having begun to write down things, Hecataeus put his treatise on paper, possibly papyrus. Only fragments have survived, but Hecataeus was widely quoted, indicating he put down a great deal. Much of it was what was called a *Periplus*, a description of the coast of the Mediterranean, and similar to a later treatise called the *Periplus of Scylax*.

Heraclitus of Ephesus, about 500 B.C., took a step toward science: he noticed changes in the material world and came to the conclusion that matter itself is constantly changing. He thus rejected Thales of Miletus' idea that there was a single, imperishable substance, which Thales thought was water, and he rejected Empedocles' view that there were 4 elements—earth, air, fire, water. For Heraclitus, everything was always in a state of flux.

In 500 B.C., Alcmaeon of Croton studied animals. He described the optic nerve and the tube from nose to ear, the Eustachian tube. He thus may have begun to direct men toward the study of biology, but what, in detail, he did, we do not know.

Anaximenes of Miletus, about 494 B.C., pondered what the universal substance was, the source of all things. He came up with *aer*—by which he meant water vapor, not ordinary air.

Five hundred years before Christ, Xenophanes of Colophon in Ionia came up with ideas that sound surprisingly modern. The sea, he said, is the source of all water; the sun sucked up moisture from it and produced rain. The land and sea, he said, changed places; fossil fish, seaweed, anchovies were found in Malta, Sicily, elsewhere. The sea is salt, he said, "because many compounds are fused together in it."

18

The Atlantic, 510 and 470 B.C.: South and North from Gibraltar

JUST AS AROUND THE MEDITERRANEAN men were busy, so were men busy in northern Europe. By about 500 B.C. they had made a series of long trips that have given us one of today's mysteries of man on the sea. By about 500 B.C. somebody had erected circular stone towers or forts, called "brochs"—the predecessors of medieval castles—at about 500 places on the Shetland islands, the Hebrides islands, the Orkney islands, and the coasts of Scotland.

A broch is almost always located near the sea. It suggests either a people who came from over the sea (perhaps Picts from Gaul), or a people who expected enemies from over the sea. In either case, the brochs suggest the existence of seamen able to navigate out of sight of land.

A writer, Pindar, who lived from about 511 to 443 B.C. mentioned the Fortunate Islands, the Isles of the Blessed, Utopia. But he had some advice for sailors who might seek such an undiscovered paradise: Do not, he said, sail west into the Atlantic. He told the sailors that neither the wise nor the unwise might go beyond the Pillars of Heracles (Strait of Gibraltar). He also wrote that no one should sail west from Gades (Cadiz, Spain).

Men promptly disregarded his advice.

The Phoenicians had established a colony, Carthage, in north Africa, about where Tunis is today—far closer to Gibraltar and to the then almost-unknown Atlantic coast of Africa than was Phoenicia.

From Carthage, sailors had not far to travel before reaching unknown seas and lands, and they soon set out to explore. Not long after 500 B.C., a Persian named Sataspes left Egypt and put into Carthage to refit and supply his expedition. He chose to ignore Pindar's warning about sailing through the Strait of Gibraltar into the almost-unknown Atlantic, and turned south down the coast of Africa.

Near the equator, he encountered (he said later) small black people who kept cattle and dressed in palm leaves. This gave weight to what Parmenides and others had said about a torrid zone that turned men black. Sataspes turned back, either forced to by unfavorable currents or frightened by the loneliness of the voyage. Or by the wind: It may have been against him. Or it may have been so favorable and so strong, right behind his square sail, that he thought the wind would blow him over the edge of the world.

Euthymenes of Massilia (modern Marseilles, France) may have been the next to go down the coast of Africa and to have reached the Senegal River. There is a tale that he did, and absolutely no more information about him.

Then from Carthage about 480 B.C., a leader named Hamilcar invaded the island of Sicily. Hamilcar had ships to spare, and two of his sons, Hanno and Himilco, soon used some of them to sail into the unknown.

About 470 B.C., Hanno chose not to take Pindar's advice to

stay on the Mediterranean side of Gibraltar. Hanno made a trip or sent someone else on a trip following the course of Sataspes through the Strait of Gibraltar and down the Atlantic coast of Africa. One account says Hanno had 60 ships, each of 50 oars, carrying 30,000 men and women plus corn and other supplies.

Hanno's expedition, away from Carthage for four or five years, established settlements that may have been in what is now Senegal and Guinea and even in Madeira and the Canary Islands. Hanno could have reached the Cape Verde Islands. His sailors saw crocodiles and hippopotamuses, probably in the Senegal River. He could have sailed to within 8 degrees of the equator, possibly to what is now Sierra Leone.

To reach any one of these places would have been amazing for the ocean explorers in their oared ships, each perhaps with a single sail, almost 500 years B.C. How amazing is shown by the fact that it would not be done again until 1,400 years after Christ, just before Columbus.

On one headland Hanno's men put down the foundations of what would be a landmark—a temple to the sea god, Poseidon. They saw great stretches of land on fire—maybe grass fires set by Africans. One dark night, drawing near land, they saw flitting lights and heard ghostly whispers in a strange language. They were frightened.

Many of the animals of Africa, including the great apes, had not been seen by Europeans or Carthaginians. Hanno or his men brought back an incredible tale of a then-unknown creature: they had heard of (or seen) savage, hairy people called "gorillas."

In the case of another then unknown animal, the expedition brought back some skins to prove it was real, skins that today we think may have been those of chimpanzees or baboons (mandrills). As long as 2,500 years ago, sailors were collecting biological specimens.

On the frieze of an ancient silver bowl from an Etruscan grave in Italy, there is the picture of a hairy, big-skulled creature, walking on two legs, throwing a stone with one hand and holding a stick with the other. It looks like a gorilla or some other great ape. One archeologist, Ludwig Curtius, believes the bowl was of Phoenician or Carthaginian origin, and that the picture on the bowl may be a result of Hanno's voyage.

Hanno said he encountered "forest people with animal skins" on the West African coast south of present-day Cameroon, "among them many men with shaggy heads whom our interpreters called gorillas."

Similar tales of wild, hairy men existed in Cyprus, Babylonia, Greece, the Orient. Man, however vaguely, was wondering about these primitive beings, wondering about his relationship to them and to other living creatures. He was already asking the question: What is man? In the 1970s he still is. Sailors have brought and continue to bring new evidence.

Hanno did not collect specimens, but he did report something else: off the coast, he said, his people saw swimming upright in the sea fish with the faces of women— the first mermaids on record, so far as I know, unless the Phoenician account of sirens that charmed sailors is considered.

At or about the same time as Hanno's voyage, 470 B.C., Hanno's brother, Himilco, sailed with another fleet from Carthage, went through the Strait of Gibraltar, and turned the other way, north. Himilco, away from Carthage for two years, may have reached northern Spain, France, Holland, Germany, Ireland, and Britain. This may be the first northern voyage of which mention is made in literature.[1]

Himilco, according to our sources, Rufus Festius Avienus in *Ora Maritima* and a mention in Pliny, described the Atlantic as the Phoenicians did, "monster-filled." Avienus quoted Himilco: "The monsters of the sea are everywhere, and keep swimming around the slow-moving ships." The monsters may have been whales.

Himilco said he found a sea filled with seaweed so "that it keeps vessels back somewhat as brush delays a man in walking." This has been quoted to show that Himilco got to an area of ocean famous today for floating seaweed—the Sargasso Sea, in the middle of the Atlantic. Columbus would encounter the weed on his first voyage across the Atlantic, in 1492. Himilco may have seen his seaweed in the Bay of Biscay, off France.

He described somewhere far out in the Atlantic a "region far towards the west," where "there are interminable swirling waters, where the sea and surge spread open far and wide. 'Nobody has visited these waters hitherto; nobody has brought ships into that wide stretch, for there no driving blasts of winds are felt upon the deep, no breath of heaven helps on a vessel; moreover dark mist shrouds the sky as with a cloak; fog at all times hides the swirling waters, and clouds last all day long in thickest gloom.' "

The Phoenicians, perhaps along with their relatives, the Carthaginians, either after Himilco's trip or much earlier, began to sail regularly to the British Isles to obtain tin. Tin they used with copper to make bronze.

Avienus said the Carthaginians traded with the Oestrum-nides, rich in tin and lead—which we think might have been either the Scilly Islands, rocky islands beyond Lands End, Britain's southwestern corner, jutting into the Atlantic, or islands off Brittany, France. Avienus said Himilco reached them four months after leaving Carthage.

Two days' sail from the Scilly Islands, said Avienus, was

the sacred island of the ancients, where the Hiberni lived—
Ireland. Also near, said Avienus, is the island of the
Albiones—Britain. He said Himilco described boats of the tin
islanders as those typical, practical seagoing craft of the
northern Europeans—"They made their ships of hides tied
together, and often traverse the vast sea with the help of
hides." The skins may have been stretched over a wicker
framework.

About the time of Hanno and Himilco, sailors on the
Mediterranean began to drop anchors. The first anchors
probably were stones with ropes tied around them. The next
ones probably were stones with holes through them for ropes.

The alphabet and the written word had led to at least a few
men being able to read. In all probability, some of the ship
captains could read. They were beginning to be able to
follow written instructions. They were reading what came to
be called "sailing directions."

What is out there? A book of sailing directions appeared
after the voyages of Hanno and Himilco into the Atlantic.
The book, the *Periplus of Scylax*, said that out there were
reefs and mud banks so near the surface that waves broke
upon them and that great tuna were stranded upon them.
The tuna were caught and shipped to Carthage. The reefs
stretched all the way from Portugal to Africa.

Out there, according to the *Periplus*, was the thick seaweed
that Himilco reported, "one hand's breadth in width."

All of this smacks of the Phoenician-Carthaginian brain-
washing of others to keep them from sailing the Atlantic. But
the *Periplus* said that the seaweed was four days' sail, in an
easterly wind, beyond Gibraltar. A puzzling and frustrating
question arises in the mind of modern man: Could the
Phoenicians actually have sailed west, into the mid-Atlantic,

into the Sargasso Sea? Could the Phoenicians or Carthaginians have reached a place we thought no one before
Columbus had reached? If so, how much farther west could
the Phoenicians or Carthaginians have traveled?

Maybe all the way to Brazil.

The *Periplus of Scylax* was a kind of work that would
become common during the centuries when so many ships
hugged the coast. It described, in order, giving distances
between them, the landmarks on the shore a sailor saw:
towns, temples, rivers, capes, mountains. It says little about
the interior of any country.

These books of sailing directions are the oldest works that
have come down to us in a science that the world's sailors
would cause to expand tremendously: geography.

In the Atlantic Ocean, the Phoenicians and/or the Carthaginians found something else besides a trade route to Britain
for tin. Conscious of dye as they were, they found in the
Atlantic a lichen, archil, that provides violet or red dye. And
on the Atlantic coast of the Iberian peninsula, the Phoenician
or Carthaginian port, Tartessus, was developing ships that
may have been the ancestors, first, of Portuguese fishing boats
that fished far away and, second, of a ship called the
"caravel," a ship in which Portuguese ocean explorers would
discover many of the lands and seas of the globe—a ship that
Columbus used to reach America.

Tartessus thus may have been a place whose ships had a
tremendously significant role as a link in the story of the
ocean explorers and, if so, this may mean that the vanished
Tartessus was a city whose importance in history was far
greater than we have known.

Once they had reached and sailed the Atlantic—or, as it
was called, Oceanus—the Phoenicians and Carthaginians

found it exactly what it is: a sea with the worst storms that sailors up to their time had faced, higher waves, winds blowing straight from the west that forced sailing ships back into harbors such as Tartessus, cold, fog, etc. Once their sailors returned, their tales of the Atlantic, which, they said, no one but themselves ever sailed, were filled with all of these hazards and with unimaginable terrors as well. To the south, they said, echoing Parmenides, were equatorial seas that boiled. If you sailed far enough, they said, you would reach the edge of the world and sail right over it and fall off.

They and other sailors went right on. Man kept on sailing beyond the next horizon, into the unknown.

19

~~~~~~~~~~~~~~

The Mediterranean, 400s B.C.:
Men Lower a Line Overboard

THE OCEAN IS DARK and hides its secrets. How deep is the sea? What is beneath the dark blue or gray or green surface, beneath Homer's "wine-dark" Mediterranean?

Some time in the fifth century before Christ, according to Herodotus (484–424 B.C.), who recounted the story of Necho's Tyrians sailing around Africa, a line was lowered from a ship to measure the depth of the water.

The line was perhaps of fibers of papyrus or twisted oxhide, and perhaps was weighted with a stone at its end. Herodotus indicates, in fact, that lowering a line was done fairly frequently. The sailor already was improving his sounding line: he was putting a lump of tallow on the underside of the weight to bring up a sample of the sea bottom, which told a sailor where he was and whether the bottom would hold an anchor. Sailors correctly concluded that the bulge of Egypt, the Nile delta protruding into the Mediterranean, is caused by mud brought to the sea and laid down by the Nile. A sounding line in 66 feet (11 fathoms) of water, lowered overboard by a ship still 60 to 100 miles (one day's sail), from the Nile, Herodotus said, brought up yellow mud like that which the Nile brings to the sea in its annual flood.

Thus sailors began to learn that, over the eons, the sea and land change places.

Fishing lines had been dropped into the sea since prehistoric times. Egyptians had measured the depth of water with poles up to ten feet long. But Herodotus' account is the first mention, in writing, of sounding by a line overboard.

Man was wondering what was beneath the dark ocean. He was asking a new question: What is down there?

Anyone who ever has dropped a fishing line into a creek, river, pond, lake, or ocean will know how the world's oceanographers have worked over the centuries: they have lowered lines overboard to measure the depth of the water and to see what they could haul up. From the dark sea they have brought up fish (the Scandinavians, cod, the Greeks, tuna), strange new animals (the sea snails of the Tyrian dye), sediments, minerals.

In the 1970s, lines dropped overboard into the water also carry instruments to record the sea's temperature, salinity, and pressure; bottles to take samples of the water; current meters to measure deep currents; clamshells and corers to take samples of the bottom; and still, motion-picture, and television cameras. The line dropped overboard still is a basic tool in oceanography.

And the line dropped overboard still measures the depth of the water and tells the sailor what the bottom is made of and therefore where he is. The sounding line still is a basic tool for the mariner.

From somewhere, perhaps from trade routes overland to the Baltic Sea, Mediterranean people had acquired the idea that in a northern land the air was full of feathers. This story was told for many years. It is a good enough description of a snowfall by a Mediterranean man seeing his first one. By Herodotus' day, snow was better understood, and Herodotus himself thought the feathers really were snow.

When Herodotus lived, the Caspian Sea was considered a leg of the northern Oceanus by a good many men. He said correctly that it was an inland sea.

He mentioned "great big fish which have no prickly bones," as dwelling in Russian rivers. These may have been sturgeon, today known to enter Russian rivers from the sea in order to spawn; they are huge (a ton or a ton and a half and up to 20 feet long) and provide caviar.

Herodotus once described a service that existed in Persia: "The Persian messengers travel with a velocity which nothing human can equal. . . . Neither snow, nor rain, nor heat, nor darkness, are permitted to obstruct their speed." This quotation became in time the one above the entrance to the main post office in New York City: "Not snow, nor rain, nor heat, nor gloom of night stays these couriers from swift completion of their appointed rounds."

When he traveled in Egypt, Herodotus saw fossil seashells and thought that at one time they must have been beneath the sea.

Called Oceanus by the Phoenicians, the frightening, unknown ocean beyond the Pillars of Heracles, Gibraltar, also had a second name, the Outer Sea. Herodotus came up with still another name. He was the first, so far as we know, to call the western ocean beyond Gibraltar after the mythical titan Atlas, *Mare Atlanticum*—the Atlantic Ocean.

20

Carthage, After 480 B.C.: Queen City of the Sea

IT TOOK HUNDREDS, even thousands of years before sailing ships got along without any oarsmen at all. Men's aching backs, legs, and arms only slowly were replaced. One reason that oarsmen lingered on was that the wind might at any time cease to blow, or it might blow the wrong way. A rower, either a galley slave, or, as in the case of Athens, a freeman out to improve the lot of his family and city, often was more dependable than the wind.

Early sailors must have experimented with their sails over the centuries, trying different sizes, shapes, materials, and riggings, and trying all of them on different vessels. With rowers still being used over the same centuries, rowed ships improved and reached their height. The number of banks of oarsmen increased. In Athens, the trireme, with three banks of oarsmen, perhaps sitting above each other, was a narrow warship about 120 feet long and 15 feet in beam. A trireme required about 170 oarsmen, rowing to a Greek flute, to propel her at a best, and very fast, speed of about 7½ knots. She carried about 30 other sailors and fighting men.

A contemporary of Herodotus, Themistocles, persuaded Athenians to build a 327-ship fleet, largely of triremes. The triremes were given projecting spurs made of wood but with teeth of bronze; they were used to ram into the sides of enemy ships. With the fleet, Themistocles won the battle of Salamis against the Persians in 480 B.C. The Persians included the Phoenicians among their allies. Salamis ended the predominance of Phoenicia on the Mediterranean, but her former colony, Carthage, managed to flourish for three and a half centuries longer.

Themistocles made a comment to which ever since man has paid attention: "He who commands the sea controls everything."

Carthage came to be queen city of the sea. Her white sails were all over the western Mediterranean. Her influence dominated from Gibraltar to Sardinia, she held Majorca and Minorca and other islands off Spain, Malta, and Sicily. Before the Roman legions arrived, there were Carthaginian settlements in Spain, where Carthage founded Cartagena, Barcelona, and Cadiz.

Cadiz is beyond Gibraltar, on the sea Herodotus had called the Atlantic, and Carthaginian ships probably sailed, as the Phoenicians did, to Britain and northern Europe. As is the case with many ancient mariners, there is a rumor, but no evidence that I know of, that Carthage's went farther than we know and that they reached the Azores.

Ocean engineering was practiced in Carthage. Her merchant ships came home into an artificial lagoon, of perhaps 60 acres, or they tied up in basins or outer harbors protected by jetties. The goods the ships brought supplied a city that eventually was wealthy, 20 miles in circumference, and, according to Strabo, of 700,000 to a million persons.

Carthage's naval ships used a 22-acre harbor surrounded by 16¼-foot-wide docks which could hold 220 vessels at a time.

This naval harbor, connected by a canal to the freight ships' lagoon, was circular. From an island in the center an admiral could inspect his entire fleet.

The Greeks about the time of their great sculptor, Phidias, and of their leader, Pericles (500–429 B.C.), had erected some striking landmarks to help guide their sailors home. At the southern tip of Attica they could see the tall marble columns of a temple to Poseidon. And as they approached Athens, they would behold high on the Acropolis the spear point and plume of a heroic statue to Athena, Athena of Battles.

Men with their own eyes could see perfectly well that the sun, moon, stars, and planets (apparently) moved around the earth, and they naturally were sure that the earth was the center of the universe. Then one man came up with a better idea, one that was not eagerly accepted. This man, nevertheless, moved toward our modern concept of the solar system.

In the 400s B.C., Philolaus of Tarentum suggested that the earth was not, as man had believed, the center of the universe, but, like other planets, revolved around a central fire. Philolaus suggested a new model of the universe to demonstrate his idea.

Another Greek, Democritus, imagined that there were in the universe countless worlds like our own. Astronomers of the 1970s accept the possible existence of other earthlike planets circling other stars similar to our sun.

Democritus put men on the trail of the atom. Everything, he said, is made of tiny, indestructible particles, atoms. He said atoms moved about in space and, making different combinations, became all things. Although everything changed form and perished, the atoms themselves, said Democritus, were eternal. Today we know how small a thing Democritus was talking about. There are more molecules (combinations of atoms) in a glass of water than there are glasses of water in all the oceans. And things do change: fewer than 2 percent of the atoms present in a human body were there the previous year.

Even the sea, Democritus said, was composed of atoms.

One thing Democritus said, inscribed today on the cornerstone of Lovett Hall at Rice University, Houston, shows an attitude vital to all science at all times and all places:

"Rather would I discover the cause of one fact than become King of the Persians."

The search for causes of facts was infectious. The sailors exploring the world sought such knowledge. So did the men who experimented with different sails on their ships. So did astronomers. Another man in another field, Hippocrates, 460–370 B.C., looked carefully for the causes of disease or other illness in human beings. He shunted aside then-prevalent superstition and looked carefully at the course run by each disease. That is, he tried to diagnose. He prescribed, as a result, mainly diet, exercise, bathing, and some drugs—rarely surgery. He realized the body possesses enormous power to heal itself. Hippocrates' search for the causes of facts would improve immeasurably the health and chances of survival of men both on land and sea.

Thucydides, *c.* 460–400 B.C., said that divers were learning, too: By 415 B.C., at the siege of Syracuse, Greek divers could stay down long enough to saw through stakes the enemy had driven into the bottom to sink Greek ships. Divers were beginning to be able to do useful work under the sea.

21

About 357 B.C.:
Plato Talks About Atlantis

In the 300s b.c., in a garden cottage in Athens, a man named Plato lectured. On sunny days he gave his talks in an olive grove, named after Academus, the Academy. Centuries afterward, the poet, Milton, wrote, "in the olive grove of Academe." Today "academe" means the world of higher education.

For Plato (?427–347 b.c.) the earth was the center of a universe that revolved about it.

One of the subjects that Plato talked about at the age of seventy was a mystery of the sea, a mystery that has interested men ever since. He mentioned a Utopian civilization (shades of the Islands of the Blessed) that had sunk beneath the waters of an ocean—the vanished country of Atlantis.

The ocean is full of mysteries; the dark sea hides beneath its surface everything that is down there, including, in the Mediterranean, a hundred or even 150 sunken cities, many covered by the waves since Plato's time. Plato is the principal source of the tale of Atlantis and, since his day, it has been one of the deepest, darkest of the ocean's mysteries. What was Atlantis, this city or country that is supposed to have been covered by the waves? Where was it? Who lived there? Did it vanish into the sea? If so, how and when?

Said the National Geographic Society in a news release: "The philosopher Plato described Atlantis in two works, *Timaeus* and *Critias*, written about 370 B.C. Plato reported that Egyptian priests told the Greek law-giver Solon, who lived two centuries earlier, that Atlantis existed as a powerful kingdom 9,000 years before Solon's birth.

"Located beyond Gibraltar, Atlantis was supposedly a country larger than Asia Minor and Libya combined; its armies overran the Mediterranean lands. One day the sea overwhelmed Atlantis, and it vanished forever.

"Plato described Atlantis as an ideal commonwealth, rich in beauty and wealth. In the minds of the ancient Greeks, Atlantis became intertwined with Elysium, the place where the righteous dwell after death. Elysium was often placed in the lower world but sometimes also in the western sea, or Atlantic, like Atlantis."

Ever since Plato, men have been speculating and guessing where Atlantis might have been. Books about Atlantis fill many feet of bookshelves. There is probably more material on Atlantis than on any other aspect of the ocean. And still nobody knows.

Guesses as to its location have ranged from the Atlantic Ocean, the Indian Ocean, the East Indies, South America, to the North Sea. There is a possibility, at least, that Atlantis could have been the city of Tartessus—the vanished city once near Cadiz, Spain, an important port to the ancient mariners.

Another possibility is that Atlantis was the Minoan civilization on the island of Crete, the civilization that developed seamen who may have been among the first to venture out of sight of land.

According to a scientist who has been investigating Crete and the neighboring island of Thera with this in mind, "The island of Thera, 100 kilometers north of Crete in the Aegean Sea, erupted with tremendous violence between 1500 and 1450 B.C. At the end of this period a large part of the island collapsed into the sea creating enormous tidal waves which caused floods and coastal damage as far away as Egypt. The roar of the explosion may have been heard as far away as Scandinavia." [1] And perhaps the island when it vanished took with it part of the Minoan civilization of King Minos of Crete.

Today we know of two other occasions, one before and one after Thera's, when volcanoes have collapsed (their tops blew off) in mighty eruptions. About 5000 B.C., the collapse of a volcano formed Oregon's Crater Lake, with its 1,000-foot-high sides, and in 1883, the most recent volcano collapse caused almost all of the island of Krakatau (Krakatoa) in Indonesia to disappear beneath the sea. That collapse set up a wave 123 feet high, the highest tidal wave (tsunami) ever to strike a beach and wreak destruction of everything upon it.

In 1966, an ocean exploring expedition found beneath the sea near Thera a cliff 700 feet high which might have been caused by the volcano collapse. A seismic record of the bottom of the sea showed debris beneath the sediment, suggesting the island had collapsed. Near Thera and beneath 1,300 feet of water, scientists found a wide moat.

A sacred island of Atlantis is supposed to have been called Metropolis; the Metropolis, according to Plato, was surrounded by a moat. One Greek scholar thinks that the finding of the moat is a convincing proof that Thera and Crete might have been Atlantis. [2]

The expedition discovered in mud on the sea bottom near Thera blocks of basalt as big as an automobile, maybe thrown up during the volcano eruption, and pumice and lava boulders up to 20 feet on a side. Widespread volcanic ash has also been recently found on the bottom of the sea near Thera and Crete.

The Minoan civilization of Crete certainly did vanish in the 1400s B.C.; history shows that. Whether or not Crete and Thera are eventually accepted as Atlantis, the volcano collapse that ended Minoan civilization was almost certainly the greatest natural catastrophe on earth during historic times.

In common with many another man who has tried to predict the future, Plato was spectacularly right on one subject, just as wrong on another.

He was right about what would be found by sailors exploring the world. He thought that Mediterranean man lived on only a small part of the globe, like "frogs round a pool; and that many other men dwell in many other parts in many regions such as ours."

On what would be the good of oceanography, of studying the depths of the sea, he could not have been more wrong: "Nothing of any worth grows in the sea, nor in effect is there anything perfect there; instead there are caverns and sand and unlimited mud and sloughs wherever there is earth, and nothing worthy of comparison in any way whatever with the beautiful things which are among us."

Listening to Plato talk at the Academy was a student who became a great astronomer. Eudoxus of Cnidus (perhaps 408–355 B.C.) later had an observatory and made the first Greek scientific explanation of the movements of the planets. He said that the planets revolved around the earth. He was incorrect, as they revolve around the sun, but his explanation was a step forward in astronomy.

Eudoxus improved the sundial. With it, he concluded that the length of a year was 365¼ days—a step towards accurate timekeeping, essential to navigation. In time his sundial would lead to an improved gnomon to measure the height of the sun, also essential to navigation.

22

Mytilene, Lesbos, 300s B.C.: Aristotle Looks at Life in the Sea

ANOTHER STUDENT of Plato, Aristotle, became known for his careful combing of his sleek hair and also for walking as he lectured. He was the son of a doctor, and his father may have observed people as carefully as did that other doctor, Hippocrates, in diagnosing their ailments. At any rate, Aristotle became a close observer himself.

He watched the sky. During an eclipse, he observed the earth's circular shadow on the moon. This proved to his satisfaction that the world was round. Another proof the globe was round, he said, was that the same constellations were not seen from everywhere on earth. Although he surmised the earth was a sphere, he believed it to be smaller than it is.

He watched the ocean. He wanted to know why it didn't overflow. Evaporation, he said. Why were there currents in the sea? Because, he said, water flows away from the higher regions in the north. Why was the sea salty? He thought something "like burnt earth" was picked up from hot, dry regions and rained down from clouds into the ocean.

Accepting a common view (perhaps held since Parmenides, born 510 B.C.), Aristotle thought that the equator made a heat barrier men could not pass.

Aristotle mentioned two tools for divers that would have helped in making observations beneath the surface: something like a hose to bring air to breathe down from the surface, and something like a helmet that, turned open side down in the water, trapped air for a diver to breathe. The implication is that divers were making some progress during Aristotle's lifetime.

Like that advocate of a big Athenian navy, Themistocles (*fl.* 480 B.C.), Aristotle saw the usefulness of the sea to men at war: "Peoples who are to survive must be capable of assisting themselves both by land and by sea . . . and, with a view to doing harm to aggressors, those who are connected with the sea will be better placed."

He saw the usefulness of the sea in trade routes: "To receive as imports all products which [men] do not happen to have themselves and to export the surplus of their own products—these are among necessities."

Aristotle spent some time at Mytilene, on the island of Lesbos, and while there he collected specimens of animals, including fish. He had a favorite hunting ground—a calm, landlocked lagoon at Pyrrha.

Looking at animals, including many creatures of the sea, Aristotle noted differences and similarities. He distinguished between vertebrates (animals with backbones or rudimentary backbones) and invertebrates. He was on the track to comparative anatomy. Using his observations of anatomy, he classified animals and named 500 species. He compiled what has been called "the first recognizable book on natural history." [1]

At one point, Aristotle came up with a vast oversimplification of the kinds of ocean animals there are: "Of marine animals, some live in the open seas, some near the shore, some on rocks."

Today marine scientists divide the coastal zone alone into 20 biotopes, or recognizable communities: the gulfside beach, mudflats, spoil lands, dunes, oyster reefs, and others. The oyster-reef biotope, to take one example, consists of all the plants, animals, fish, and other organisms that live specifically around oyster reefs.[2]

So far as we know, Aristotle was the first man to write to any extent about fish. "Of water animals," he said, "the genus of fishes constitutes a single group apart from the rest, and including many diverse forms."

It certainly does. With perhaps 30,000 to 40,000 species by today's figures, fish are far and away the most common vertebrates in the world.

"There is no doubt," he said, "but that fishes have the sense of taste, for a great number of them delight in special flavors; and fishes freely take the hook if it be baited with a piece of flesh from a tunny or from any fat fish, obviously enjoying the taste and the eating of food of this kind." Fish, he said, "are observed to run away from any loud noise, such as would be made by the rowing of a galley, so as to become easy of capture in their holes; for, by the way, though a sound be very slight in the open air, it has a loud and alarming resonance to creatures that hear under water."

He understood a basic fact of life in the sea: many fish deposit eggs by hundreds of thousands, and yet few small fish survive to maturity. "If all the eggs were preserved, each species would be infinite in number."

Some fishing boats stayed at sea so long their catches had to be salted down, Aristotle said, an indication that deep-sea fishing was being carried on.

Aristotle thought that fish sleep: "Very often it is possible to take a fish off its guard so far as to catch hold of it or to give

it a blow unawares; and all the while that you are preparing
to catch or strike it, the fish is quite still but for a slight
motion of the tail. And it is quite obvious that the animal is
sleeping from its movements if any disturbance be made
during its repose; for it moves just as you would expect in a
creature suddenly awakened. Further, owing to their being
asleep, fish may be captured by torchlight. The watchmen in
the tunny-fishery often take advantage of the fish being
asleep to envelop them in a circle of nets; and it is quite
obvious that they were thus sleeping by their lying still and
allowing the glistening underparts of their bodies to become
visible, while the capture is taking place. They sleep in the
night-time more than during the day; and so soundly at night
that you may cast the net without making them stir. Fish, as a
general rule, sleep close to the ground, or to the sand or to
a stone at the bottom, or after concealing themselves under a
rock or the ground. Flat fish go to sleep in the sand; and they
can be distinguished by the outlines of their shapes in the
sand. . . . Cartilaginous fish sleep at times so soundly that
they may be caught by hand. The dolphin [porpoise] and the
whale, and all such as are furnished with a blow-hole, sleep
with the blow-hole over the surface of the water, and breathe
through the blow-hole while they keep up a quiet flapping of
their fins; indeed, some mariners assure us that they have
actually heard the dolphin snoring." Aristotle said, and
scientists today agree, that some fish sleep, hibernate, or hide
during winter or summer.

Among other observations, today's scientists have learned
that a parrot fish secretes a blanket of slime around itself to
protect it as it sleeps. A wrasse lies on its side and covers itself
with sand. Sole and flounders lie flat on the bottom. Some fish
sleep in crevices in coral. Some balance in mid-depth. Russian
scientists have observed shoals of thousands of herring,
floating in all kinds of positions including belly up, apparently

sleeping or lying still after eating. Fish that hibernate during the winter or rest on the bottom include the basking shark (which may weigh 4½ tons and reach 45 feet in length), the pencil-size pipefish, and the 4-inch-long seahorse.

Aristotle knew that fish make noises—the gurnard "a grunting kind of noise," the chalcis "a sort of piping-sound." The cuckoo fish, he wrote, "makes a sound greatly like the cry of the cuckoo, and is nicknamed from the circumstance. The apparent voice in all these fishes is a sound caused in some cases by a rubbing motion of their gills, which by the way are prickly." He said the scallop and the flying fish made whizzing sounds.

That every fish makes a noise is understood as a result of modern research.[3] During the spawning season, croakers and drums gather at the entrance to Chesapeake Bay. Scientists listening through hydrophones found the noise almost deafening. The sounds of ships' propellers were drowned out. For their spawning runs the croakers, which weigh up to 300 pounds and are up to 6½ feet long, and the drums separate themselves into proper species by their noises. Spawning causes fish to make many of their sounds.

A few of the other fish that make noises that man has ascertained include the ocean sunfish, a disk-shaped animal 8 or 10 feet or even more in diameter, which grunts or growls for defense and also gnashes its teeth. So does another giant, the bluefin tuna, which may weigh over 1,000 pounds.

The sea robin groans, clicks, and cracks. Burrfish and puffers whine. The toadfish honks, toots, growls, and croaks out a message containing 150 pulses a second—a surprising ability. There is a mystery in the toadfish's vocal ability: "It's such a low-frequency sound that for us to duplicate it would take all kinds of sophisticated equipment."[4]

Fish with swim bladders can make drumming noises or sound like foghorns. The grunter grunts or hums by vibrating its swim bladder, and is therefore known as the singing fish. By displacing water or by quickly changing direction or speed, fish even make noises in the water as they swim. Small parrot fish eat by reaping algae from hard surfaces—a crunch. Somewhat larger parrot fish bite hard substrates—a scrape.[5]

From 50 feet below the surface off Grand Bahama Island, scientists listened to reef fish make sounds they described as pops, rumbles, staccatos, and quacks. They also listened to the dusky damselfish make pops, croaks, fluttering tremolos, and mechanical crunches—all audible above the background of shrimp and water noises.

It has been suggested that the whispers of herring keep them together in deep shoals. And even the seahorse, which is a true fish, makes a noise, a monotonous but somewhat musical sound.

"With regard to the crustaceans," wrote Aristotle, "one species is that of the crawfish, and a second, resembling the first, is that of the lobster; the lobster differing from the crawfish in having claws, and in a few other respects as well. . . . All these animals "have their hard and shelly part outside, where the skin is in other animals, and the fleshy part inside."

Aristotle knew that the hermit crab borrows a shell from another animal, and that it can lay the borrowed shell aside: "It does not adhere to its shell like the purple murex . . . but can easily slip out of it."

Today we have gradually collected more facts on crustaceans. Crabs, lobsters, and other crustaceans, mostly very tiny, are arthropods, animals with jointed legs. The crabs and lobsters have 10 legs and therefore are called "decapods." Land arthropods include insects (6 legs), spiders (8 legs), centipedes (30 to 346 legs), and millipedes (up to 784 legs).

Water-dwelling crustaceans are arthropods which breathe by means of gills and have two pairs of antennas.

There are perhaps two million species of animals on earth, on land and in the sea. Of these, the arthropods alone number over one million species. The teeming insects on land and the teeming crustaceans in the ocean are the most numerous animals on the globe, millions and millions of them, in thousands of species (750,000 species of insects alone); the individual arthropods account altogether for perhaps four-fifths of all animals on earth. The most common arthropods in the sea are copepods, small, ¼-inch-long to less than pinhead-size or shrimplike creatures that weigh as little as 1/140,000 of an ounce and are spindle-shaped with a forked tail. Red, black, or sparkling in color, copepods scull along on 5 or 6 pairs of legs and graze on plants among the plankton of the sea, which they catch with special bristles that are better strainers than any man-made net. The copepods for the most part eat tiny, microscopic sea grass. The plants they graze on are called "diatoms"; a copepod may eat 130,000 diatoms a day. Existing by the quadrillion, the copepods, not cattle or sheep, are the world's most common grazing animal. In turn, the copepods are gobbled up by sharks, birds (storm petrels), jellyfish, arrowworms (transparent fish-shaped animals of the plankton), the young of many species of fish, and the adults of the mackerel and the herring of the enormous herring fisheries of northwestern Europe. One herring may have in its belly 60,000 copepods.

The land animals which approach closest in numbers to the copepods are arthropods and all are insects. They probably are either the ants, of which there may be more individuals than there are of any other animal; or the beetles, of which there are 250,000 species; or the mosquitoes, which are so numerous their total weight may exceed that of all other animals on the globe.

Yet the copepod may outnumber any of these. Seven-
tenths of the world is under the sea, where land insects
cannot live. And here the unfamiliar and frequently invisible
copepod grazes and multiplies and again grazes on the
microscopic grasses of the ocean.

In striking contrast to the tiny copepods, some of the
jointed-leg animals in the ocean are big. A Japanese spider
crab with a 10-foot leg span lives on the continental slope to
the abyss of the ocean off Japan. A 10-pound king crab from
the bottom of Alaskan waters may have a leg span of nearly 5
feet. An isopod, *Bathynomus giganteus*, 14 inches long and 6
inches across, from over 1,000 feet down in the Gulf of
Mexico, resembles "an armadillo crossed with a centipede." It
is at least 20 times longer than its cousin on land, the common
sow bug, found under rocks and logs.

Aristotle mistakenly believed that some animals were born
as a result of what is now called "spontaneous generation."
For thousands of years ancient man had thought that some
creatures, including many insects and worms, sprang to life
out of mud, slime, decaying bodies of men or animals, or their
dung. This was understandable. Egyptians along the Nile had
noticed that in summer, when the Nile rose and overflowed
its banks, the warm, humid soil left behind caused their grain
and fruit to grow, filled their marshes with lotus flowers, and
turned the marshes green with papyrus—and also produced
lots of insects, by means, they thought, of spontaneous
generation.

Aristotle thought shellfish spontaneously spring to life in
mud, oysters in slime, cockles on sandy bottoms, and
barnacles and limpets in the hollows of rocks. "The hermit
crab," he said, "grows spontaneously out of soil and slime,
and finds its way into untenanted shells."

One reason Aristotle and other ancient scientists believed

in spontaneous generation was that without microscopes there was no way to observe and understand larvae. A larva is the immature, early form of an animal, often tiny at first. It does not resemble its parents or the adult it will become. A tadpole, for example, is the larva of a frog. A wriggler is the larva of a mosquito. A caterpillar is the larva of a butterfly or moth. The grub is the larva of a beetle. The maggot is the larva of a fly. A transparent, leaf-shaped larva will turn into a snake-shaped eel. From any of the 4 million eggs a female spiny lobster may lay in one spring and summer, a larva may come that will at one stage look like a leaf with long, fringed legs and long, stalked eyes; before it becomes an adult, the young spiny lobster will go through the bewildering number of 20 to 25 different larval stages.

Aristotle knew of three species of sponges, and he told of the use of one for man: "As a lining to helmets . . . for the purpose of deadening the sound of the blow." He wrote: "Sponges grow spontaneously either attached to a rock or on sea beaches, and they get their nutrient in slime: a proof of this statement is the fact that when they are first secured they are found to be full of slime." The sponge "is at its best when found in deep water close to shore," where it is protected from stormy winds and excessive heat.

After Aristotle, up until the 1700s, men argued over whether a sponge was a plant, the home of a marine worm, or a sea insect. Aristotle, 300 years before Christ, said accurately that the sponge is an animal.

Of the 8-armed octopus Aristotle wrote: "The head comes after the feet, in the middle of the feet that are called arms or feelers. There is here situated a mouth . . . and . . . two large eyes, and betwixt the eyes a small cartilage enclosing a small brain."

He knew that, when frightened, the octopus, the cuttlefish, and the 10-armed squid discharge an ink (he called it a juice) into the water which blinds or distracts their enemies. Artists were using this ink not long after Aristotle's life; they are using it today.

He described the birth of octopuses: "The eggs, when the female has laid them, are clustered around the sides of [a] hole. They are so numerous that, if they be removed, they suffice to fill a vessel much larger than the animal's body in which they were contained. Some fifty days later, the eggs burst and the little polypuses creep out, like little spiders, in great numbers; the characteristic form of their limbs is not yet to be discerned in detail, but their general outline is clear enough. And, by the way, they are so small and helpless that the greatest number perish." The female octopus, he said, "at times sits brooding over her eggs, and at other times squats in front of her hole, stretching out her tentacles on guard."

Aristotle had not seen the mating of eels or their eggs. Not till the 1920s would scientists discover that eels breed in the middle of the Atlantic, beneath the seaweed-filled Sargasso Sea, and then travel, aided by the Gulf Stream, to Europe and North America.[6]

But taking the word of what other men thought they had seen, Aristotle went spectacularly wrong: "Eels have at times been seen to emerge out of . . . earthworms, and on other occasions have been rendered visible when the earthworms were laid open by either scraping or cutting."

"There are also sea-serpents," Aristotle said; they resembled snakes or eels. "There are several kinds of sea-serpent, and the different kinds differ in color." In this he was right. They may be black or yellow-bellied or ringed or dark above and light below.

According to marine biologists of the 1970s, there are about 60 species of sea snakes. Usually 4 to 5 feet long, sea snakes can reach 7 to 9 feet. One grows thick as a man's forearm. They breathe air, but, some believe, can close their nasal passages underwater. They have sacs to store air, can cut their pulse rate in half, and therefore they can stay submerged 2 to perhaps 8 hours.

They have been seen 100 to 150 miles from shore. In the Balboa harbor in Panama, thousands of black and white sea snakes surrounded a swimming man. Though they possess venom far more toxic than that of their relative, the cobra, they inject it in far smaller amounts and the swimmer was unharmed.

Aristotle wrote that the porpoise had been a pet of boys along the shore. Today there are a number of documented instances of porpoises coming repeatedly into shallow water and playing with youngsters and never harming them.

He wrote that, when a porpoise was caught and wounded by fishermen, other porpoises came and surrounded the fishing boat until the captive was set free. A few years ago, when a porpoise caught in a trawler's net and apparently dead was tossed back into the sea, other porpoises rubbed against its side and helped it regain consciousness.

Aristotle described adult porpoises trying to support a little dead porpoise on the surface. The porpoise, he commented, "is remarkable for the strength of its personal affection." Today we have many verified eyewitness accounts of mother porpoises trying to keep babies breathing the air they must have and nudging them to the surface.

He said the porpoise could leap over a ship's mast. At aquariums in the United States today, porpoises routinely leap about 18 feet out of the water—about the height an Olympic champion pole vaulter achieves.

Again agreeing with modern scientists, Aristotle knew that porpoises could squeak and moan. These sounds today have been recorded on tape. He knew that porpoises, whales, and seals were mammals, and not big fish; that they were warm-blooded, have hair, and suckle their young. He knew porpoises could dive deep fast. He did not know why they sometimes strand themselves—swimming onto shallow beaches from which they then cannot get free. It is still not known why they do it.

Aristotle knew that there were during his lifetime unknown animals in the ocean: "Furthermore, there are some strange creatures to be found in the sea, which from their rarity we are unable to classify. Experienced fishermen affirm, some that they have at times seen in the sea animals like sticks, black, rounded, and of the same thickness throughout; others that they have seen creatures resembling shields, red in color, and furnished with fins packed close together."

In 1964, an example of what Aristotle had called "some strange creatures to be found in the sea" was hauled up in a plankton net from 1,000 to 6,000 feet beneath the Sargasso Sea. It was black, an inch long, with big eyes, and as part of its physique, a long, stringlike filament streamed behind. At the end of the filament leafy appendages swept the water, like a trawl. No such method of capturing prey, if that is what it is, ever had been observed by scientists before.

Named *Kasidoron edom*, the new fish not only was among Aristotle's "strange creatures," but it was a new genus and a new family of fish.[7]

Today, in the last half of the twentieth century, not a year goes by without scientists' hauling out of the sea creatures they have never seen before.

Aristotle on disease in fish: "We know of no pestilential malady attacking fishes . . . but fishes do seem to suffer from sickness; and fishermen infer this from the fact that at times fishes in poor condition, and looking as though they were sick, and of altered color, are caught in a large haul of well-conditioned fish of their own species." In the 1970s, diseases in fish are one of the fields opening for marine biologists and a subject man today has a great deal to learn about.

Aristotle on turtles: "The sea-turtle lays on the ground eggs just like the eggs of domesticated birds, buries the eggs in the ground, and broods over them in the night-time. It lays a very great number of eggs, amounting at times to one hundred."

On parasites: "There are some snail-shells which have inside them creatures resembling those little crayfish that are also found in fresh water."

On the migration of birds: "The crane . . . migrates from one end of the world to the other." He said the crane flew from Scythia to the marshlands south of Egypt.

On movements of sea animals: "Of shell-fish and fish that are finless, the scallop moves with greatest force and to the greatest distance." On the scallops, which are bivalves (that is, with two-part, hinged shells): They can "fly. . . . They often jump right out of the apparatus by means of which they are caught." And on the snails that provided the purple dye of the Phoenicians: "The murex or purple-fish and others that resemble it, move hardly at all."

Aristotle knew a great deal more of the sea anemone than might be expected. He knew that it can move. Even today this flower-like animal, with its thick stalk, is thought of as remaining fixed in place. But some sea anemones can move slowly on their bases. Said Aristotle: "The sea-nettle or sea-anemone, clings to rocks . . . but at times relaxes its hold." One sea anemone, he said, "roams freely ahead." He said that its waving tentacles captured little fish, scallops, and sea urchins for food; the mouth is in the center of the body amid the tentacles.

Aristotle followed Thales of Miletus, the man who had rubbed amber and discovered static electricity, in trying to explain things scientifically and not by myths. So insistent

was he on careful observation that he has become known as
the father of scientific inquiry.

Aristotle recorded his lectures on animals in two books, the
world's first known natural history, *The History of Animals,*
and *On the Parts of Animals,* which stressed comparative
anatomy.

In the light of modern biological knowledge, Aristotle
made errors; in the light of his day, he was astonishingly
accurate. Said a modern scientist: "For centuries afterward it
was judged almost heretical to question any of the Greek
philosopher's statements. Even where he had obviously erred,
as in reporting that the housefly has eight legs, medieval
scholars inclined to trust the master's testimony rather than
their own eyes." [8]

Another tribute today is paid to Aristotle. A basketlike
structure that holds the teeth (and their muscles) of the sea
urchin is named after him. It is called "Aristotle's lantern."

23

From Macedon, After 336 B.C.: An Army Explores

ARISTOTLE HAD a student named Alexander, born in the year of the 106th Olympic games, 356 B.C. Alexander, who would be an explorer of both land and sea, wore a purple cloak. He was the son of King Philip II and Queen Olympias of Macedon, in northern Greece. His mother started him off to what for those days was a heavily scientific education. It included reading, writing, arithmetic, geometry, medicine, astronomy, biology, and the works of the poet, Homer.

Alexander joined the army at age sixteen, took it over when his father died in 336 B.C., and with it conquered the eastern end of the Mediterranean (although he did not reach Italy), and everything else out to India. He subdued (in chronological order) Greece, Thebes (where he spared Pindar's house), Sardis, Miletus, Halicarnassus, Lycia, Phrygia, Western Cilicia, Syria, Tyre in Phoenicia, Egypt, Persia under King Darius. He twice crossed the high, frigid Hindu Kush Mountains, marched through the Khyber Pass to the Indus River in India. He reached what is today West Pakistan. He saw the world's tallest mountains, the Himalayas. He had marched off the map of the world as the Greeks knew it. He wanted to push on from the Beas River to the Ganges River, which he considered the end of the earth, but his army was too tired and forced him to turn back.

Alexander had something he may have acquired from Aristotle, "the insatiable curiosity and the untiring persistence of a scientist or explorer." [1] He took along with his army a scientific staff. His engineers surveyed distances with measuring wheels. His physicians learned new diseases and new methods of cures. His stargazers observed constellations of stars at night and learned what information astronomers in the countries they passed through had obtained. His armies are even said to have carried plants from place to place during campaigns either for food, as medicines, or simply because they were beautiful. His intelligence officers asked questions about everything.

At Ecbatana, in Persia, the Zoroastrians showed Alexander a dark liquid that came out of cracks in the earth and would burn. The substance earlier had been used to bond bricks in the Tower of Babel, by the Egyptians for embalming their dead, and by the Phoenicians for caulking their ships. Alexander's scientists were looking at something for which other men would find thousands of other uses—petroleum.

In India Alexander and his men saw, rode on, and used elephants. As elephants were known from Africa, this led, logically enough, to the idea that India and Africa were closer together than they are and that they might even be joined. In the Indus River they saw crocodiles, also known from the Nile and Africa, and he wrote to his mother, Olympias, that he had found the springs of the Nile. Later he knew better.

Two centuries earlier, according to Herodotus (who had lived in the century before Alexander), a Greek, Skylax of Caryanda, had sailed down the Indus River for King Darius of Persia, and then had sailed west for 30 months till he reached the Red Sea and "the port from which the Egyptian king [Necho, around 600 B.C.] had once sent out the Phoenicians . . . to circumnavigate Africa."

Alexander, who may have read about Skylax, wanted to follow the Indus River to the sea, which he called "Ocean." Said Arrian, a historian who wrote about it much later in *The Anabasis of Alexander*: Alexander "gave order for the bugle to sound departure." His fleet started—80 thirty-oared vessels and up to 2,000 transports, galleys, and boats thrown together for the occasion. "Never was there a sound like that of the fleet rowing all together, with the coxswains crying the strokes and the oarsmen chanting as they struck the swirling water in unison."

After 500 miles, Alexander's army was near the coast. Accustomed to the almost tideless Mediterranean, they were startled by the high tides near the mouth of the Indus. When a tide rushed in, it knocked together ships or hurled them against the shore. When a tide ebbed, it left the whole fleet stranded.

Alexander could not wait to sail the Indian Ocean. He took, Arrian reported, his fastest sailing ships, some of one and a half banks of oars, and the thirty-oared vessels. "On the day after they set out, a storm arose and the wind blew contrary to the river current, making troughs wherein the craft were shaken, so that most of the ships were damaged and some of the thirty-oared vessels completely came asunder."

Alexander sacrificed bulls to appease the sea god Poseidon.

One of Alexander's admirals was a man from the island of Crete, Nearchus. Nearchus sailed down the Indus with Alexander, then along the Indian coast, homeward-bound toward Greece, while Alexander and his army trudged along the coast.

On the way back, Nearchus charted coasts and harbors—a

step toward hydrography. According to Arrian, one day Nearchus reported a strange sight: "Water was seen being blown upward from the sea as though from bellows." Experienced pilots said this was from whales. Inexperienced sailors were startled and oars fell from their hands. Nearchus ordered one ship's crew to man catapults, to row directly at the monsters, to shout, to splash with their oars, and to blow bugles. The spouting whales dived or swam away and the sailors applauded and praised Nearchus "for his courage and intelligence."

Sometimes whales were stranded along this coast. The inhabitants used their rib bones as beams for houses and their jawbones as door frames. These people lived almost entirely on fish which were stranded or caught just off the beach in hand nets.

Halfway between the Indus River and the entrance to the Persian Gulf was an island, Ashtola. One of the sailors' horror tales about the Indian Ocean concerned this island. It was said that whenever a ship put in there, its crew vanished without a trace. It was also said that a mermaid changed sailors into fish. When one of Nearchus' ships disappeared near the island, his sailors said it had unwittingly touched the shore and the island's evil magic had worked. To prove this was only a superstition, Nearchus sailed to the island and with some of his crew went ashore. They all survived.

After a hard voyage that lasted 80 days, the fleet reached its goal, the mouth of the Euphrates River. Only four ships had been lost.

The city of Tyre in Phoenicia was located on an island; to attack Tyre, Alexander built a causeway. When Tyrian divers cut the anchor ropes of his oar-propelled warships, Alexander substituted chains—perhaps the first use of anchor chains. He also used divers to destroy booms—underwater obstacles.

There is a story that, after his capture of Tyre, Alexander had some months to loaf along the shore and watch the merchant ships and warships. Perhaps influenced by divers for sponges in the Mediterranean or by divers for pearls in the Persian Gulf or Red Sea, Alexander decided to go beneath the sea for a look himself. According to another story, he was the first person to have descended into the sea in a diving chamber of any kind; the first to have had himself lowered by a line into the water so he could see with his own eyes what was there.

If this story is true, Alexander, after the pearl and sponge divers, made the next logical step in man's journey beneath the sea.

The story, in a thirteenth-century manuscript, *La Vrai Histoire D'Alexandre*, says that Alexander got into a glass barrel and, with glowing lamps, was lowered to the sea floor, presumably in shallow water. The glass barrel was called a *colimpha*—a device that kept a man dry but at the same time, admitted light. To breathe, he must have had some kind of snorkel arrangement.[2]

Two other ancient manuscripts, one French, one Arab, say Alexander was accompanied by two other persons.[3] The Arab source says the diving chamber was built of wood, caulked with resin, wax, and other substances, and lowered between two ships into the sea.

Alexander, with or without his two companions, was the first man of whom we have any account who stayed down for a long period—longer than a man could hold his breath, longer than he could breathe with a leather bag of air or a primitive snorkel.

Alexander saw, he himself said afterwards, "many fish that

had the form of beasts that live on land and walk on legs . . . and many other wonders that are unbelievable." He was said to have seen a monster that took three days to swim past his glass barrel. That tale has been repeated to show that there might be such things as sea serpents—far longer than the sea snakes that both Aristotle and modern marine biologists have described.

In Egypt in 332–21 B.C., Alexander established one of 13 towns he founded that were called Alexandria. This one would last. In a few decades its library, established by Ptolemy I, would become the center of the world's learning. It would be built up by its superintendent, Demetrios Phalareos, to be the world's largest collection of manuscripts before the introduction of printing—Chaldean, Persian, Jewish, Ethiopian, Greek, Latin, Egyptian, and others. Alexandria was called the "Mother of Books."

The city became the center of the world's science. There, men following in the footsteps of Hippocrates made some of the earliest dissections of human bodies. They also dissected animals and discovered the functions of the heart and brain and traced the nerve system.

According to a legend that may not be true, throughout his travels Alexander kept sending back to his old teacher, Aristotle, astronomical observations and biological specimens: plants, animal skins, shellfish, insects, birds. His specimens could have been used when Aristotle wrote his *History of Animals* and *On the Parts of Animals*.

Alexander also sent, at different times, three captains— Hiero from Soli, Archiis, and Androsthenes—to try to sail around Arabia. None made it.

Alexander died in Babylon in 323 B.C. He was thirty-two years and eight months old. He died either of a fever that may have been malaria or possibly from poison. Whatever it was, he probably also was physically exhausted. One hundred years after his death men would begin to call him Alexander the Great.

In 322 B.C., the next year, Aristotle died at age sixty-three. For a long time some of his works were lost; over 200 years later they were to turn up in the cellar of a house in Scepsis. Meanwhile, other ideas of his spread to the Phoenicians, after their conquest by Alexander. Eventually all of Aristotle's works were in the library at Alexandria. The Phoenicians and the library at Alexandria passed Aristotle's thoughts on to the Arabs, who, in the course of time, spread them in Europe. Aristotle became the most accepted philosopher in Christian Europe. By the 1200s A.D., Aristotle would be taught at the Universities of Paris, Oxford, and Cambridge, which the Arabs never reached. In the 1400s A.D. in Spain, which the Arabs had reached, Aristotle was widely read. Seventeen hundred years after his death, his idea of a round earth, smaller than it is—an earth on which a man might sail west to reach the Orient—would stick in the mind of an obscure sailor aboard cargo ships that touched at Mediterranean, Portuguese, Spanish, and northern European ports, Christopher Columbus.

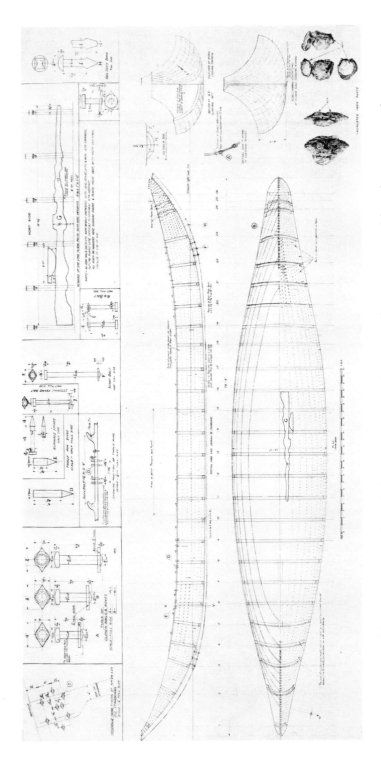

Architectural construction of the huge open rowing boat of 650–525 B.C., driven by 40 oars, whose impression was found at Sutton Hoo, England, in 1939. No timber survived. (British Crown Copyright, The Science Museum, London)

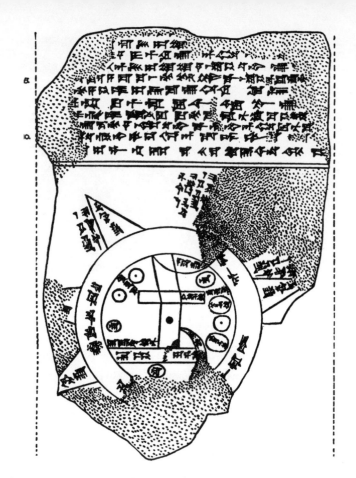

ABOVE Inscribed on a tablet is what may be the oldest-known map of the world, the Babylonian "Mappa Mundi" from 600 B.C. It shows the land surrounded by the sea and, at center, Babylon and the Euphrates River. (The British Museum)

BELOW An ancient astronomical instrument, found in Ireland, and dating perhaps from 500 B.C. (From *The Pictorial History of England*, 1838)

In the 300s B.C., Alexander of Macedon conquered Tyre in Phoenicia, and had himself lowered in a glass barrel to observe life in sea. This fanciful illustration is from a thirteenth-century manuscript now in Burgundy Library, Brussels. (Electric Boat Division, General Dynamics Corporation)

ABOVE Strange men for centuries were rumored to exist in faraway places, as sailors gradually explored the earth. Since the 300s B.C., false tales were of men with big feet, one eye, two heads, no head, and dog head. (From *Margarita philosophica*, 1517)

BELOW As the sailor became more proficient, his ships became more elaborate and larger. Under Ptolemy IV Philopator of Egypt, 220–204 B.C., there was built a 42-foot-long ship that required 4,000 rowers. She may have looked like this. (New York Public Library)

ABOVE By 100 A.D., the Romans decorated the bows of their ships as shown on these Roman coins. (New York Public Library)

BELOW By 200 B.C., skin-covered boats on frameworks had been made thoroughly seaworthy, as in this model of an Irish craft. (British Crown Copyright, The Science Museum, London)

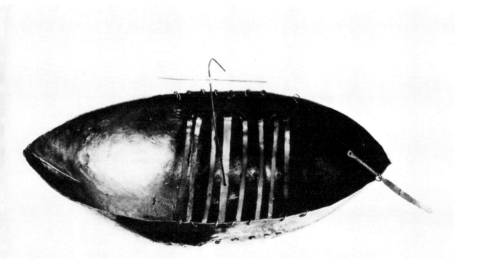

ABOVE By the time of Christ, geography was far along, as is shown by the detail in this map of Spain, 70 A.D., by a Roman geographer, Pomponius Mela. Note that he shows ships out on the Atlantic. (Copyright, The British Library)

BELOW A drawing of a Roman ship of around 79 A.D., taken from a painting found at Pompeii. (New York Public Library)

ABOVE By 200 A.D., Roman merchant ships (shown here in a bas-relief) had grown much larger and were capable of carrying great loads of grain from Egypt to Rome. (The Science Museum, London)

BELOW A model of a Roman merchant ship, similar to the one pictured in the bas-relief. (British Crown Copyright, The Science Museum, London, and New York Public Library)

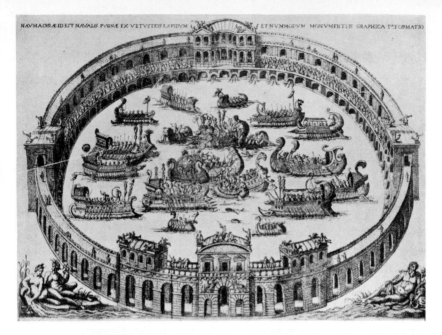

In Rome around 80 A.D., mock naval battles were fought on land to show the public what went on at sea. As shown on this drawing and on two coins, great reservoirs were dug and surrounded by amphitheaters. There is a record of one 1,800 feet long and 1,200 feet wide. As many as 30 ships and 3,000 fighting men took part. (From *Ships and Ways of Other Days*, New York Public Library Picture Collection)

24

To the Arctic, 330 Years B.C.: Ultima Thule

WHAT IS out there? A contemporary of Aristotle and Alexander, a Greek astronomer named Pytheas, fitted out a sailing ship with auxiliary oars, and sailed into the unknown Atlantic and northwards to answer the question.

What he accomplished, perhaps from 330 to 325 years before Christ, over 1,800 years before Columbus' discoveries of 1492, was nothing less than an expedition to the Arctic.

The Greeks of Pytheas' time thought that the earth was divided into 5 zones—one hot (around the equator), 2 moderate, 2 cold. Men could live only in the moderate zones. Land around the equator, too close to the sun, was fatally hot, with burning rocks and boiling water. In the frozen and silent north, and far south, too far from the sun, men would find no animal or sea life at all, nor could they survive there. The Arctic north was regarded as located just above Britain. The Greeks did not believe the Phoenicians ever had reached, or sailed across, or could cross, the burning tropics, the Torrid Zone. Nor did they believe a man could live in the frigid north. But Pytheas was to make the journey north—and to come back alive.

Pytheas lived in a Greek colony, Massilia (present-day Marseilles), on the Mediterranean coast of France. Massilia is a Phoenician word meaning "settlement"; the town may have been a Phoenician trading post. It was later taken over by the capable sailors of Phocaean Greece.

At the mouth of the Rhone River, Massilia for long had been on an important overland trade route for lead and tin from Britain and for amber from northern Europe.

Tin came overland from French Atlantic ports. It was mined in the Tin Islands, or Cassiterides, off France or Britain or both (we are not positive; the merchants of Massilia at the time either did not know or were vague).

By Pytheas' day, amber was worn not only as jewelry, but also as charms, by Egyptian pharaohs, Greek philosophers, Roman aristocrats, and others. Accordingly, when it was washed ashore during storms along the Baltic coast, it was picked up and shipped to the known world. And inside the golden, maroon, or brown blobs of amber, trapped by the amber itself after it had oozed from its pine tree, creatures or small objects were preserved—a fly, a spider, a beetle, a snail, an earthworm, a small lizard, a bird's feather, a bit of a reptile's skin, a hair, or a flea.

Business in amber was brisk. The Massilia merchants were sending ships past Gibraltar into the Atlantic and north. They probably supported Pytheas and paid for his ship and trip.

Pytheas may have been looking for the sea route to Britain discovered in 470 B.C. by Himilco of Carthage—but kept secret ever since. The Carthaginians kept their mouths shut as tight as had their forefathers, the Phoenicians. How secretive they were about their route to Britain is indicated by an incident reported by the Greek Strabo. A Carthaginian ship, pursued by a Roman vessel trying to learn the way, was deliberately run aground and sunk by her master with the intention that the Roman captain would follow behind and do the same thing. When the Carthaginian captain returned home, he was reimbursed for the value of his cargo by the Carthaginian senate out of the treasury.

Pytheas probably had learned some of his astronomy from Eudoxus of Cnidus, the Greek stargazer and improver of the sundial or gnomon. Using a gnomon to calculate the height of the sun by the length of the shadow it cast, Pytheas worked out a way to determine latitude, and accurately located Massilia, his point of departure and return.

Vilhjalmur Stefansson says Pytheas was the first who applied astronomy to geography to locate a point on the earth.[1]

Pytheas learned that the North Pole was not marked by a star, but that it was a small place in the sky with three stars near it. He learned that the stars Beata Ursae Minoris and Alpha Draconis were very close to the pole, and he selected one as his polestar, a star to steer by. Sir Clements Markham commented: "It is probable that there was no other man, in the days of Alexander the Great, who could have prepared for a voyage of discovery by fixing the exact latitude of his point of departure, and by selecting correctly the star by which he should shape his course." [2]

His ship, if she was one of the typical Greek Massilia merchant vessels of those days, would have been 150 to 170 feet long, in beam one-fourth of her length, with a hold 25 to 26 feet deep. She probably drew 10 to 12 feet of water and had a tonnage of 400 to 500. She probably could travel about 50 or perhaps 70 or even 100 miles a day. She was twice as long and about as fast as the vessels in which the Vikings

sailed the North Atlantic 1,200 years later and planted a
colony in Iceland—the first westward movement by Europeans.

She was probably a larger and a more seaworthy ship than
the *Santa Maria*, the largest of Columbus' three vessels which
crossed the Atlantic over 1,800 years after Pytheas. She may
have had other ships to keep her company. In all probability
she had oarsmen in addition to sails. Including the rowers for
two banks of oars if she was a bireme, she might have had a
crew of 100 or more men. Or, counting the rowers for three
banks of oars if she was a trireme, she might have had a crew
of 200.

On his Arctic journey, Pytheas sailed in the spring,
perhaps April, through the Pillars of Heracles at Gibraltar,
turned north, and arrived off present-day Cape St. Vincent,
Portugal, in those days the end of the world known to the
Greeks.

Cape St. Vincent was a tall cape, highly visible, which
could be seen, and was, by sailors for centuries after Pytheas,
from as far away as 50 miles. From Pytheas onwards it would
be a landmark indicating to any returning sailor on the
Atlantic that home port was not far away.

As had the first mariners to sail out of sight of land,
Pytheas, when he passed Cape St. Vincent, went beyond
unknown horizons into unknown seas.

About the latitude of modern Oporto, Portugal, he noticed
that the longest day was about 15 hours. He sailed north
along the coasts of Spain and France. He measured the depths
of the Bay of Biscay. In Britain he reached both Kent and
Land's End. He described tin mining. He probably saw
boats, or coracles, made of willow branches covered with
hides.

He may have circumnavigated Britain, because he seems to
have learned the rough shape of the island, and he seems to

have learned of the Orkney (ancient Orcades) Islands, north of Scotland, for which the black and white killer whale *Orca* is named. For one section of Britain, he recorded a longest day of 17 hours; that would be near Flamborough Head, a cape on the east coast of Yorkshire. He discovered a fermented beverage that Britons made from barley: beer. In contrast to the slight tides of the Mediterranean, he saw the high tides of northwest Europe. They were as new to him as the high tides of the Indian Ocean were, at almost exactly the same time, to that other Mediterranean adventurer, Alexander of Macedon. Pytheas was the first Greek to connect the tides with the moon. In contrast to the sunshine of the Mediterranean, he encountered the rain, clouds, and mist of northern Europe.

Sailing back to the continent of Europe, he traveled beyond the Rhine River and reached an island—never positively identified—where amber was to be obtained. It could have been North Prussia or somewhere in the borderland between Denmark and Germany, off the Schleswig coast.

We do not know how far north Pytheas reached. We know he arrived, after 6 days' sail into the unknown seas, at a place north of Britain he called Thule. Jutland? The Faeroes? The Orkneys? Iceland? Even Greenland—almost to North America? He mentions a spot having its longest day 19 hours long. In the Shetland Islands? Norway is another possibility.

In Scotland or in the Orkney Islands, Pytheas might have heard of an inhabited land still further north, "the land of the midnight sun," and he might have set out to find it. If he did hear this, there already must have been contact by sea between northern Britain or the Orkneys and Iceland or Norway a thousand years before the age of the Vikings.

Pytheas said he saw an ocean that was sluggish and thick like a jellyfish. He could have been referring either to mushy ice or to an explosion of life of some kind of plankton, the tiny drifting plants and animals that sometimes multiply so much they stain the sea red or another color or form a slime. If Pytheas meant plankton, his is one of the earliest references to it.

We believe Pytheas reached the Arctic because he described a "congealed, frozen" ocean, maybe ice sludge or pancake ice, or maybe actually even the edge of the Arctic ice sheet. He called it "a curdled sea." Fog, sea, and sky, he said, were so gray you could not tell them apart. A frequent condition in northern or Arctic mists, this is exactly what the area north of Iceland often looks like.

More evidence that Pytheas reached the Arctic lies in the fact that he seems to have reached the land of the summer midnight sun. He came to a region, or heard of a region near him, where the day lasted 21 or 22 hours in midsummer. This could be northern Norway or at the edge of the Arctic ice pack north of Iceland.

A modern Arctic explorer, Vilhjalmur Stefansson, believed Pytheas' Thule was Iceland. He thought that either Scots or people in the Orkneys might have been impressed by the power of Pytheas' oarsmen, in calms or against the wind, and might have volunteered to guide his ship to Iceland or Norway or both.

According to Stefansson, ancient man and his boats were perfectly able to reach Iceland from Britain. Large leather-covered or wooden boats or ships could have done it—and did do it, perhaps even long before Pytheas.

It is his theory that man had boats and ships two, four, or five times as long ago as any archeological records ever found indicate. Norwegian Bronze Age rock carvings show boats that look as though they could be oceangoing, so by the Bronze Age ships perhaps regularly traveled the route to and from Scotland—the Orkneys, the Shetlands, Norway.[3]

And if man was a capable sailor in the Bronze Age, he must have been also in the earlier Stone Age. Stone Age implements found in Cornwall and Brittany show the same culture from 3000 B.C. or earlier, which meant contact across a broad stretch of sea.[4] Similar cromlechs, or tombs, in the Mediterranean-Atlantic coast of Europe and the British Isles suggest that men at the same time were sailing the Bay of Biscay, crossing the wide end of the English Channel, and crossing the Irish Sea.

There was no technical reason that ancient northern European man should not have reached Iceland. He had the knowledge—in boats and ships, stars, and wind in the sails.

As ancient man was discovering the Orkney and Shetland Islands, he was actually rediscovering them, as archeology shows, after other, more ancient sailors. Once he discovered the Faeroe Islands, 100 miles from the Shetlands, Iceland was only 240 more miles of sea farther. And in southwest Iceland there is a volcano, the 6,952-foot-high Mount Öraefajökull, a fine landmark that a sailor sights from a day's sailing (about 100 miles) away. Thus a sailor from the Faeroes would be in sight of Iceland for almost half his trip. In the summer, daylight around Iceland lasts a long time. This and the fact that mirages are common near Iceland would help.[5] Men have seen Iceland from 240 miles away or farther, and mirages could have beckoned ancient sailors.

The same reasons—good ships, frequent islands, short journeys, long daylight, high visibility—would help northern European sailors, the Norsemen or Vikings, to cross 1,300 years later the Atlantic first to Iceland and then, in two more short trips, on to Greenland and North America.

Today, many ancient voyages have been linked with the discovery of America, and there is even a tale, probably false, that, after leaving his Ultima Thule, Pytheas sailed southwest to North America. With Pytheas' own records lost, there is no way to check this story.

What we do know about Pytheas comes from Timaeus, born about 346 B.C.; and from the later Polybius, Eratosthenes, Hipparchus, Strabo, and Pliny. Pytheas was also known to a pupil of Aristotle named Dicaearchus, who died about 285 B.C.

On all of the legs of this trip Pytheas could have sailed along the coast, always in sight of land, except on his way (if he made it) to Iceland, Norway, or other northern islands.

He took from eight months to two years for his round trip; estimates vary. After he returned home to Massilia, he apparently published *The Periplus*, a book of sailing directions for coastal pilots on such a trip.

Whether or not he reached Iceland, Norway, or both, or somewhere else, Pytheas' name "Thule" came to mean the northernmost point of Europe. The phrase "Ultima Thule" came to mean the farthest limit possible.

Pytheas has been credited with "the first voyage of discovery with scientific importance." [6] After Pytheas, there are no further records of Greek voyages to Britain, Thule, or anywhere north.

Pytheas, said Fritjdof Nansen, an authority both on the Arctic and on Pytheas, was "the first of whom we have certain record to sail along the coasts of northern Gaul and Germany." For men who lived around the Mediterranean, he was the discoverer, following the Phoenicians and Carthaginians, of Great Britain, Scottish islands and Shetland, and of Thule or Iceland or Norway as far north as the Arctic Circle. Nansen on Pytheas' significance: "No other single traveler known to history has made such far-reaching and important discoveries." [7]

Whatever else may be said of Pytheas' trip, one thing is sure: Pytheas' ship showed she could sail far north in one of the world's roughest oceans, the North Atlantic. She showed how able ships had become, how far advanced they were, since the day, thousands of years before, when someone made the little model ship found in the sands of Egypt.

By Pytheas' day, the Phoenicians, Carthaginians, Greeks, and Romans had developed ships as able as his. That was why Pytheas had one. Also, by Pytheas' day, northern Europeans had developed oceangoing craft. From his day onwards, man would be an open-sea sailor. He could make any passage.

25

Around 300 B.C.:
Drifting Bottles,
Voyages to India

PLATO HAD TAUGHT Aristotle. At his school in Athens, the Lyceum, Aristotle taught a student named Theophrastus. Some time before 300 B.C., Theophrastus began tossing bottles and marked seaweed into the sea to see where they would drift. Theophrastus showed that the Mediterranean receives most of its water from the Atlantic.

Today men aboard a single oceanographic ship on a single cruise will toss overboard as many as 10,000 beer bottles, each of which contains a message asking its finder to let it be known where he found it. Today U.S. marine biologists with the help of thousands of commercial and sports fishermen tag fish and toss them back into the ocean. Their tags, like the messages in the bottles, ask the finders to report.

Another student of Plato, Heraclides of Pontus (*c.* 388 to 312 B.C.), said to Aristotle that the world turns on its own axis from west to east in 24 hours. It does. That explained, he said, why distant stars appeared to move around the earth. He

156

said that Venus and Mercury revolve around the sun. They
do.

A Greek, Megasthenes, traveled to the Ganges River in
India—he probably was the first Greek to reach its banks—
and around 300 B.C. his reports began to spread. He said that
an Indian king who had helped Alexander, Sandracottus, or
Chandraguptra, was attended and guarded in his palace only
by women. Megasthenes reported accurately that India had
cotton (which he called "tree wool"), sugar cane, rice, and
spices, and that the country possessed elephants, tigers, large
snakes (pythons), rhinoceroses, crocodiles, fierce wild dogs,
parrots, monkeys, and peacocks. He said that the nearby
island of Taprobane (Ceylon) had elephants, gold, and pearls.
    Megasthenes heard and mistakenly believed some tall tales:
ants as big as foxes, ants that dug gold; unicorns (the
rhinoceros?); snakes and scorpions with wings; men with
their hands or feet turned backwards; men with ears like
dogs'; men with one eye in the center of the forehead;
floppy-eared men who lay down on their ears to sleep. For
centuries these nonexistent animals and people were part of
the fairy tales men believed.
    The spices and other goods from India and the rest of Asia
came by ships—following the route of Alexander's admiral,
Nearchos—to Red Sea ports in East Africa. One of the Red
Sea ports, Myos-Hormus, became the main port for trading
with India. The products of Asia next could be transported
overland by camel to Mediterranean ports to be transshipped.
    From Alexandria, the spices and other products of India
and Asia were again transshipped. Alexandria's harbor was
not in the center of the Nile delta and so did not fill up with
sand. The harbor continually was improved and made
spacious and safe for ships. The Greeks named Alexandria

Eunostos, "the safe return." The merchants of Alexandria had right at hand sailors they promptly hired, the Phoenicians, who already had their own skilled navigators and captains, and trading posts, and trade routes around the Mediterranean and beyond in the Atlantic—that is, around the known world.

On the Red Sea coast of Egypt, a brand-new port, Ptolemaïs Epitheris, was established with just one purpose. It was to ship African elephants north to Egypt to be trained for war. The idea was to give the rulers of Egypt an inexhaustible supply of a formidable war weapon, the tank or truck of its day.

Greek captains, planted in the Red Sea by Alexander, were interested in the East African coast all the way south along the Red Sea and beyond into the Gulf of Aden and to the easternmost point of Africa, Cape Guardafui. Here, as on the opposite coast of Arabia, they could obtain frankincense and myrrh. (Punt, the goal of the fleet of Queen Hatshepsut, quite possibly was near here.) And on the East African coast the Greeks could obtain so much of another spice that the coast was named for it, the Land of Cinnamon.

As they moved ever farther south down the East African coast, Greeks set up landmarks bearing the names of the captains who reached each successive point south: Pytholaus, Lichis, Pythangelus, Leon, and Charimortus. These captains were exploring East Africa exactly as, in the 1400s, the Portuguese captains would explore West Africa and so prepare the way for Columbus and his age of exploration. And these Greek captains themselves prepared the way for a golden age of Arab sailing ships, including a type that would become famous, the dhows.

Men also continued to believe in the existence of the

Fortunate Isles, the Islands of the Blessed, the Utopia on earth. Sailors kept looking for them. The unknown author of *De Mirabilibus*, about 300 B.C., said the Carthaginians had sailed into the Atlantic from Gibraltar and, after several days, reached a wooded island—and he was probably quoting Timaeus; a man named Diodorus repeated the story. The island was fertile. It is now thought to have been Madeira.

The same unknown author mentioned the Rhine River and said the Germans lived beside it—the first mention of the Germans in writing we know of.

Also around 300 B.C., in what is today Germany, the Saxons reached the mouth of the Elbe River and proceeded to the sea. They had the common northern European boats of willow framework covered with skins and keels of oak. Without compasses or charts of any kind, the Saxons managed to get to the Orkney Islands.

26

Alexandria, About 280 B.C.:
A Light on the Shore

IN THE CENTURIES before Christ, man built seven structures that became known as the Seven Wonders of the World. They show how capable ancient man was at engineering, a science that helped him improve his ships. Five of the wonders were tombs or memorials: A 40-foot-high statue of Zeus in his temple at Olympia, Greece, with flesh of ivory and a coat of beaten gold. The statue was created about 432 B.C. by Greece's greatest sculptor, Phidias.

A marble temple larger than a modern football field, the largest and richest one of ancient times (from the 300s B.C), the temple of Artemis, or Diana, at Ephesus (south of today's Izmir, Turkey). It had 106 forty-foot-tall columns to support its roof.

The hanging gardens of Babylon (in what is now Iraq), built about 600 B.C. by King Nebuchadnezzar. They were great stone terraces filled with fruit trees and tropical flowers. One tale says that there were 5 terraces, each 50 feet above the one below. There were even woods on the terraces like those in Media—home of a wife of Nebuchadnezzar. (Babylon, a city built over successive ages, had also two other sights sometimes but not always classed among the Seven Wonders: the palace, 8 miles in circumference, and the Tower of Babel, according to Strabo a little higher than the highest pyramid, which may have been an astronomical observatory. It contained, said Herodotus, statues of solid gold.)

The 5,000-year-old pyramids of Egypt (their age is speculative), 700 of them. The Great Pyramid at Giza, where the largest are, was up to 754.5 feet on each side, 481 feet high, and covered 20 acres. The pyramids are the only ancient wonder still in existence.

The square marble skyscraper tomb of King Mausolus (who died 353 B.C.) at Halicarnassus (modern Bodrum, Turkey). Erected by his widowed queen, Artemisia, it contained colossal statues of horses, lions, men, women, gods, and goddesses.

The sixth wonder, the Colossus, was neither a tomb nor a memorial, but a 105-foot-high (maybe 117 feet) hollow bronze statue of Helios, or Apollo, the Greek god of light and the sun, on the Aegean island of Rhodes. (The Statue of Liberty in New York harbor is 117 feet from heel to top of the head, but the extended arm bearing a torch increases the total height.) The Colossus' legs may have spanned a ship channel. A ship in full sail is supposed to have been able to pass through the legs. The Colossus, made over 12 years, 292–280 B.C., by the sculptor Charles of Lindus, may have held aloft a burning torch. Mariners could see the Colossus from far off. About 224 B.C. an earthquake (according to the later writers Strabo and Pliny) shattered it to the ground.

Alexander had seen and been impressed by the towering tomb of Mausolus at Halicarnassus. As a result, he had planned to replace a small pillar serving as a lighthouse at Alexandria with an immense lighthouse. (Lighthouses had begun to be built along the coast of Egypt around 600 B.C.)

The site he chose was on the island of Pharos, near the narrow entrance to the harbor of Alexandria, where sandbars and reefs were dangerous. The lighthouse was started by Ptolemy I, or Soter, perhaps a half-brother of Alexander, who had become ruler of Egypt, and was finished by its architect, Sostratus of Cnidus, about 280 B.C., under Ptolemy II, or Philadelphus. At the base, it was 100 feet square. It may have been 200 feet (20 stories), 450 feet, or even 600 feet tall. Windows at its top faced the sea and behind them, fires were lighted and kept burning with perhaps logs or a pitch, or a petroleum. The smoke by day and fire by night guided mariners. The lighthouse—possibly the first of its kind— could be seen as far as 30 miles. It gave its name to lighthouses that were to come after: the Pharos.

Strabo said part of an inscription on it read: "for the sake of the mariners." The Pharos stood until 1375 A.D., when, like the Colossus of Rhodes, it was destroyed by an earthquake. It became the seventh Wonder of the World.

27

The Mediterranean, 200s B.C.: Travelers on the Sea

THERE ONCE LIVED in Gath-hepher (later Galilee) a man known as Jonas, or Jonah, who went on a trip. At Joppa he paid the fare and went aboard a ship going to Tarshish. That makes him one of the first ship passengers whose name we know. The ship sailed, and a great storm arose.

The sailors cast lots to learn who aboard the ship had incurred the wrath of the Lord and thereby caused the storm. The choice fell on Jonah. The vessel apparently had oars, for the Bible says the oarsmen tried with might and main to reach the shore. When they could not, Jonah asked the crew to throw him into the sea. He was tossed overboard.

The Old Testament book of Jonah (perhaps written in the third century B.C.) says that "a great fish" swallowed him. "And Jonah was in the belly of the fish three days and three nights." Then, after Jonah prayed with all his heart, the fish vomited him out upon dry land. Jonah had reached the depths of despair; a force greater than he had saved his life.

Later books of the Bible refer to the story: Matthew 12:39, 40, 41; 16:4; Luke 11:29, 30; and, in the Apocrypha, Tobit

14:4, 8. In the three-day-long episode of the great fish, Christians later were to see a foreshadowing of Christ's death, descent, and resurrection.

About the time when Jonah's story circulated, there appeared on the sea in large numbers a new kind of ocean traveler, something different from the sailor, explorer, fisherman, or naval man. One result of the conquests of Alexander the Great and his admiral, Nearchus, had been to unify the eastern Mediterranean and the islands in it. They were safer for visitors, accordingly, and people might go to see the pyramid at Giza or one of the other Seven Wonders or other sights. The tourist came into existence.

Soon some big ships crowded aboard as many as a thousand sightseeing passengers. Tourists set out to see what they could see.

Also in the 200s B.C., a few huge luxury ships appeared, owned by kings of Sicily and Macedonia and pharaohs in Alexandria. They had luxurious deckhouses, covered walks along the decks, marbled rooms, mosaics, statues, and paintings, and private bronze baths.

One of the kings in Sicily, Hiero II of Syracuse, built a great ship we know about, although we have no dimensions for her. We do know she had several decks. On the lowest freight was carried (corn, Sicilian salted fish, wool, etc.). On the middle deck was a dining room and space for soldiers; and the top deck had a promenade deck and officers' quarters. Inside floors were mosaic work of colored marble. The dining salon contained an ivory and gold temple dedicated to Venus. The ship's mainmast, probably short and for a single sail, was said to be from a single tree trunk.

From about 310 to 230 B.C. there lived Aristarchus of Samos (the city and island of Pythagoras). In an age when

the sun and stars were still supposed by many people to orbit the earth, Aristarchus said—as had Heraclides of Pontus
in the 300s B.C.—that they did not. Aristarchus believed that
all the known planets, including the earth, revolved around
the sun in circular orbits. Thus, as had Philolaus of Tarentum, he gave man a concept of the solar system. The sun,
he believed, was the center of the universe. (It is not.) The
sun, he believed, stood still. (It does not; the sun orbits part of
our constellation, the Milky Way, at 155 miles, or 250
kilometers, a second, and requires 100,000 or more light
years to complete its orbit.)

Aristarchus also said—again as had Heraclides of Pontus—
that the earth made a complete revolution on its own axis
each day, thus causing day and night. Aristarchus also found a
way to compare sizes and distances of the moon and the sun.
As a result, man began to have a new idea: the universe was
far more immense than he had suspected.

Aristarchus was so far ahead of his time that people did not
take him seriously. Seventeen hundred years after him,
Copernicus, after the telescope had been invented, based his
researches on Aristarchus' ideas. Copernicus published his
opinions in 1543, and these influenced Johannes Kepler, and
so modern astronomy came into existence.

A sister institution to the library at Alexandria was the
museum. It was more than a museum. It has been called the
first research establishment in the world. It possessed three
rare developments for the time: laboratories, a botanical
garden, and a zoo. Its scientists dissected specimens. Pupils of
Aristotle's school, in particular scientists, taught there.

The head of the mathematics department, about 300 B.C.,
wrote a new math book. He was Euclid, and his *Elements of
Geometry* has been called "the greatest mathematical treatise
ever written." [1]

Long before Euclid, Thales of Miletus, who had predicted an eclipse of the sun, had also had the idea of proving mathematical statements. Euclid, following Thales, insisted that if you can't prove it, you don't know it. Ever since mathematicians have been trying to prove their propositions from basic axioms. The concept that there can be certain proof was another giant leap for mankind—such as sailing out of sight of land or such as Aristarchus' conclusion that the earth was not the center of the universe. Navigating a ship requires mathematics and astronomy. Euclid's contribution to navigation, including maps and charts, would be enormous.

Mathematics would contribute to astronomy, geography, oceanography, physics, chemistry, engineering, meteorology, and hundreds of other sciences.

About 260 B.C., a student at the Euclidean school at the museum was Archimedes of Syracuse, 287–212 B.C., who learned the basic principles of the pulley, the screw, and the lever. These are all simple, basic machines, and his work was a step toward the science of mechanics. To illustrate the principle of the lever, he said to the ruler of Syracuse, Hieron: "Give me a place to stand and I will move the world." (There are only two other basic machines—the wheel and axle and the inclined plane. All of today's complicated machines are combinations of the principles of the pulley, the screw, the lever, the wheel and axle, and/or the inclined plane.)

Archimedes was credited with the Archimedean screw, a cylinder with a continuous screw inside it; when the screw is turned, water is raised for irrigation or to drain sumps. He also invented hydrostatics, the science of fluids at rest. Any solid body lighter than water, said he, would float, but some of it would be submerged—it would displace water equal in weight to its own weight. In other words, a floating body displaces its own weight in a liquid. The principle is used in determining the displacement of ships.

In *The Sand Reckoner*, Archimedes figured that the universe was thousands of millions of miles across—in men's minds, after Archimedes and Aristarchus, the universe would grow even larger. Back of all Archimedes' thinking was the approach of Thales and Euclid: Archimedes was a man who proved his mathematics.

Archimedes could have left more records of his work. Exactly as did the Phoenician and Carthaginian sailors, many Greek scientists left few records. One reason was that a common attitude of early times was for people to look down their noses at anything useful or practical, and there was little public interest in descriptions of scientific work or in the work itself.

In 240 B.C. a flaming object appeared in the sky. Over 1,900 years later, in 1682, an Englishman, Edmund Halley, would identify such an object in the sky as a comet and trace its orbit. It would become known as Halley's comet—one that makes a complete orbit every 76 years. It is the most faithful of comets. In 1986 it will return to the vicinity of the sun. Halley's comet has been traced back to 240 B.C.—it was what men saw then.

About 230 B.C., Apollonius of Perga, working in the mathematics school at Alexandria, proved the mathematics that, 1,800 years later, Johannes Kepler would use to show that each planet orbits the sun in an ellipse, not in a circle. Later, Isaac Newton's theory of gravity would show that other celestial orbits had to be ellipses.

Apollonius also developed the astrolabe, a device to navigate by the polestar, Polaris, or by the sun.[2] A graduated circular disk with a movable sighting device, the astrolabe was a new tool to measure the height of star or sun and thus to help determine a ship's position. It gave man a new tool to answer the questions, Where am I? Which way should I go? The astrolabe was one of the earliest navigating instruments, the first one for many a sailor. Only a long pole or a line to measure the depth of the water could have preceded it as an aid to navigation. Strange and fairly awkward, a bit hard to use, the astrolabe was not at once enthusiastically received and mastered by sailors, but it would creep slowly into use.

28

Alexandria, 200s B.C.: A Man Measures the Earth

THE RULING PTOLEMIES of Egypt taxed ships trading at their ports. To avoid payment, Carthaginian ships are believed to have sailed—or attempted to—from the Cadiz region of Spain (Gades, that is, or Tartessus) all the way around Africa to reach and trade on its eastern coast.

A man who worked for Ptolemy II, the king who finished the lighthouse (Pharos) at Alexandria, was to follow the Carthaginians. He was Eudoxus the Navigator (not the same as the earlier Eudoxus of Cnidos), and he came from Cyzicus, in what is now Turkey.

Eudoxus became what Pytheas of Massilia in the previous century had become: an ocean explorer. Ptolemy II sent him on a trading voyage from Egypt to India. Eudoxus' guide already had been the only survivor of a shipwreck in the Red Sea.

Eudoxus brought back precious stones and perfumes. He also brought back information of the kind ocean explorers collect: knowledge of the monsoon winds of the Indian Ocean. On his return, a monsoon wind drove him far south to a point on the African shore south of Ethiopia. Here he found the figurehead of a Phoenician ship. It could have been from the Phoenician voyage for Egypt's Pharaoh Necho back in 600 B.C. In any case, it convinced Eudoxus that a man might sail all around Africa. Accordingly, he made three separate efforts to do so—from the Atlantic side, as the Carthaginians were doing. All his three trips were unsuccessful. On one of them he carried music girls along. No one knows what happened to the girls.

Eudoxus himself did not return from his last trip.

Not until the late 1400s, and Bartholomew Diaz of Portugal, would European man sail around Africa.

At the Alexandria library and the museum, much work was done in the fields of astronomy and navigation. Here a man named Timosthenes became, as Pytheas of Massilia had in the previous century, both a scientist and knowledgeable about navigation. He learned so well he became chief pilot (equivalent to admiral) in the navy of Ptolemy II.

Timosthenes wrote sailing directions, 10 volumes. He described cities and harbors on the Mediterranean, their bearings and positions, and distances between them.

To do this accurately, Timosthenes figured he had to have more than the 8 directions from which winds blew that were used by the Greeks. Timosthenes came up with 12. He, too, used directions from which winds came.

He placed Ethiopia and the Red Sea in the south-southeast. The wind from this direction was Phoenix.

The Celts he placed in the north-northwest, whose wind was Thrascias.

Timosthenes' 12 wind directions went onto a chart, called a "wind rose." Eventually his directions became points on the face of the compass, the "compass rose."

Timosthenes was widely quoted. Among men who used

his writings were Hipparchus, Posidonius, Strabo, and Pliny, and a young librarian at Alexandria, Eratosthenes.

A Greek born about 276 B.C., Eratosthenes came from Athens to preside over the library under Ptolemy III. A friend of mathematics expert Archimedes, Eratosthenes became capable in mathematics, geometry, and astronomy. At the neighboring museum, he used these skills in determining the distance around the world.

He believed the world was round.

He learned that, at noon on midsummer day the sun was directly overhead at Aswan, Egypt. He measured the angular distance of the sun at Alexandria at the same moment. It was $\frac{1}{50}$ of a circle.

Eratosthenes asked Ptolemy III to command state surveyors to determine the distance between the two places. Men trained to walk in uniform steps counted their steps and found the distance was 5,000 stadia, perhaps 500 miles. If that was the distance between Aswan and Alexandria, then the whole circle, the circumference of the globe, must be 50 times as great, or 250,000 stadia, increased later to 252,000—roughly equivalent to 24,867 miles. A 1962 figure from the International Union of Geodesy and Geophysics, based on earlier figures from the International Astronomical Union: the circumference of the earth at the equator is 24,901.55 miles.

Eratosthenes had figured the distance around the world with an error of only 1 percent.

He never knew it. He himself considered his figures much more approximate and much less accurate than they were.

It was Eratosthenes' greatest achievement, but not his only one. The papyrus rolls at the Alexandria library included hundreds written by early travelers over land and sea. They included the geographical and scientific information collected on Alexander's marches, reports from Alexander's admiral,

Nearchus, and accounts of ocean explorers, including Pytheas of Massilia. Eratosthenes went through these travelers' tales and put their information into organized descriptions of known countries. He made a map showing towns, mountains, rivers, lakes, seas, climates. His map included more of the world than had been known earlier. It extended from the Atlantic shores of Europe and Africa past India and Ceylon. (He was the first to mention the Chinese.) There was more of the Near East. Distorted, but shown, were India and Russia. The British Isles were outlined, and France was shown jutting into the sea as it does. Basing his information about northern regions mainly on Pytheas' account, Eratosthenes showed Ultima Thule, locating it where Norway is.

He mistakenly depicted the Caspian Sea as a bay of the ocean, although both Aristotle and Herodotus had said it was an inland sea, as it is.

Eratosthenes noticed that similar high tides had been reported by Alexander and Nearchus in the Indian Ocean and by Pytheas in the Atlantic. From this, he concluded that the Atlantic and Indian Oceans were one—the world ocean. "The ocean encompasses the land," he said.

There being one ocean surrounding the land, you could, Eratosthenes thought, sail west from Europe to Asia: "If the extent of the Atlantic Ocean were not an obstacle, we might easily pass by sea from Iberia [Spain and Portugal] to India, keeping in the same parallel." Seventeen hundred years after Eratosthenes, Columbus would try to do that—sail west from Spain across the Atlantic to India.

Another conclusion of Eratosthenes was that Spain and North Africa once had been joined by a strip of land. In 1970 samples of the bottom of the Mediterranean, obtained by oceanographers, showed that indeed this had been the case.

To locate places accurately on his maps, Eratosthenes drew

cross lines—one of the first rough systems of latitude and longitude. (Pytheas of Massilia had had something similar.)

He included in his geography the circumference of the earth, which, in the first place, he had had to determine to give a scale to his map of the world.

Eratosthenes died in 196 B.C. What he had done when he coordinated his information into a geography and when he had measured the circumference of the globe was to make another of man's giant leaps: he had established geography as a science.

The library at Alexandria built up the world's largest collection of rolls of manuscripts, 100,000 at first, eventually 700,000, on papyrus or parchment. A roll, or scroll, wrapped around a wooden stick was held in the right hand while the left slowly unrolled it to reveal the next column of writing. A scroll telling the story of the pharaoh Ramses III was 135 feet long.

Among the treasures collected by the Alexandria library were all of Aristotle's library's scrolls, and the *Iliad* of Homer—a copy Alexander had taken on his later marches. At night he had laid it, along with his dagger, under his wooden headrest. The library established a new policy: making copies of manuscripts. Not just copies for a few scholars, many copies, for a wide public. Knowledge was to be spread around.

All had been leaps forward for man: Aristotle's natural history, Euclid's mathematics, Eratosthenes' measuring the circumference of the earth and founding the science of geography. No leap ever was more important for man than the spread of knowledge, multiplying manuscripts. That would lead in time to multiplied charts, maps, and sailing directions, it would help sailors and oceanographers, and it would lead to the printed word in books, papers, and magazines, and eventually to the concept of education and literacy for all. On sea and on land, modern man is influenced by what was done at Alexandria.

29

222–51 B.C.:
Incredible Rowboats, Unknown Continents

CALM DAYS, without wind, are frequent in the Mediterranean. Therefore, while man was making so much progress in science, he kept right on rowing some of his ships. In fact, man used his brain, hands, and eyes to develop oared ships far beyond the triremes of Athens. Alexander had used quadriremes (four banks of oars) to overcome the Phoenicians, and ancient records tell of ships with 5, 6, 7 (Alexander again), 8, 11 (Demetrios in Cyprus), 12, 15, and 16 banks of oars. So far as I know, no modern man has figured out how any vessel could possibly have had so many banks of rowers. I do not think we are even sure what ancient man meant when he referred to what we translate as a "bank."

From 222–204 B.C., in the reign of a big-navy king, Ptolemy IV (Philopator) of Egypt, Alexander's historian, Callisthenes, recorded what must have been the hugest and most elaborate rowed ship of all, a vessel 420 feet long, 57 feet in beam, 72 feet from keel to the highest point of the poop deck. She needed 4,000 oarsmen. Her oars were supposed to be so perfectly balanced that a child could move one. We have no idea what the arrangement of oars and oarsmen could have been, or what such a ship could possibly have been like.

The next Ptolemy, also according to Callisthenes, built a vessel 300 feet long, 40 feet in beam, and 60 feet from keel to top deck. The ship was called the *Thalamagus*. She had hanging gardens, marble stairs, and colonnades.

The warships of Carthage, with improved rams to smash into the sides of enemy vessels, worried a Roman citizen, Caius Duilius. He invented a grappling iron to hang onto enemy ships. With the grappling iron and with gangplanks the Romans could put their soldiers, or legionnaires, the best hand-to-hand fighters, aboard the Carthaginian vessels. The Romans also used tree-trunk-size harpoons to harpoon a ship, then haul her in and board her. With these weapons, the Romans, in 201 B.C., reduced the power of Carthage. In that war, so many rowers were required that the Roman and Carthaginian fleets each carried about 150,000 men.

In 200 B.C., according to one source, the Romans actually attempted to sail across the top of Russia and succeeded. They are said to have followed Pytheas' route through Gibraltar north, passed the Shetland Islands, and Norway, then sailed across Russia to the Bering Strait, then, after visiting China, sailed south around Asia home. In China they could have seen cable drilling for oil; it was being done there.[1]

In the second century B.C., Seleucus of Seleucia, on the Tigris, noticed a correlation between phases of the moon and the tides, as had Pytheas in the 300s B.C.

Working on latitude and longitude was Hipparchus of Nicaea. Hipparchus devised trigonometry and so laid the basis for some map projections.

Hipparchus made a list accurately locating 1000 fixed stars. Fixed stars are so far from the earth that, unlike the swift planets, they require long, precise observations to determine their movements. His observations have stood up until today.[2]

He thought (after Anaxagoras in 500 B.C. and Aristarchus of Samos in 260 B.C.) that the earth orbited the sun. He tried to determine the distance from the earth to the moon, and his estimate, 33 times the diameter of the earth, was remarkably close.

Measurements were crude and inexact. Hipparchus took a step to make measurements more accurate. He divided a circle into degrees, minutes, and seconds. This made measurements more accurate and resulted also in more accurate astronomy and navigation. He measured the length of the lunar month and missed it by 1 second. Fifteen hundred years before the telescope was invented, when men watched the stars with their eyes alone, he figured the length of the year and filed his result at the library at Alexandria: his estimate of the length of a year was 6 minutes 14 seconds in error.

In 150 B.C. Crates of Mallos, in Cilicia, a commentator on Homer, made, so far as we know, the first globe to represent the earth. His globe was exhibited at the time in the Greek city (today in Turkey) of Pergamum, where he was librarian. It included the known world of the Mediterranean and the unknown opposite side of the world. On the opposite side he put three other continents. (Earlier, Pythagoras had believed in land masses on the opposite side of the globe from the Mediterranean world.) Undiscovered, these continents were added by Crates apparently to balance his globe and give it symmetry.

Long after Crates and after the discovery of North and South America, men kept seeking a missing continent in the Pacific Ocean, until the 1700s A.D. and Captain James Cook.

Captain Cook found the eastern coast of Australia. In the 1800s, others outlined the Antarctic.

From 135 to 51 B.C. was the lifetime of the geographer Posidonius of Apamea in Syria. He was born among the Phoenicians and lived some time on the island of Rhodes. As others had before him, he thought a ship sailing through Gibraltar, with an east wind in her sails, would go straight to India. His calculation of the circumference of the earth was less than Eratosthenes' figure. Posidonius estimated the circumference at 17,000 or 18,000 miles, about 7,000 miles less than it is. This figure was accepted by a later astronomer (not a pharaoh), Ptolemy, and still later impressed Columbus.

Posidonius himself traveled to the area of present-day Cadiz, Spain (perhaps to the lost city of Tartessus), to measure the tides. He linked the tides with the moon, and he noticed that their monthly period corresponded with the full moon.

30

Sea of Sardinia, 100 B.C.: How Deep Is the Ocean?

EVER SINCE MEN had been sailing the open sea, they must have wondered about its depth. But they had to battle or at least work like galley slaves to make their way from port to port, and there was little opportunity to find out.

The only early record of sounding the deep sea that I have been able to locate was that of Herodotus in the 400s B.C., and I do not know what depth was found.

About 100 B.C. one of the startling discoveries of the ancient world was made, an important discovery for oceanography. Lowering a line into the dark sea, just as fishermen had done for centuries, sailors lowered and kept lowering the line till they had measured a depth of over a mile, or 6,000 feet. It was the first time men ever had discovered any such depth.

Strabo, who was a contemporary of Christ, reported it: "The sea of Sardinia, than which a deeper sea has never been sounded, measuring, as it does, according to Posidonius, about 1,000 fathoms."

What Posidonius was talking about was the first recorded

sounding of the deep sea, away from shore, anywhere. Besides diving for oysters, sponges, and pearls, man's exploration of the depths started right here, with the unknown sailors of whom we are told by Posidonius through Strabo.

A mechanical device dating from 80 B.C. has been discovered. In 1900 sponge divers found an astronomical calculator in a ship carrying bronze and marble statues that had gone down off the Greek island of Antikýthēra. The astronomical calculator told the date and movements of heavenly bodies.[1] Its setting was correct for the year 80 B.C.

The Greeks apparently were more mechanical than we knew. To produce a device as complicated as this one, they must have known something about the uses of gears, pulleys, and levers which Archimedes had worked on in Alexandria. Man was taking steps in the direction of his eventual machines, engines, and motors.

Even after Timosthenes in Alexandria had used the 12 directions from which winds blew in making his wind rose, the Greeks stuck to 8 directions for winds. In the first century B.C. a Greek astronomer, Andronicus of Cyrrhus, or Andronicus Cyrrhestes, erected the Tower to the Winds. He gave it 8 sides, for the 8 winds: the cold north wind, Boreas (Aquilo to the Romans); the dry, cool east wind, Eurus or Euros; the warm south wind, Notos or Notus (Auster to the Romans); the mild west wind, Favonicus or Zephyrus; the frigid northeast wind, called the true Boreas; a dry, hot wind from the southeast; a moist, hot wind from the southwest; and a wind called Argestes, bringing hail and rain from the northwest.

On top of his tower Andronicus placed a large bronze figure of Triton, a demigod of the sea. The figure turned in the wind so that it pointed with a rod in the direction from which the wind blew—the first wind vane.

In 55 B.C., a Mediterranean man, Julius Caesar, received a lesson he did not want to learn. He was used to insignificant tides. He ran into a high one. Or a high one ran into him.

Caesar had just reached Britain, near Dover and the white cliffs, and had beached some of his ships for the night. When the moon was full, he learned, the tide was highest—"a fact at that time wholly unknown to the Romans," Caesar sadly commented.

There was a storm. Caesar is believed to have been able to swim, and once to have saved himself in a storm—this one or another—by swimming. His ships were not saved; a 20-foot spring tide swamped those on the beach. The storm piled up large ships, at anchor, dashed them to pieces, and sank them. The next year, 54 B.C., another storm sank 40 of Caesar's ships and left others almost wrecks.

The Romans called the Atlantic *Mare Tenebrosum,* or Dark Sea, because of its hazards. The name turned into the Arabs' name for the Atlantic, the Green Sea of Darkness. It caused men to dread the Atlantic and to avoid it for a thousand years after Caesar, until the Norsemen or Vikings came along and sailed west and farther west.

In Britain Caesar saw enemy ships that he said were better in northern waters than his own. High prows and sterns protected them against storms and waves, flat bottoms made them better in shallow water (at low tide) and easier to beach. They were strong—of oak—and had crossbeams. Their sails were leather or skins because canvas or cloth would not last in northern gales. Julius Caesar had described the forerunners of the Norsemen's ships of a millennium later.

About 40 B.C. Juba, King of Mauretania, in north Africa where Morocco and part of Algeria are today, made an expedition and reached some islands off the northwest coast of Africa that he called Canaria, or the Canaries, because of the "multitude of dogs of great size" found on the islands. (Phoenicians or Carthaginians, including Hanno in 480 B.C., might previously have reached the Canaries.) Juba's account told the Romans about the islands and was preserved by Pliny the Elder. Almost 1,500 years afterwards, the Canaries would be a base for explorers of the wide ocean, just as important as islands less than 25 miles apart had been to eastern Mediterranean oarsmen. The Canaries, for example, would launch Columbus on an exploratory trip west across the Atlantic.

In 31 B.C. Antony and the daughter of Ptolemy XII, Cleopatra, used the Tyrians' purple dye. Near Alexandria they sailed into the Battle of Actium in a ship with sails dyed purple. They lost the battle to Octavius, or Octavian, who became Augustus Caesar, emperor of Rome—that is, the known world. The Greeks, who had backed Antony, went down with him. The *Pax Romana*—Roman peace—then prevailed in the Mediterranean.

After the Battle of Actium, Vergil read to Augustus Caesar parts of a long poem, the *Aeneid*. In the poem Vergil gave names to ships—the *Chimaera, Scylla, Centaur, Pristus, Tiger,* and *Triton*. These ships, along with the *Argo* of Jason, are among the first ships on any record to be given names.

One line in Vergil mentions that early form of boat, the hollow log: "Rivers then first the hollowed alder felt."

Another Roman poet, Horace, died in 8 B.C. as the pre-Christian era was ending. Horace was singing the courage of men who went to sea and was appreciating the first men to dare to, such as those who sailed in hollow logs, when he wrote: "He had round his heart a breastplate of oak and a triple armor of bronze, he who was the first to entrust to the angry waves a fragile boat."

31

Roman Empire,
63 B.C.–21 A.D.:
A Man of Christ's Time

ONE OF THE MOST IMPORTANT ancient geographers was a Greek, Strabo, who lived in the Roman Empire. His work summed up what educated men—of whom there were very few—knew about geography and the land and seas of the world at the time of Christ.

Strabo was born about 63 B.C. in what today is Turkey. In 29 B.C. he went to Corinth, Greece, when Augustus Caesar was there; from 25 to 24 B.C. he traveled up the Nile; he traveled altogether about 15,000 miles in the Mediterranean area; and he could have seen the Star in the East.

As did Eratosthenes and so many others, Strabo worked in Alexandria. He described the lighthouse as a tower of white marble built "for the safety of mariners." Under Augustus Caesar, he helped organize the government of the Roman Empire. Following in the footsteps of Herodotus, Eratosthenes, and Posidonius, Strabo wrote a geography. It appeared, presumably on 30 or so scrolls, in 18 or 19 A.D., or two or three years before Strabo died, about 21 A.D. It was published in English for the first time in 1844.

It shows that geographers at the start of the Christian era were well advanced. Strabo knew the world was round, and in his geography he credited sailors with thinking so. For centuries, with the wind in the sails of their ships, they had gone out on the open sea far from sight of land, then slowly approached the shore from afar. Strabo wrote that a shoreline gradually increased in height as the sailor approached it from the sea. Furthermore, if someone stood on shore and looked out to sea, he saw first the ship's mast, then her higher parts, then her hull. And from high on a mast of a ship, a sailor could see things he could not see from the deck.

Quoting Homer that a sailor "lifted up on the vast wave from the deck quickly beheld afar," Strabo wrote, "we shall assume that the earth is spheroidal." And he concluded: "The evidence of the senses and common observation are alone requisite."

As had Herodotus (484–424 B.C.), Strabo knew something that one might logically have expected to have been only recently discovered. "Everyone will admit," he wrote, "that formerly at various periods a great portion of the mainland has been covered and again left bare by the sea." His evidence included a quotation from Eratosthenes that mussel, oyster, and scallop shells are found far inland, as are salt beds and salt springs, and the fact that fossil seashells had been found beneath the sands of Egypt. Strabo said the level of the Mediterranean Sea had varied at different times and he told of cities that had sunk into that sea following volcanic eruptions or earthquakes.

He echoed Herodotus in saying that other rivers, like the Nile, keep converting to land the channels where they empty into the sea.

A comment from a modern geologist: "In fact, most sedimentary rocks studied by geologists were deposited in the sea, which is not surprising if we remember that every part of the earth was under water at least once. Most places have been inundated many times in the planet's four or five billion years of history." [1] A recent estimate of the time the earth has existed is from 4¾ to 5 billion years—considerably longer than man has been around as a hunter, fisherman, or berry gatherer. But something alive has been on earth 3½ billion years. Fossils this old of living organisms such as algae and bacteria, or plants or protists (but certainly living things), creatures so tiny it would take a million to fill a thimble,[2] and other microfossils 3.1 billion years old, perhaps ancestors of modern blue-green algae,[3] have been discovered in South Africa in recent times.

Strabo thought that Sicily might have been pushed up above the sea by the fires of a volcano, Mount Aetna. He said that a small island had indeed been thrust up by a volcano. For this kind of geological insight, he would be praised in the 1800s by a geologist who influenced Charles Darwin, Sir Charles Lyell.

To Strabo, said E. H. Bunbury, "the voyage of the Argonauts (and Jason) to Colchis was as real as that of Columbus or Vasco da Gama to ourselves." [4] Yet that Black Sea trip after the golden fleece may have been only a myth.

Like Aristotle, Strabo knew the importance of studying biology, of observing "the occupants of the ocean." Geography to him embraced "the history of the animals, plants, and other different productions of the earth and sea, whether serviceable or useless." Birds flying overhead had both encouraged men to explore and helped show them the way to new places. For instance, watching cranes showed they flew south from Europe for the winter. Strabo also said geography includes the study of "the occupants of the ocean." A man whom he consulted at Alexandria, Polybius, described fishing for swordfish in the Straits of Messina and said that a swordfish could drive its sword through a boat. Swordfish still drive their swords through wooden hulls. Strabo wrote about whales in the Persian Gulf, and of how, in the sea off Spain, there abounded whales, large eels, shellfish, and "shoals of rich fat tunny [tuna]," cuttlefish, and squid.

Although Strabo knew something about Africa for some distance south, he said both coasts of Africa still were hazardous: "All those who have sailed along the coast of Africa, whether starting from the Red Sea, or the Strait of Gibraltar, after proceeding a certain distance, have been obliged to turn back again on account of a variety of accidents." Almost no one, at least since Pharaoh Necho's Tyrians in 600 B.C. or Carthage's Hanno in 480 B.C., had tried to sail south along either coast of Africa. The "variety of accidents"—winds, storms, leaky ships, disease (particularly scurvy and dysentery), torrid equatorial weather, shoals, ignorance—would make the African coast inaccessible for sailors for almost 1,500 years after Strabo. In other words, almost three-quarters of all the time between Strabo and Christ and today would pass before ocean explorers from Europe would move even a little distance down the west coast of Africa. Not till the 1400s, shortly before Columbus, and under Prince Henry of Portugal, would sailors begin to explore Africa's Atlantic coast.

Strabo saw the Red Sea as the dividing line between Africa and Asia. From his travels and from Roman and Greek vessels that went to India and to the ivory-tortoise-shell-and-peacock island of Ceylon, he picked up information about Asia. The ships' main port of departure was Myos-hormus on the Red Sea, which Strabo visited: "I found one hundred and twenty ships sail . . . to India."

He knew about Britain, even to the tiny, rocky Scilly Isles off the southwest tip. He said Britain exported iron, corn, cattle, hides, gold, silver, and excellent hunting dogs. He also knew of Ireland. He said the Sacred Promontory—present-

day Cape St. Vincent, Portugal—was the westernmost point
of the continent of Europe. (Actually, the Cabo da Boca, near
Lisbon, is.) He described Gaul (France), Italy, the Danube,
and the Black Sea. And he had some information about
Germany, Russia, the Scandinavian countries, and the Arctic
Circle. Strabo credited what he knew about the Baltic Sea
region to Pytheas. He believed the Arctic to be covered, as it
is, by an ocean.

Strabo missed one thing in his geography. Rome and
Augustus Caesar were building roads throughout Europe—
good roads, often straight, suitable for the improved wheels
on improved carriages, as man made mechanical progress.
The roads were too new to be included by Strabo.

He criticized some exaggerated tales by earlier men: "No
faith whatever can be placed in Demiachus and Megasthenes" [who had been in India following Alexander]. They
coined the fables concerning men with arms long enough to
sleep in, men without any mouths, without noses, with only
one eye, with spider-legs, and with figures bent backward.
. . . They told of ants digging for gold, of Pans with
wedge-shaped heads, or serpents swallowing down oxen and
stags, horns and all." But Strabo himself followed the idea
that eels and lampreys became oysters, and that tuna eat "sea
oak," perhaps the great seaweed reported by the Carthaginian Himilco.

Roman cartographers during Strabo's working life were
sketching on a linen material—mappa—and from this came
the word "map." The Romans drew up what they called
"itineraries"—routes for travelers, showing distances and
stopping places. Strabo went farther. Food was being spread
around the Mediterranean by ship, food in good supply; men
were eating better. So Strabo's geography was surprisingly
modern in one detail, as complete as a guidebook of the

1970s. He even included a list of recommended eating places in Mediterranean ports where the food was good.

Strabo's sources, many of them consulted at the library at Alexandria, included the travels of Alexander of Macedon and, perhaps for such things as Red Sea whales, Alexander's admiral, Nearchus. He used the journey of a Greek, Artemidorus (140 B.C.) around the Mediterranean for information about its coasts. For a description of Gaul, he relied on the commentaries of Julius Caesar. Pytheas provided his Arctic information. Among his sources was Ephorus, a writer who lived before Alexander and is believed to have written 30 scrolls of the most accurate geography in the ancient world, all lost to us today.

Strabo knew the importance of astronomy and mathematics to navigation and geography, although he did incorrectly believe that the stars moved around the earth. He credited the Phoenicians' "night-sailings" to their knowledge of astronomy, and he said they were the first sailors to navigate by the Great Bear.

As had Aristotle, he concluded that, because the world was round, a sailor could reach the Orient by sailing west. He came to another conclusion after some figuring. He estimated the extent of the then-known inhabited world. He accepted Eratosthenes' almost exactly correct estimate of the circumference of the globe. He saw at once that the known world was only about a third of the total circumference of the globe in the temperate zone. Therefore two-thirds was unknown. This might be all water, an ocean that encircled land, in which case there would be a very long journey for sailors traveling west to Asia. Or—said Strabo, who knew nothing of the Americas, the Antarctic continent, Australia, or the Pacific Ocean—there might well exist other continents. Inhabited by men. There might be men and continents unknown to the Greeks and the Romans.

It was an idea that would linger in the minds of men.

Sailors of Strabo's day had no way of measuring distances at sea, yet somehow they learned to tell quite accurately how far they had sailed. They could estimate within a fifth of the correct distance. In the case of frequently used routes, this led to fairly accurate knowledge of distance traveled. Sailors also determined very accurately the locations of ports they often visited. In such practical matters, the sailors (with the help of astronomers who could locate towns, like Pytheas of Massilia) were ahead of the geographers.

Neither the sailors nor Strabo located for us one land he wrote about, Turdetania. We do not know where it was. It may have been on Spain's Atlantic coast, and may have contained the now lost port of Tartessus. From Turdetania, Strabo wrote, there came the largest ships that entered the ports of Rome, Ostia and Dicaearchia, and these vessels carried corn, wine, wool, honey, and salted fish. They probably carried back olives and olive oil from as far away as the Garden of Gethsemane and Lebanon, some of it from olive trees still alive today, 2,000 years later. Those trees are among the oldest of all living things.

At the time of Strabo, most ships still sailed the relatively calm Mediterranean. But if Turdetania was an Atlantic port, her sailors, for some of the time and some distance at least, had to battle Atlantic winds, waves, swells, and storms.

Out of this land entirely lost to history, out of this port that has disappeared, from these nameless seamen, there would over the centuries develop men and deep-sea ships capable of crossing the widest ocean and sailing beyond the farthest horizon. What is out there? Strabo and his contemporaries could not tell us what was beyond their known world, but later men, whose names we do know—Diaz, Da Gama, Columbus, and Magellan—would take ships from the same southwest corner of Europe where we believe Turdetania lay, and sail south along West Africa and east to the Orient, but mostly west and farther west and still farther west, to find the continents that Strabo thought might be out there somewhere. From Portugal and Spain, from where Europe juts farthest into the Atlantic, men and ships, with the wind in their sails, would sail forth till they had spanned all the oceans and reached the ends of the earth.

That would not in the least have surprised Strabo, who saw the importance of geography to men. Once a man had studied it, he commented, he "will not be satisfied with anything less than the whole world." He understood the importance of the sea to men—for trade routes, for exploration. He could be said to have had an insight that one day ocean science—oceanography—would be vital to men. Said he: "We are in a certain sense amphibious, not exclusively connected with the land, but with the sea as well."

32

First Century A.D.:
Roman Ships and Sailors

In 5 A.D., Augustus Caesar sent out a Roman fleet that reached Germany, Jutland, and the Danish islands. Augustus was proud of it: "Before that time no Roman had penetrated [so far] either by land or sea."

Roman freight ships grew large, up to 1,000 tons, and 180 feet long. One type used a single square sail and gave up oarsmen entirely. Their greatest cargoes: food, which had brought man the land animal onto the sea in the first place. Wheat and barley came to Rome from Sardinia, Sicily, Carthage in North Africa, and Egypt's Nile valley in great fleets of grain ships that had evolved from the freight ships of Phoenicia, Crete, and Greece. Of all the Roman vessels, the most important were the great corn ships. And of all the Mediterranean trade routes of the times, the most important was from the grain port of Alexandria to Ostia, Rome's port at the mouth of the Tiber. Alexandria's lighthouse, the Pharos, three-quarters of a mile offshore, became the most important landmark for the Mediterranean sailor. The lighthouse guided him, through reefs and shallows, into the flat

Nile delta and what the sailor called the "Harbour of Good Homecoming."

Other cargoes of Roman freighters were olive oil and wine (in large jars called "amphoras," the shipping casks of the Romans and Greeks), jewelry, flax, linen cloth, dates, fruits, and vegetables. Roman vessels carried entire cargoes of works of art—bronze and marble statues, busts of Dionysius, Ariadne, Aphrodite; and lamps that provided glimmers of light when much of the world was dark after nightfall. These cargoes and the size of the ships we know from Roman ships sunk in the Mediterranean and recently found by archeologists.

Roman sailors dropped lines overboard into the dark ocean to see how deep it was or what fish they might catch. They often drew up bare hooks or empty nets or no samples of the bottom and so collected little information or caught nothing. Sometimes currents washed away their lines.

On the Sea of Galilee, a fisherman, Simon Peter, lowered his net all night, pulled it up, and had nothing to show. Christ said, "Cast ye the net on the right side of the ship, and ye shall find." Peter did so and of fish he caught "a great multitude" (Luke 5:6). It was difficult to haul up the net (Luke 5; John 21). There is no way of counting the infinite number of fishermen who since then have cast their nets over the right side.

During the smooth seas of the summers, the large Roman freighters carried sightseers from Naples to Athens in a week, from Athens to Asia Minor in a few more days. There were only a few cabins or staterooms for important people, and almost all passengers remained on deck. There were no dining rooms, and the passengers ate food they had brought with them. The ship provided only one thing: drinking water. One of the principal sights was the pyramids of Egypt. Touring, uncomfortable as it might be, was booming.

Touring was luxurious for some. By 37–41 A.D., the Roman emperor Caligula built two galleys fitted with saloons, art galleries, and baths. Sailing along the coast of Italy in one of the ships, Caligula was entertained by dancers and musicians. Two galleys, found in Italy's Lake Nemi and excavated piece by piece from the 1500s to the 1900s, appear to have been Caligula's. One was of the enormous length of 450 feet, about 192 broad, and 51 feet from keel to deck. Some of her decks were covered with tiles and red marble.

All of man's sailing vessels until about Roman times of the first century A.D. had carried single masts and sails. Then something new appeared upon the seas: above the single square sail of a Roman merchant ship was the first superimposed sail, a triangular topsail. Then the Romans and the Etruscans, who also lived on the Italian peninsula, began using two-masted ships.

A Roman two-masted ship might have a foremast slanted toward the bow and carried a small, single sail, the artemon, that helped her sail a little against the wind. She might have a mainmast with a large square sail displaying a wolf suckling Romulus and Remus. Such a ship is shown on a marble relief located at Ostia. And according to one writer, some of the biggest Roman ships had a mizzen mast with a third square sail.[1]

With ships and cargoes flourishing, there were sinkings, and the profession of salvaging grew. On the island of Rhodes, said Livy, a contemporary of Strabo, a diver shared in any sunken property he recovered: from a depth of 36 inches, 10 percent; from 12 feet deep, 33 percent; from 24 feet deep, one-half. Man slowly was learning to work beneath the sea.

When Claudius I was emperor of Rome, 41–54 A.D., a Roman fleet was based in Boulogne, France, on the English Channel. The fleet circumnavigated England, and thus proved something the Romans were not sure of, that Britain was an island. As ocean explorers always do, they encountered islands new to them, in this case, the Orkneys.

In 42 A.D., Claudius and his general, Plautius, invaded Britain. For centuries, to guard against attack from the ocean, it was considered wise to establish a town a short distance upriver and not right at the edge of the sea. Claudius and Plautius fortified a small town up a river and called it Londinium. It became London.

About 43 A.D., Pomponius Mela of Tingentera, Spain, in the earliest known Roman geography (counting Strabo as a Greek) was the first to mention the Orkney Islands: "thirty in number." Diodorus had spoken of the Orkneys but had not labeled them as islands. Mela also was first to mention the Shetlands as islands and said there were seven of them. Mela was the first man to tell of an "immense bay"—probably the Kattegat, an arm of the North Sea. Mela mentioned Thule (probably from Pytheas); "There the nights in any case are short."

One thing that ships were bringing less of was the dye, Tyrian purple. The man who succeeded Claudius as emperor of Rome, Nero, who ruled from 54 to 68 A.D., decreed that only he could wear Tyrian purple. So valuable did the dye become that a pound of purple wool reached the equivalent of $150.

About 61 A.D., a Roman grain ship from Alexandria, carrying St. Paul and 275 other persons, passed through a storm, approaching what is today the island of Malta. A sailor lowered a line overboard: "And sounded, and found it 20 fathoms and when they had gone a little further, they sounded again and found it then 15 fathoms." (Acts of the

Apostles, XXVII:28). The vessel had two masts, perhaps an oxhide sail, carried a small boat, one of the earliest lifeboats on record, and one estimate is that she was 100 feet long, 25 or 30 in beam, 10 in draft.

Sailors, like those aboard St. Paul's ship, when they hauled in a line overboard, stretched out their hands and each time brought up the length of rope they could reach with their hands with arms outstretched. This was roughly 6 feet 1 inch. A sailor then counted the number of lengths he brought aboard. This gave him the depth of the water: so many lengths, or fathoms. A fathom in time became exactly 6 feet, as it is today.

From the Red Sea, Greek captains sailing for Rome explored western and northern India. They, and perhaps Phoenicians and others, sailed around India and reached Burma, Malaya, and Indonesia. They brought back pepper. A Greek captain named Alexander, about whom virtually nothing is known, is supposed to have sailed around the Malay Peninsula and to have reached what is now Laos, Vietnam, and even southern China. The Greeks called Malaya the "Golden Peninsula."

Fourteen hundred years afterwards, the Portuguese would sail around Africa and reach the same places.

One Greek, Hippalus or Hippalos, learned that the monsoon winds blow east or west across the Indian Ocean, according to the seasons. Instead of hugging the coast from Arabia to India, as other navigators had done, he sailed out of sight of land directly across the Indian Ocean from Cape Fartak in Arabia to the southwest coast of India. The southwest monsoon was named for him: the hippalos.

The monsoon gave the skipper a break. The steadiness and direction of a monsoon enabled him to keep on course simply by running directly before the wind. Thus, monsoons made possible long voyages out of sight of land.

What is out there?

A Roman playwright, Seneca, who lived from *c.* 4 B.C. to 65 A.D. and who may have been influenced by the work of Strabo, made a prophecy that some day ocean explorers would find something if they sailed west. He foresaw that a vast, unknown land beyond the then-uncrossed Atlantic would be discovered. The forecast occurred in Seneca's play, *Medea*; earlier, the Greek Euripides had also written a play titled *Medea,* and Seneca based his work on Euripides'. Medea was the lover of Jason, the sailor who led the Argonauts into the Black Sea in search of the golden fleece.

In his play, a tragedy, Seneca praises the first sailors out of sight of land. He describes as "venturesome" the man "who in frail barque first cleft the treacherous seas and, with one last look behind him at the well-known shore, trusted his life to the fickle winds; who, ploughing the waters on an unknown course, could trust to a single plank, stretching too slight a boundary between the ways of life and death."

Seneca said sailing ships had improved the lot of men. Before them, "every man inactive kept to his own shores and lived to an old age on ancestral fields . . . with but little, knowing no wealth save what the home soil had yielded."

The men of Seneca's day knew much more than before man had sailed the seas. In ancient times, he said, "not yet could any read the sky and see the stars with which the heavens are spangled . . . not yet did Boreas [the north wind], not yet did Zephyrus [the west wind] have names." Sailors had long known how to set their sails sideways to catch cross winds. Sailing was safer: "Any little craft now wanders at will upon the deep." The long-distance sailing ship, he said, had joined together nations that once were separated and had made something of one world of the known world.

Seneca went on to utter his prophecy, one that has been regarded ever since as a forecast of the discovery of a New World, specifically, by Columbus. New continents would be found, he predicted. "There will come an age in the far-off years when Ocean shall unloose the bonds of things, when the whole broad earth shall be revealed, when [a new mariner] shall disclose new worlds and Thule not be the last of the land."

At the museum in Alexandria about 65 A.D., there was a Greek, Hero, who built a small steam engine that demonstrated that the power of steam could move the parts of a machine. It was only a toy. It would be a hefty 1,800 years before steam would be used to operate ship engines on a scale wide enough to replace wind in the sails. But Hero's toy was every bit as much a prophecy of things to come as were Seneca's words.

33

Italy, 79 A.D.:
A Man Watches a Volcano

Two or three years after Strabo's death, in 23 or 24 A.D., there was born a boy named Pliny, who in time would become known as Pliny the Elder to distinguish him from his nephew, Pliny the Younger. Pliny the Elder was another who believed the earth was round, for, he said, if the world was flat, as many men still believed, the ocean that surrounds the land would drain off right over the edge. Pliny did not think that men on the opposite side of a round earth would have trouble walking around even if, as some men then argued, their feet were above their heads. He thought that people anywhere on earth would stand with their feet toward its center.

He mentioned divers who breathed through their mouths by means of a tube whose end was attached to a float on the surface, so divers must have been making progress.

There was an ocean, Pliny concluded, all the way across the top of Russia and the top of the world. He gave as his reasons for this belief Arctic voyages from both Atlantic and Pacific that may or may not have been made. We are uncertain. But if Greek captains such as Alexander reached China, they might have sailed on north. And Pliny was an admiral in the navy of the emperor Vespasian and he should have known.

For another emperor, Augustus Caesar, Pliny said, a Roman fleet had sailed part way across the Arctic from the Atlantic, and its men saw nothing ahead but more sea. This may have been on the voyage when Augustus' vessels reached Jutland.

Pliny had an inkling of something else startling for his time: the depth of the sea. He quoted Fabian as saying the ocean reached two miles deep. Why the ocean did not overflow was a subject much discussed in those days. Aristotle had said the cause was evaporation. Four hundred years after Aristotle, it was Pliny's opinion that water from the sea slipped into veins in the earth and came out again in springs and wells.

According to Pliny, men from the British Isles had crossed the ocean to a land 6 days' sail away, perhaps Iceland, and they had done it in boats "covered with sewed hides," a type of seafaring craft found in northwestern Europe since time immemorial. Pliny knew of the Orkney, Shetland, and Hebrides islands, and is the first known writer to tell of the last. He was the first to use a word that would come to designate a northern European area—Scatinavia, or Scandinavia.

At one point Pliny told of a voyage from Egypt to India. Passengers started right after the rising of the dog star, Sirius, the second week in July. In 30 days they reached Ocelis, just outside the Strait of Bab el Mandeb, between the Red Sea and the Gulf of Aden. The hippalos, or southwest monsoon of the Indian Ocean, could then blow them to the Malabar Coast of India in another 40 days.

According to a book of sailing directions contemporary with Pliny, the *Periplus of the Erythrean Sea* (Indian Ocean), a sailor approaching the Indus River saw the water change color far out to sea. The sailor also saw many sea snakes, such as Aristotle had described and which we know of today, off the Indian coast. The sea snakes were bright green or gold, and seeing them, the sailor knew that land was near.

The *Periplus* described sandbanks, currents, very high tides in the Indian Ocean—which Alexander of Macedon had encountered. One port, Barygaza (Broach), had fishermen act as pilots for incoming ships—the first mention of local pilots to bring vessels into port.

The only work of Pliny to survive was his *Natural History*. And how it survived: it was popular until the nineteenth century. Composed of 37 volumes, it was the second natural history, after Aristotle's 400 years earlier, and was compiled from 2,000 works by 326 Greek writers and 146 Roman writers. When his *Natural History* came out, Pliny knew of 176 sea animals—four fewer than Aristotle had mentioned. It is hard to believe in this day when hundreds of thousands of marine animals are known, but Pliny thought he had them all: "By Hercules!" he said, "in the sea and in the Ocean, vast as it is, there exists nothing that is unknown to us."

Pliny's volume on land animals opened with the largest, the elephant, and he put in some animals that were entirely imaginary.

He described the turtles of the Indian Ocean as being large enough so that one of their shells could be the roof of a cottage. Considering the size of land tortoises of the Indian Ocean's Aldabra Islands and some of the turtles that live in the ocean, this was only a slight exaggeration.

One subject that Pliny investigated—volcanoes—would

become vital to the study of islands, of the seas, and of the forming and continual changing of the earth itself by the 1970s.

On a day in 79 A.D., Pliny's sister Plinia noticed a cloud of smoke shaped like a pine tree rising above a mountain. She pointed it out to her brother. Pliny, who then was in command of a fleet in the Bay of Naples, ordered that its galleys try to rescue people on the coast. He had the sailors of a small vessel steer toward the smoke. As they did, he wrote down every movement and every change that he noticed, the first recorded eruption of the volcano Vesuvius. "The ashes," his nephew, Pliny the Younger, later wrote to Tacitus, "were now falling fast upon the vessels, hotter and more and more thickly the nearer they approached the shore; showers of pumice, too, intermingled with black stones, calcined and broken by the action of the flames."

Lava from the volcano made it impossible for Pliny to reach the shore; he sailed, instead, to a place called Stabiae. That night the mountain cast up vast sheets of flame. In an apartment on shore, Pliny saw the courtyard outside the apartment filled with cinders and pumice stones. He left his shelter, placing a pillow over his head "by way of protection against the falling stones and ashes." He tried to reach the shore and his ships, but could not through the storm of hot rocks, cinders, sand, and fine white ash. He lay down and took a drink of water. Aroused by flames and sulphurous fumes, he got up and, leaning on two servants, attempted to go on, but he fell, and amid the darkness of the eruption, perhaps asphyxiated by the fumes, Pliny the Elder died.

The eruption went on for eight days and nights till the shore and nearby area were buried 20 to 65 feet deep. Later, when a deluge of rain came into contact with the fine white ash, the ash turned into a claylike material that formed molds around the dead bodies of the people who had been trapped in it. One man's body was found with arms upraised; the roof of his house, weighted by lava, may have fallen in on him. Another man's body was found over a gate; he had a key out and a large amount of money which he must have been trying to save. Another person was carrying a number of silver vases when life ended; others had snatched up jewels, or documents. Five people were buried standing up. An old woman apparently had lain down quietly. A girl had her dress held round her head. A heavy man in a short tunic lay upon his back calmly; the ashes even preserved the record of his mustache. Many took to cellars they shut tight. The dust and ash found a way in through every chink and crack and buried them all until the preserved molds of their bodies— 700 altogether—were discovered, beginning in 1748.

The ash, cinders, and rocks destroyed two towns, Herculaneum and Pompeii, so that they never could be rebuilt. The ash, cinders, and rocks, buried many mosaics, including some at Pompeii that showed men apparently using a dog-paddle stroke, apparently swimming. That skill, although it had been possessed by Julius Caesar, was known to very few men, including very few sailors, but it may have been spreading.

Pliny himself was found several days after his death, his nephew, Pliny the Younger, wrote, "untouched and without a wound; there was no change to be perceived in the clothes, and [the body's] appearance was rather that of a person asleep than of a corpse."

Pliny and Seneca both showed how capable at exploring the land men had become in the Roman Empire. One expedition sent by the Roman emperor Nero made a long trip up the Nile. The objective was to locate the headwaters of the Nile. Far inland after a difficult journey, the men reached immense marshes so full of mud and plants that they could only be penetrated by small, one-man boats. These marshes, on the White Nile, would not be rediscovered until explorers reached them 1,800 years later, in 1839 and 1840.

The trek by Nero's explorers was made not to obtain food or to lay out a trade route or to fight a battle—it was made to obtain knowledge, knowledge for its own sake. That was its significance. Ancient man was becoming aware that he needed information—a step toward science. This was one of the most important steps forward that man ever has taken.

34

Late First Century A.D.: A Voyage to India

THE MAN who lived at the time of Pliny, or possibly just after, and who produced the *Periplus of the Erythrean Sea* is unknown. We believe he was a Greek merchant in Alexandria. His *Periplus* seems to have been partly the result of his own experience, and it is one of the most accurate works on geography that we have from the days of Greece or Rome. Covering the Indian Ocean from the port of Myos-hormus on the Red Sea, the Strait of Bab el Mandeb and the coast of East Africa all the way past Arabia and India to China, it adds to what was known by Eratosthenes, Strabo, and Pliny.

By the time of the *Periplus*, sailors regularly were reaching as far south as 6 degrees past the equator on the coast of East Africa. They probably called at the land of Punt, the goal of Queen Hatshepsut in 1500 B.C.

The *Periplus* said that Africa was entirely surrounded by ocean, and men could sail around it. This was widely believed at the time, although nobody was doing it. The eastern side of the Arabian Sea the *Periplus* pictured as hazardous to seamen. Its rocks and shoals and the absence of harbors caused ships to founder. The sailors were robbed and enslaved. Sailors avoided that coast and went down the center of the Red Sea.

The *Periplus* provided both landmarks and other hints for sailors. High Cape Fartak, visible 60 miles away on a clear day, was where ships bound for India headed into the open sea. The Indus River in India had 7 mouths, but only one, the middle one, was navigable.

The gulf called Barace, now the Gulf of Cutch, had black sea snakes marking its approach; if a sailor saw snakes that were green or gold, and smaller, he had gone too far.

Behind India's Malabar Coast, near Calicut, the best pepper in India was produced. The pepper and other spices of Asia were to be sought by men for the next 2,000 years. They made palatable food that had been kept for a long time without refrigeration, and so spices were extremely important in feeding a family. The *Periplus* told of Hippalus' discovery of the monsoon wind that sent ships across the Indian Ocean to get those spices.

"The whole [trip to India] was formerly performed in small vessels, which followed the coast: A pilot named Hippalus was the first, who, from observing the position of the ports, and the configuration of the sea, discovered the mode of sailing right across the open sea; from whom the name Hippalus is given to the local wind which blows steadily from the southwest, in the Indian seas." Big ships replaced small ones for the 40-day, 1,800-mile open-ocean passage to India.

The *Periplus* described the coast of India to its southern promontory, Cape Comorin, on to Taprobane (Ceylon), and the east coast of India up to the mouths of the Ganges. But the description becomes more and more vague. The Greeks and Romans did not often sail so far as the east coast of India.

The author told of the pearl fisheries near Cape Comorin

and off Ceylon. He said that beyond the Ganges a place called Thinae sent silks by two overland trade routes to India. Thinae he had no details about, but it was China, and this is Western man's first mention of China in writing.

A man of the same period who probably studied and worked in Alexandria, Dionysius Periegetes, wrote that the seas around Ceylon were infested with sea monsters that could swallow a ship and all her crew.

In 80 A.D., at Rome, the 45,000-seat Colosseum, one of a number of amphitheaters the Romans built, was opened. For the occasion the emperor Titus flooded the 281-by-177-foot arena, and, upon the artificial lake thus created, ships fought mock naval battles.

A Roman, Plutarch, said that the moon had caves and ruptures, believed that it was like the earth, did not doubt that life could live upon it, and said that life on the moon was no harder to believe in than life in the sea.

In 84 A.D., the Roman general Julius Agricola defeated the Scots but failed to conquer Scotland. He sent a fleet around Caithness and Cape Wrath in northernmost Scotland. Cornelius Tacitus, Agricola's son-in-law, who reported the trip in 98 A.D., said the sailors saw the Orkneys and that they glimpsed Pytheas' Thule, "which had lain concealed in gloom and eternal snows." He said that the sea there was "a sluggish mass of stagnant water, hardly yielding to the stroke of the oar, and never agitated by wind or storms." As winter was drawing near, the men had orders not to go farther toward Thule. "This Thule," according to a modern authority, "must have been Fair island or the Shetland isles, and this is the most northern point reached by the Romans, so far as is known." [1]

As the fleet sailed down the west coast of Britain, its sailors picked up information about Ireland that soon would add details to Ptolemy's maps. The fleet sailed to Land's End and through the English Channel to Sandwich—another voyage (after Claudius' about 42 A.D.) all the way around the British Isles.

Between the ocean and the Rhine, in western Germany, Tacitus described a people called the Frisians, who lived around lakes that Roman ships sailed upon, perhaps a string of shallow lakes near the sea. The Frisians later were to become great fishermen, particularly for herring, and great sailors and long-distance traders.

Tacitus mentioned one tribe of people, the Angli, without saying where they lived, although it was probably in what is Germany today. This was the first time we know of that the people who were to give their name to England were mentioned in writing.

Unlike Pliny, Tacitus did not use the name of Scandinavia, but he did know of rumored lands to the north of the Baltic Sea, which he called the "Northern Ocean," which would turn out to be Sweden.

He mentioned the Suiones—apparently the Swedes—who, he said, "were mighty . . . in ships." Their ships had raised ends—high bows and sterns—and instead of the holes for oars that the Romans used, the Swedes used oarlocks. Like Julius Caesar, Tacitus thus described a forerunner of the much later Viking vessels. A 70-foot-long ship of the third century after Christ, dug up at Nydam, bears out Tacitus' description.

35

Alexandria, 150 A.D.:
Ptolemy and His Geography

FROM 96 TO 180 A.D., during the reigns of the emperors from Domitian to Marcus Aurelius, the Roman Empire reached its high point of prosperity and power. The sailing ship had helped spread the empire to its greatest extent. It included northern Africa and all other shores of the Mediterranean, as well as Britain, northwest Germany, France, Spain, Portugal, Italy, Greece, Turkey, the Middle East, and the Arabian peninsula.

During the reign of the Emperor Hadrian, 107–138 A.D., Flavius Arrianus of Nicomedia, who wrote a history of Alexander the Great, also wrote the *Periplus of the Euxine Sea*, the Black Sea. Arrian, as he was known, himself visited the coast, including Sebastopol, the easternmost outpost of Hadrian's Roman Empire. His *Periplus* amounted to a survey or summary for navigators of the geography of the Black Sea, in case the Romans needed it for military reasons. Painstaking and trustworthy, it gives distances that are close to accurate, headlands, rivers, and towns.

In the second century A.D., the geographer Marinus of

Tyre tried to locate on a map, according to latitude and longitude, every place on earth.

From Roman marches over land south into Africa—the Romans actually had succeeded in crossing the Sahara Desert in two months—he knew that Africa stretched farther south than men had previously believed. But Marinus made the opposite mistake. He concluded Africa stretched too far south.

He thought, as had Posidonius, that Asia reached farther east than most men previously had believed, but he made it stretch farther east than it does. One reason was that he had heard many travelers' tales of journeys by land or sea so very slow that distances sounded longer than they were.

He knew nothing of the Americas or the Pacific Ocean, and instead of accepting Eratosthenes' accurate estimate of the circumference of the globe, he took Posidonius' smaller estimate. Therefore, Asia must be a place that jutted far out into a small ocean, toward Europe. Man might reach it fairly quickly by sailing across the Atlantic, which Marinus thought of as a narrow ocean.

Wrong though he was about Asia, Marinus was the first geographer to recognize, or even to suspect, Asia's vast sweep eastward. Only 50 years before him, the *Periplus of the Indian Ocean* by an unknown geographer described in detail the west coast of India and named China, but had no concept of Asia's size.

Marinus influenced a Greek-Egyptian astronomer and geographer named Claudius Ptolemaeus—Ptolemy—who lived about 73 to 151 A.D., worked at Alexandria, and used, among other sources, Alexander of Macedon's journals and the work left by Marinus of Tyre. He collected all that was known, or guessed, about astronomy and put it into a book with an Arab title, *Almagest* (The Great Work).

Ptolemy developed his astronomy from Hipparchus' work

on movements of the fixed stars and the planets, and gave credit to him as his chief authority. Nevertheless, Hipparchus had earth, moon, and planets revolving around the sun, while Ptolemy thought the sun, moon, and planets revolved about the stationary earth at a uniform rate. The earth obviously did not spin, Ptolemy said; if it did, it would toss into the air animals and other objects and leave them behind.

Ptolemy was not as correct as, in the previous century, Aristarchus of Samos had been in describing the solar system. Ptolemy had done some complicated thinking to back up his ideas, but his thinking unfortunately was mistaken. It was good enough, however, so that there was no way of proving him wrong until telescopes were invented. His ideas about astronomy were believed in Europe for 1,300 years. The Ptolemaic universe would not be proved wrong until Nicholas Copernicus (1473–1543), Johannes Kepler (1571–1630), and Galileo Galilei (1564–1642).

Ptolemy put together everything that the sailors had learned and mapped the known world, often inaccurately, from Ireland and Londinium east to the Orient. It required 26 maps in an atlas for him to show the locations of 8,000 principal places.

In Ireland he named rivers, bays, headlands, and cities. One city, Eblana to Ptolemy, is today Dublin.

In southwest Britain he named the two important headlands, Land's End and The Lizard, and he knew the difference between them.

He knew almost exactly the width of the English Channel between The Lizard and France.

Pytheas of Massilia, in the 300s B.C. had been able to make the astronomical observations that allowed him to assign to his own city a definite and accurate location. But even in Ptolemy's time no such observations had been made for most cities of the Mediterranean or of most places in the rest of the world, so on his maps he could locate them only inexactly. This caused him to distort Italy and stretch the heel of Italy's boot to the east. Among other errors, he mapped the north shore of Africa as almost a straight line.

In Africa, the origin of the Nile River was correctly placed beyond the great marshes, choked with papyrus, found by the Roman expedition under Nero.

Two high snow-covered mountains, Kilimanjaro and Kenya, not far from the source of the Nile, were somehow known to Ptolemy. He mistakenly supposed that they were part of a range. The range does not exist, but the name he gave it still does—Mountains of the Moon.

Thule Ptolemy placed well south of the Arctic Circle—he apparently followed Julius Agricola and Tacitus in saying the Roman fleet had sighted it. Ptolemy apparently identified Thule as the largest of the Shetland Islands, Mainland.

Both Marinus of Tyre and Ptolemy had the ocean extending, as it does, across the top of Europe. Ptolemy, however, figured that Russia was larger than it is and thought it extended farther north and east than it does. Above India, he knew of the high Pamir Mountains—the word means "roof of the world"—of Russia. They run into the Himalayas.

Unlike many of his day, Ptolemy knew where Ceylon was, and he knew a lot about it—ports, rivers, capes, coasts, even its people, but he made it far larger than it is.

Greek mariners had given Ptolemy and, before him, Marinus of Tyre information on a peninsula the sailors called the Golden Chersonese—the Malay Peninsula. Beyond the Golden Chersonese, still farther east, Ptolemy located a land and city called Sinae, a city with walls of brass. From the inexact maps that resulted, it is difficult to tell just what the sailors had reached: it may have been Hanoi, Indochina (now

Vietnam). On Ptolemy's maps the coasts and countries shown are unrecognizable.

But one thing is clear: the Greek sailors had gone beyond new horizons, past the limits of the land previously known to European man.

They may, in fact, have known of the island of Java and told Ptolemy about it; but he seems not to have had any notion of the great archipelago of the East Indies.

Ptolemy's maps showed unexplored land running solidly from southern Africa all the way across to China and stretching to the Antarctic. This supposed but actually nonexistent land bordered the Indian Ocean on the south and east and incorrectly made the Indian Ocean a lake.

Ptolemy knew that the Caspian Sea was an inland sea, a vast lake, as indeed it is—the largest in the world. This information he had received from Herodotus and from Marinus of Tyre. In Marinus, also, Ptolemy found the first mention of two rivers, the Ural and the Volga.

On two Ptolemy manuscripts the maps are credited to Agathodaemon of Alexandria, who may have been a contemporary.[1] This is the first time an artist or mapmaker is given credit, so far as I know.

Ptolemy's grid of latitude and longitude for a spherical earth led to a method of projecting it onto a flat surface. His map of the world was the best for a thousand years.

He did not use Eratosthenes' nearly correct estimate of the circumference of the earth, but—as Posidonius had in 150 B.C. and as had the Phoenician, Marinus of Tyre—he used a smaller figure, about 17,600 miles. And he showed Eurasia (the continent of Europe and Asia) extending halfway around the world instead of one-third of the way, as it does. Thus his idea was that the earth was smaller than it is, land area greater than it is, and area covered by sea was far less than it is.

Ptolemy would be restudied in the late 1400s. His idea that upon a small sea on a small earth sailors could cross an Atlantic of reasonably short span and reach Asia would encourage Columbus. It would also encourage John Cabot and others who would look for a northwest passage from Europe to Asia.

36

150–500 A.D.:
As Rome Fades,
Men Sail On—and On

FROM PTOLEMY ON for several hundred years, which included the decline of the Roman Empire, the story of European man was so full of turmoil, trouble, wars, and rumors of wars that most histories tell of little else. Nevertheless, struggling man still was capable. And in the centuries after Ptolemy man achieved a number of things that helped him know his world better and aided mariners. In this same period, men obtained some of their most durable legends. Their achievements, their new knowledge, and their legends came from widely scattered places. One achievement was that northern Europeans—the ancestors of the Vikings—reached into the Mediterranean. Other developments, important and unimportant, actually came from all over Europe and from many men on the sea.

In 166 A.D. under the Roman emperor Marcus Aurelius, a Roman ambassador arrived at the court of the Chinese emperor, Hiwanti. The diplomat, Antoninus, traveled there we know not how or whether by sea or by land, but the

Romans later had a wider knowledge of eastern Asia, knowledge that must have come from this period.

In 180 A.D., a Roman lawyer, Minucius Felix, was on the way toward knowing something of the warmth that one of the Atlantic currents, the Gulf Stream, brings to northern Europe: "Britain is deficient in sunshine," Felix noted, "but it is refreshed by the warmth of the sea that flows around it."

Early Christians made an acrostic from the Greek for "Jesus Christ, God's Son, Saviour": *Iosous Christos, Theou Uios Soter.* The initials spell *Ichthus,* Greek for "fish." Among the Christians, the fish became a symbol for Jesus, and they used the symbol on rings and tombstones and in literature and art.

In 196 A.D., during a siege of Byzantium, divers played a role by cutting ships' cables.

A *Stadiasmus of the Great Sea* (the Mediterranean) described its coasts. A practical guide for the navigator, the *Stadiasmus* was one of the sailor's best tools yet. Beneath names of places there were explanations: "A place of anchorage," "a roadstead," "a port." Landmarks were given: "A lofty tower." A sailor was told how to approach Carthage and other major ports. He was told where water could be found, especially important on dry shores of northern Africa.

Solinus was a Roman of the third century A.D., who liked to point to the wonders that he learned about and to say, "Gee, whiz!" about them. As might be expected, he recorded that Ireland was free of snakes. He gave a new name to the sea between Africa and Europe: the Mediterranean.

By about the year 240, northern Europeans—Franks, Saxons, Germans, others—had learned enough about the sea to be proficient sailors. One group of Franks (freemen) helped needle the Romans. After capturing a fleet in the Black Sea, which they had reached overland, they sailed through the Bosporus and Hellespont into the Mediterranean to pillage the shores of the Roman Empire—Asia, Greece, Africa. They sacked Syracuse, sailed out past Gibraltar into the Atlantic, sailed up the coasts of Spain and France and through the English Channel to German or northern Holland shores. This success encouraged northern Europeans from then on to minimize the dangers of the sea and to think about its advantages.

The Saxons did indeed think about the advantages of the ocean. They were raiding their northern European neighbors. Edward Gibbon, who wrote *The Decline and Fall of the Roman Empire*, said they went to sea in ships you can hardly believe—big versions of currachs or coracles, skin-covered baskets: "Large flat-bottomed boats with sides and upper works consisting only of wicker, with a covering of strong hides. . . . But the daring spirit of the pirates braved the perils both of the sea and of the shore. . . . The meanest of their mariners was alike capable of handling an oar, of rearing a sail, or of conducting a vessel; and the Saxons rejoiced in the appearance of a tempest, which concealed their designs, and dispersed the fleets of the enemy."

These were among the forefathers of the later Vikings.

Around 287 A.D., these Saxon pirates—as well as Scandinavians—appeared off the coasts of Britain and France. Rome appointed a sailor who may have been one of them, Carausius, to do something. Carausius, who was either a Belgian or a Briton, did something. He beat the pirates, took over their ill-gotten treasure, and practically became a pirate himself. He was sentenced to death by Rome, but instead went with his fleet to Britain, of which he became ruler. Rome bought peace by naming him emperor of Britain. He then recruited the pirates for his ships, which became something entirely new at that time in history: a British navy. It controlled the sea from the Rhine to the Strait of Gibraltar.

Carausius' rule lasted seven years. He died in 294.

If the Phoenician alphabet, which made us all readers and writers of the printed word, was a surprising gift from the sea, so was something else—the legend of Santa Claus. About 300 A.D., a man named Nicholas, supposedly born in Asia Minor, near Myra, in today's Turkey, was ordained a priest. One of the stories told of him is that, on a trip to the Holy Land, high waves buffeted his ship. When he spoke to the storm, it subsided. As a result, Nicholas became the patron saint of travelers, sailors, and sponge divers. He was said to be able to restore a drowned sailor to life. He appeared to countless storm-tossed crews. His image, in countless seaports, often was a painting with an anchor or ship in the background.

Under Constantine the Great, he became bishop and archbishop of Myra, a seaside town. From there, he probably traveled by boat on his rounds.

He became the patron saint of Greece, Sicily, and Russia. After Nicholas saved the lives of three children, he became the patron saint of little children. He once gave dowries of gold so a poor nobleman's three daughters might marry. This gave him a reputation for giving gifts.

St. Nicholas' feast, 6 December, possibly the day he died in perhaps the year 340, became the children's holiday. Its nearness to Christmas gradually caused the legend of Nicholas to be incorporated into the Christmas season.

The Germans gave him his red cloak. The Dutch brought his story to New Amsterdam (New York) and called him Sijterklaas. St. Nicholas, or St. Claus, or Santa Claus, over the centuries became the figure we know today.

In 1087 his body was moved from Myra to Bari, Italy. At Bari, Crusaders prayed at his church. Today girls pray for husbands there, and fishermen and sailors pray for fair weather.

On the high roads laid down in Europe by the Romans, the best ones suitable for wheeled vehicles, there were milestones marking measured distances. For use on the roads, there were issued itineraries, the road maps of their day, which included the distances between points. The most important, *The Itinerary of Antoninus*, the emperor at the time, showed a series of routes through all provinces of the Roman Empire up to Hadrian's wall in Britain. Such itineraries and accurate distances, continually corrected and brought up to date, furnished the information for a map of the Roman roads made by Agrippa. The itineraries and accurate distances also helped bring about better maps for the sailor and better answers to a sailor's questions: Where am I? Which way should I go?

The sailing ships that by Roman and early Christian days often brought passengers home safely, had become a kind of symbol of security amid troubled waters—as Noah's Ark had been long before. The ship, accordingly, came to have a symbolic meaning for Christians—a refuge in the stormy sea of life, something to carry you through. In the fourth century St. Ambrose compared the Church to a ship and the Cross to a mast. The ship also became the symbol or attribute of some saints, including St. Julian, St. Vincent, and St. Nicholas of Myra.

In 375, in *De Re Militari*, Flavius Vegetius Renatus reported that divers had new equipment, a hood and a leather bag around the neck, with a tube to provide breathing air from the bag, which floated on the surface. Vegetius' book would be reprinted almost 1,200 years afterwards, in 1511, this time with a picture of the diving apparatus.

In the 400s A.D., Orosius described, near Britain, an island inhabited by Scots: the Isle of Man.

Man was finding his world.

By about 434 A.D., how a sailor did his job was described by *Mu'allium* (Pilot), a sort of guide for ships' officers in the Arabian Sea. It was written in Sanskrit, a language of India: "He knows the course of the stars and can always orient himself; he knows the value of signs, both regular, accidental, and abnormal, of good and bad weather; he distinguishes the region of the ocean by the fish, the color of the water, the nature of the bottom, the birds, the mountains, and other indications."

By the fifth century, the Saxons and other ancestors of the Vikings were going to sea in improved, stout vessels—the Baltic, the North Sea, the English Channel, the Bay of Biscay. As Edward Gibbon would later, Suetonius noted their lack of fear of storms: "Tempests which [frighten] other men fill them with joy." The Saxons lived in what today is Germany, Belgium, Holland. They and the Scandinavians began a love of the sea that persists in northern Europe to this day.

A German people called Vandals, mentioned by Pliny, left home along the Baltic Sea, crossed Germany, France, the Pyrenees, and Spain, and then by sail into North Africa. With never more than 15,000 warriors, they conquered North Africa. On 14 October 439, under King Gaiseric, the Vandals captured Carthage. They occupied it for the next 94 years. Their ships now crossed and crisscrossed the Mediterranean. From Carthage they sailed west to Cartagena, Spain, and the Balearic Islands; northwards to Sardinia, Corsica, Italy; east to Sicily and Italy. From Carthage, Gaiseric's ships sallied forth as pirates; they plundered, according to themselves, "the dwellings of men with whom God was angry." In 455 they sacked Rome.

In 533 the armies of Emperor Justinian, from Constantinople, defeated the Vandals. Today the title of the king of Sweden is King of the Swedes, the Goths, and the Vandals.

By 455 Italy was reached by the sailing ships of the Eroli, a sparse Scandinavian people, also among the ancestors of the Vikings who would make voyages across the Atlantic and into the Arctic Ocean a few hundred years later on.

About 525 A.D., a Roman astronomer and abbot, Dionysius Exiguus, introduced the system of dates as B.C. (before Christ) and A.D. (Anno Domini).

In the time of Saint Columba (521–597 A.D.), a man named Cormac is thought to have sailed from Ireland three times in search of an unknown island. Columba was a missionary. He brought Christianity to Scotland, is said to have seen a mysterious water beast in Loch Ness—a monster that by 1975 no one had identified—and became a saint. His contemporary, Cormac, may have been looking for Iceland— it might have faded from man's knowledge since Pytheas of Massilia reached it, if he did reach it. Cormac might have been looking for Thule. Cormac may have reached Iceland; if so, he could have been among the Irish who are believed to have preceded the Norsemen there. What is out there? From Cormac over the next 1,500 years—or until today—the sailors of Europe would explore the seas and the world till they had mapped the entire globe.

The Roman Empire declined, cities slid beneath the waves (about 150 Mediterranean cities have sunk since Roman times), but men in the Mediterranean continued to sail their ships for food and other goods for their families. Trade continued in wines, cereals, spices, honey, olive oil, fish, other

foods, earthenware, coins, arms, metal goods, precious stones
and pearls, perfumes, the purple dye of the Tyrians, bronze
and marble statues and busts, brocades, silks, muslin, linen,
timber, wax, whalebone, leather, wool, hides, and skins. In
northern Europe, similarly, men kept busy at sea.

European man, since the first hunter rode down the first
river on the first log, had come a long way in learning about
the ocean. European man, both northern and southern, since
he first fished along the shore, had come a long way in using
the ocean to increase his well-being. European man, since the
time of the little model boat found in the sands of the Fayum,
Egypt, had come a long way in developing the power of wind
in the sails.

Empires would rise and fade. Wars would come and go.
Nations would be born and die. But men would stay at sea.
They would keep going, continuously, right until today, and
they would observe and study the sea and develop today's
oceanography. Sailors are the one group of men who never
looked back.[1]

37

Postscript:
What Came After

THE SAILOR NEVER LOOKED BACK.
This silent, uncommunicative, unknown man sailed on and on. What he did would shape our world. What he did would establish expanding oceanography.

Almost 2,000 years have passed since the day of Christ and Strabo. Five hundred of those years had passed when the Roman Empire faded, when northern Europeans, including Norsemen or Vikings, came into the Mediterranean and harassed Roman vessels.

Almost 600 years had passed when Ireland's St. Brendan, with 16 other men, made a real or legendary voyage in an ox-skin-covered curragh to what may have been Iceland. Seven hundred and fifty years had passed when the Muhammadan Empire, the next great one after Rome's, had spread over the Mediterranean and, in Africa, Spain, and Portugal, had reached the Atlantic. This ocean they dreaded, and called the Green Sea of Darkness. One thousand years since Strabo had passed when the Vikings or Norsemen, in open boats each with a single, square woolen or walrus-hide sail, dared the frosty, choppy North Atlantic, reached Iceland, where they found Irish relics—and in Europe's first westward migration founded a colony—went on to Greenland, and almost certainly got to Canada. They could do what they did because they were the most advanced of ancient oceanographers. They learned to use a prevailing west wind to cross the ocean. They answered "Where am I?" "Which way should I go?" by watching sun, stars, and birds when they could see them. When they could not, in the frequent fogs, they found their way by the feel of the water on their hands, its smell, drifting tree branches, samples of bottom mud, and noticing what sea animals there were.

Eleven hundred of the two thousand years since Strabo had gone by when Norsemen and other Europeans sailed into the Mediterranean on the Crusades. They looked at the Mediterranean ships and added cabins at the bow and stern of theirs. With appetites for new tastes, they also looked at Mediterranean food and plants and took back to northern Europe oranges, lemons, pomegranates, olives, tulips, myrtles, and cedars of Lebanon. Twelve hundred years—three-fifths of all the time since Strabo—had elapsed before scientific sailors borrowed their wives' treasured sewing needles (a woman probably had only one), floated them on corks, and watched the way they pointed—the first steel compass needles, another answer to the questions "Where am I?" "Which way should I go?"

Fourteen hundred of those years had gone by—seven-tenths of all the time between Strabo and today—before, in Portugal, Prince Henry brought together map-makers, compass-makers, astronomers, and captains of the improved two- or three-masted (still square-rigged) sailing ships that had resulted from the Crusades and suggested they venture on the Green Sea of Darkness, the Atlantic. By bringing together all kinds of experts on the sea, Prince Henry took the science of oceanography a big step ahead. His captains, as a result, became the first since Hanno (470 B.C.) to move south along Africa's Atlantic coast.

Almost 1,500 years—three-fourths of the time since Strabo—had elapsed when Bartolemeu Diaz, for Portugal, went from the Atlantic around the tip of Africa into the Indian Ocean, the first sailor we know of since the Egyptian Pharaoh Necho's Tyrians (in 600 B.C.), to go around the Cape of Good Hope. After Diaz returned, a man sailed in the opposite direction: to the west. This man had been a sailor, and sailed down the African coast in Portuguese ships, and also followed Carthage's Himilco (470 B.C.) and went in the other direction to Britain. He may have reached Iceland as a crew member on a freight ship, and he may have heard of a continent westward of Greenland. He went back to Portugal, looked at Ptolemy's atlas, and thought the westward continent was Asia. So on behalf of Spain he sailed to reach it. In the midocean Sargasso Sea on his first trip, Christopher Columbus saw great expanses of seaweed such as Himilco had described.

Just over 1,500 years after Strabo, two sailors, Ferdinand Magellan and Sebastián del Cano, between them would get a sailing ship, the *Victoria*, around the world. That, in the 1500s, would be the first round-the-world trip any vessel ever had made. It would prove what Parmenides of Elea, 570 years before Christ, had concluded—that the earth was round. Not only was it the first round-the-world voyage for a ship, it was the first time any men at all that we know of had traveled around the globe. Magellan himself died on the way. In 1580, Francis Drake, who made maps and charts and sounded the depths and otherwise furthered oceanography every league of the way, became the first captain to sail around the world and himself return alive.

Four-fifths of the time since Strabo had passed when men

in square-rigged, three-masted sailing ships, the *Sarah (Susan) Constant*, the *Discovery*, and the *Good Speed*, landed on an unknown shore and founded what would become Virginia and the United States. The year was 1607. In 1620 others landed from another square-rigged ship, the *Mayflower*, on a cool rockbound coast and established Plymouth colony and Massachusetts and New England. The ships at Virginia and Plymouth Rock were much smaller than the Roman corn ships, and probably much smaller than the one Pytheas had sailed from Massilia north to the Arctic in the fourth century B.C. over 1,900 years before.

Aristarchus of Samos, 310–230 B.C., had said that the sun was the center of the solar system. But in the early 1600s, when the telescope, which eventually would prove that, was only in the process of being invented, ships were being sailed and the American colonies were established by men who still did not know for certain that the earth revolved around the sun.

By the time of the first New World colonies, the 1600s, and even before, the fishing fleets of Portugal, Britain, France, Holland, and other European countries were continually traveling to the Grand Banks off Canada, hauling in cod by the ton and doing exactly what the earliest sailors of all had done—trying to feed their families and everyone else in the colonies. So vital was fish to Europeans that some of the time there were five fish-days a week instead of just one, Friday.

Over 1,750 years—seven-eighths of the time since Strabo—had passed, and the American Revolution was underway, when Britain's Captain James Cook in sailing ships explored the Pacific and filled in details of the world's vastest ocean. Cook had artists sketch coastlines, took along scientists to identify new sea and land creatures, measured the depths, discovered the east coast of Australia, sailed among icebergs, rediscovered Hawaii (the Spaniards apparently had been there, then lost its location), and tried to find (but could not) a passage above Alaska back to Europe. Captain Cook was the first to report the largest shark, the up-to-13-ton, white spotted whale shark.

Not until after nine-tenths of all the time between Strabo and our day—in 1818—would Britain's Captain John Ross, in a wooden square-rigged sailing ship, the *Isabella*, lower a line overboard and find a spot in the sea as deep as the 6,000 feet located about 100 B.C. in the Sea of Sardinia and reported by Posidonius and Strabo. Captain Ross lowered a hemp line overboard and learned that the water was 6,000 feet deep in Baffin Bay between northeast Canada and Greenland, Viking waters. From 4,800 feet, he brought up a Medusa-like, writhing, many-armed starfish. The very deep sea thereby was shown for the first time to hold living creatures; it would have far more strange animals than Aristotle or Pliny had imagined.

Not till the 1830s would the United States and Britain develop the highest form of sailing ship, the clippers, with their skyscraper masts, six sails to a mast. The clippers cut weeks from the trip from Britain to Australia or New York to San Francisco. Not till 1838, when the United States had hundreds of sailing ships pursuing the largest whales, whose oil lighted lamps that made it easier to study after dark, would U.S. Navy Lieutenant Charles Wilkes set sail on an unusual voyage: the first American ocean-exploring expedition in history. Wilkes went to the Canary Islands, then to Brazil (sending back specimens), to the southern tip of South America, saw icebergs in the Antarctic, saw mountains there and became the first to be sure that Antarctica was a continent. He explored South Pacific island waters so well that his charts were used by U.S. armed forces in World War II.

Simultaneously with clippers, whaling ships, and Wilkes, a naval lieutenant from Virginia, Matthew Fontaine Maury, was mapping the best whaling grounds; was delineating winds and currents and finding the best routes for the clippers and so enabling them to break speed records. Maury also was measuring the depths and sampling the bottom of the Atlantic Ocean as part of the preparations for the laying of an electric cable across the ocean—a way of communication that would transmit messages across in minutes, instead of the two or more weeks of a sailing ship.

Not till nineteen-twentieths of all the time between Strabo and our era had gone by would men in Britain's *Challenger* and the U.S.'s *Tuscarora* lower lines overboard in the Pacific and find depths of around five miles. They would bring up thousands of unknown living things from the depths of the sea: glowing fish, blind octopuses, strange sharks and sea cucumbers, sea lilies, and thousands of living and fossilized species of the tiny plants and animals of the plankton— drifting life in the sea that can be seen almost always only with a microscope. John Ross, Charles Wilkes, Matthew Fontaine Maury, and the *Challenger* and the *Tuscarora* had established modern oceanography.

The *Challenger* used sails to cruise, but she had an auxiliary engine. The *Tuscarora*, too, had sails. But, after almost 1,900 of the 2,000 years after Strabo, man was getting another source of energy besides wind in the sails. The sailing ship would be shoved aside, and the coal-, petroleum-, and today nuclear-powered ship would take its place. But the sailing ship lives on in rivers and lakes and harbors of Europe and the United States, at ponds where boys sail toy boats, in thousands of mariner's museums, in thousands of pictures, and as models inside bottles.

The sailing ship at last, at the end of all the 2,000 years since Strabo, has ceased to do the heavy work at sea. But the sailors who, after Rome fell, never turned back have not turned back this time either. Oceanographers have been defined as sailors who use big words. The sailors who use big words these days are at sea studying physics, chemistry, biology, and geology of the oceans and their basins, and studying meteorology—the weather above it.

Only since World War II has progress in oceanography been amazing, and that is why the field of sciences that composes oceanography is mushrooming today. Men today need food, just as much as in the days of prehistory or ancient Greece; since World War II, marine biologists have helped increase the catch from the world's oceans by 200 percent.

But that is only one detail. What today's scientists of the sea are doing is nothing less than what men on the land did thousands of years ago when they learned to plant seeds, grow crops, and raise animals instead of hunting, fishing, and gathering nuts and berries. Men learned to use the land, and today oceanographers are learning how men can use the ocean.

Two thousand years ago Strabo had said man was in a sense amphibious, connected with the sea. A few years ago, the commander of the U.S. Naval Oceanographic Office, Captain T. K. Treadwell, echoed Strabo: "Oceanography and the marine sciences that compose it are preparing to play a major role in the history of mankind."

Instead of depending entirely on catching fish where they find them, men are beginning, after centuries of failure, to raise fish as food crops. Rainbow trout have been raised, and so have salmon, to pan-size. The trout have been improved to produce more eggs and to grow faster. Only within the last six years have universities and laboratories learned how to raise fish and shellfish and squid from egg to adult—dozens of species, more than we knew how to raise in all the centuries of effort before.

The purple dye of the Phoenicians, Tyrian purple, was wealth from the sea. At least 2,000 kinds of fish and shellfish right now are being tested for chemicals and for medicines against cancer and a host of human ailments. Seaweed, long known for iodine, provides algin, used in paper sizing, textile printing, cosmetics, paints, explosives, and drugs. Another substance from seaweed, carrageenin, goes into ice cream and chocolate milk. Sheep and cows and chickens eat seaweed, and so do people the world around; Icelanders have a red seaweed salad they enjoy. In recent years, Canada has become a country with a large seaweed industry. And kelp, the largest seaweed, whose fronds grow longer than the boles of the California redwood trees, is harvested as a crop in Australia and California.

The Pacific floor, in many places, is carpeted with what are called manganese nodules, potato-sized rocks that contain manganese (essential in making steel), cobalt, iron, nickel, and copper (man's first metal after gold, and the one that ended the Stone Age). Engineers are beginning to suck them up through giant vacuum hoses. In the sea sailed by ancient Greeks and Arabs, the Red Sea, there has been discovered, on the deep bottom, a hot slurry rich in minerals. Beneath the bottom of the ocean just offshore of the continents, man since World War II has learned how to locate and obtain one-fifth of his petroleum—oil and natural gas—and the percentage is rising. In addition to the oil wells offshore, some are already out of sight of land. In shallow water just offshore, man obtains sulfur, phosphates and other fertilizers, and sand and gravel.

The sea contains 97 percent of the globe's water; men on land are using only 1 percent. Plants to obtain fresh water

from the sea are multiplying. The process is not far from
being economically feasible.

The diseases that Aristotle only knew fish had are today
being studied at a number of laboratories. The noises fish
make are listened to. The Navy needs to know all about
sounds made in the sea, and what makes them. How the eel
can migrate (Aristotle did not know it did) from Europe and
the United States to its spawning grounds in the mid-Atlantic
Sargasso Sea is being studied. A theory is that it is sensitive
to, and guided by, electric fields generated by movement of
ocean currents. Fish, including the 1,000-pound bluefin tuna,
make migrations as long and as intriguing as the flights of
birds over oceans, which oceanographers also observe.

As the ship with the wind in its sail was a new type of
vehicle that took men to new places, so since the 1960s men
have had deep-diving vehicles—bathyscaphes and submarines—that convey them to the greatest depths and allow
them to look into the sea through windows, assisted by lights.
On January 6, 1960, Jacques Piccard and U.S. Navy
Lieutenant Don Walsh reached the bottom almost seven
miles down (35,800 feet) in the Challenger Deep of the
Pacific's Mariana Trench—the deepest known place in the
ocean. As Alexander of Macedon had done in a glass chamber
in shallow seas in the fourth century B.C., Piccard and Walsh
gazed into the water. Seven miles down they saw living
things—a red shrimp and a foot-and-a-half-long flatfish. This
was the first, and so far the only, eyewitness proof that
advanced living things could exist in the cold, pressure, and
darkness of the greatest depths. In 1975, scientists who had
been dropping cameras to the bottom of the Pacific off
California said that their deep pictures showed far more
life—vertebrate and invertebrate—on the bottom than had
been suspected. Big sharks and teeming shrimp were discovered in many places.

As man in prehistoric times tamed wild animals and made them his helpers, so today he is for the first time making progress at taming wild ocean animals. Some historians believe that the dog was man's first domesticated animal on land, and that when he obtained the dog to help him, man took the step that made him supreme on earth over all other creatures. Already assisting men in the sea are porpoises, seals, sea lions, and whales. Porpoises, friendly to men since Aristotle's time, drive away sharks. Porpoises, seals, and sea lions, some not on leashes, recover sunken weapons. Even a pilot whale has been trained as a servant to men.

A surprising animal help to men was created in 1975 by improving the breed—nothing less than a super microbe that, spread in the sea, can digest petroleum and convert it into food for marine life. Combining genes of four bacteria, the super microbe may one day clean up oil spills or pollution at sea.

Columbus, on the way home from his first trip in 1492, put down so well the details of a hurricane that he qualified as a meteorologist. Today men watch hurricanes with planes and satellites and radar, and detail their paths so well that people ahead of them are warned and thousands of lives formerly lost are saved.

Because the fossils of marine animals were discovered far inland, Strabo had concluded the land and the sea changed places. Many more fossils have been found; today we know much of the land once was covered by the sea. In the 1960s and 1970s the theory was accepted that the continents themselves. move over the sea bottom, an inch or several inches a year. Dakar, Africa, is about 60 feet farther from South America than it was in Columbus' day. Drilling into the Mediterranean sea floor and analyzing the sediments has shown that the Mediterranean has been alternately a sea, dry desert-like land, and land dotted with ponds. Today, near

Greece and Crete, sea-bottom sediments are thickening and piling up; a new mountain range may be forming.

Only today, since World War II, has the advent and wide use of sonar to measure the ocean's depths made it possible to map the bottom, and this is currently being done. The map will show that the sea is not a bowl or teacup, but has a rugged floor beneath its dark surface. There are dunes, hills, mountains standing alone—one of them almost as tall as Mount Everest—mountain ranges, great canyons, or trenches, deeper than the Grand Canyon. At one place on the Pacific bottom there is the greatest spread of lava on earth, indicating an unimaginable flow of lava at some past date. Also on the Pacific floor, there are plains spreading wider than the great plains of the central United States that provide so much of the world's food.

The sea holds so much promise for man today that Great Britain, Russia, France, the Scandinavian countries, Japan, Monaco, West Germany, even inland Switzerland (no coast, no navy, no merchant ships) are among the nations learning how to use the sea. Jacques Cousteau is at Monaco.

In the United States, over the past few decades, the beginnings were made by the U.S. Naval Oceanographic Office and the National Ocean Survey (of the National Oceanic and Atmospheric Administration, Department of Commerce). And by the Woods Hole Oceanographic Institution on Cape Cod; the Scripps Institution of Oceanography, La Jolla, California; and the Lamont-Doherty Geological Observatory of Columbia University.

A hundred years ago in the United States the land-grant colleges were established to study agriculture, and their research stations found the means to improve American farms till the nation could feed and provide fiber to all its people and many others. Today, the first sea-grant universities—Washington, Rhode Island, Oregon State, Hawaii, Wisconsin,

Texas A&M, and the University of California system—all have their own oceanographic ships; some of them have fleets. The sea-grant universities receive federal funds to enable them to study and teach oceanography. The Naval Academy, the Coast Guard Academy, and the maritime academies have added oceanography to their curriculums. Hundreds of other universities, from Miami to Southern California and Stanford, from Louisiana State and the University of Texas to Yale and Connecticut, teach oceanography. So do junior colleges and high schools, in particular in every state on the coasts.

Today's oceanographers, teaching men how to use the sea, may well make as significant a change in the world as did those much earlier men who taught others how to use the land, for agriculture.

Today's ocean explorers know full well how much they owe to ancient men. For some of them, today's men on the sea have named a number of features on the bottom.

For the Greek who in the sixth century B.C. mapped the known world, oceanographers have named the Anaximander Mountains below the wine-dark surface of the eastern Mediterranean.

For the philosopher who in the fourth century B.C. told a tale which he heard from Egypt of the sunken civilization of Atlantis, there is Plato Seamount, submerged south of the Azores islands.

For the man who circa 260 B.C. invented hydrostatics, the science of fluids, there is Archimedes Seamount.

For the geographer who, at the time of Jesus, described the known world—a world that had been found by the ancient mariners—there is Strabo Trench in the floor of the Mediterranean.

For the Roman admiral who studied volcanoes and observed the eruption of Mount Vesuvius, there is the Pliny Trench in the bottom of the Mediterranean.

For the Alexandrian whose atlas showed the world without the Americas and the Pacific Ocean, and encouraged Columbus to sail west across the Atlantic, looking for Asia, there are on the bottom of the sea near the island of Crete the Ptolemy Mountains.

Man's journey toward today's oceanography, and the future's, began with many for whom nothing can be named—they were anonymous. There was the prehistoric man who drifted down a river on a log. There were those who hollowed out logs for dugout canoes, or who built rafts, or who went to sea in either. There were those who captured fish and crustaceans near the mouth of Portugal's Tagus River, or who put a small sail onto a boat on the Nile.

For today's oceanography, and the future's, men were headed when they first deliberately sailed out of sight of land. For today's oceanography they were headed when Hatshepsut sent her fleet to Punt, and Pytheas explored the Arctic in 300 B.C.

For today's oceanography, men were headed as long ago as when, before anyone at all had dared the sea, perhaps lost while hunting in the desert or jungle, perhaps simply squatting or lying awake in the entrance to a cave, a man looked upwards at the sky and the stars.

Notes

CHAPTER 1

1. Dr. Carl Johanson, quoted in *Science Digest*, February 1975.
2. The Harvard Museum of Comparative Zoology announced Bryan Patterson's discovery of African fossils on January 13, 1967.

CHAPTER 2

1. Eric H. Warmington, *Greek Geography*, London and Toronto: J. M. Dent & Sons, Ltd.; New York: E. P. Dutton & Co., Inc.

CHAPTER 3

1. Dr. Meyer Rubin and Harold E. Reade of the U. S. Geological Survey made the discovery of Ice Age tools and fossils near Puebla, Mexico, on May 27, 1962. The Associated Press reported the event.

2. Information about the Santa Rosa people is in N. J. Berrill's book, *Journey into Wonder* (New York: Dodd, Mead & Company, 1951); paperback edition, Collier Books, The Crowell-Collier Publishing Company, 1961.

3. Edward P. Lanning, an anthropologist at Columbia University, is the authority on the Peru coast dwellers of 8500 B.C.

4. The quotation is by Leon La Porte in the April 1972 issue of *NOAA* (National Oceanic and Atmospheric Administration of the U.S. Department of Commerce).

CHAPTER 4

1. The source of information about oars in Denmark about 7000 B.C. is James B. Sweeney, formerly of the United States Naval Oceanographic Office.

CHAPTER 5

1. Geoffrey Parsons, *The Stream of History* (New York: Charles Scribner's Sons, 1923), index at end of Volume 4.

CHAPTER 6

1. Douglas Phillips-Birt, *A History of Seamanship* (Garden City, New York: Doubleday & Company, Inc., 1971), apparently speaking of this same amphora, says that it is "now considered to be more like 4000–3000 B.C."

CHAPTER 7

1. This impression of cart wheels is in the Field Museum of Natural History, Chicago.

2. James Dugan, *Man Under the Sea* (New York: Harper & Row, 1956); paperback edition, New York: Collier Books, 1965.

3. The source of this is James Sweeney of the U. S. Naval Oceanographic Office.

CHAPTER 8

1. Lionel Casson, *The Ancient Mariners* (New York:The Macmillan Company, 1959).
2. *Ibid.*

CHAPTER 9

1. The Right Reverend R. Cumberland, D.D., Bishop of Peterborough, in *Sanchoniato of Byblus*, a Phoenician history translated by Dr. Cumberland (London: W.B. for R. Wilkin, 1720). New York Society Library.
2. *Ibid.*
3. Philo Herennius of Byblus, a Phoenician historian.
4. *Ibid.*
5. Viljhalmur Steffanson, *Ultima Thule* (New York: The Macmillan Company, 1949).
6. Lionel Casson, *The Ancient Mariners* (New York: The Macmillan Company, 1959).
7. *The Columbia Encyclopedia.*
8. C. W. Ceram, *Gods, Graves and Scholars* (New York: Alfred A. Knopf, 1956).
9. The archaeologists of the Smithsonian were Dr. Betty J. Meggers and Clifford Evans. They were quoted in a Smithsonian news release December 3, 1963. Original information on the Valdivia pottery came from the Museo Victor Emilio Estrada of Guayaquil, Ecuador, and from Dr. Emilio Estrada of the museum.
10. News release, December 3, 1963, of the Smithsonian Institution, Washington, D.C.
11. The shell-mound skulls in Alabama have been studied since 1942 by Dr. Albert Casey of the University of Alabama.
12. Dr. A. W. Brogger of Oslo, Norway.

CHAPTER 10

1. Commodore R. St. B. Collins, Royal Navy (who served
   1955–60 as hydrographer of the British Navy) in the 1955
   foreword to E. C. R. Taylor's *The Haven-Finding Art* (New
   York: American Elsivier Publishing Company, Inc., 1971).
2. August Erman and Aylward M. Blackman, *The Literature of
   the Ancient Egyptians.* Reprinted by Harper & Row as
   Ancient Egyptians: A Sourcebook of Their Writings.
3. Elizabeth Goudge, *Island Magic.* Reprinted 1975, New York:
   Pyramid Publications (paperback).

CHAPTER 11

1. Nicholas C. Flemming, *Cities in the Sea* (Garden City, New
   York: Doubleday & Company, Inc. 1971).

CHAPTER 12

1. Dr. Pritchard is with the University of Pennsylvania Museum. He was sponsored by the Ford Foundation and the
   National Geographic magazine.

CHAPTER 13

1. Diving with George F. Bass of the University of Pennsylvania
   Museum for the Phoenician wreck were Peter Throckmor-
   ton, Honor Frost, and Frederic Dumas. Helping ashore was
   Joan du Plat Taylor.
2. J. W. Buel, *Heroes of Unknown Seas and Savage Lands*
   (Philadelphia: World Publishing Co., 1891) credits this tale
   of Menelaus to the Greek geographer who lived in the Roman
   Empire at the time of Christ, Strabo.
3. Lionel Casson, *The Ancient Mariners* (New York: The
   Macmillan Company, 1959).

CHAPTER 15

1. The 1958–59 expedition was led by Nicholas C. Flemming of the University of Cambridge, England.

CHAPTER 16

1. Dave Marra, *Naval Oceanographic Office Bulletin*, Suitland, Maryland, 3 March 1972.
2. Professor Cynes H. Gordon of Brandeis University.
3. J. W. Buel, *Heroes of Unknown Seas and Savage Lands* (Philadelphia: World Publishing Co., 1891).

CHAPTER 17

1. Will Durant, *The Life of Greece* (New York: Simon and Schuster, 1939).
2. Åke Wallenquist, *Dictionary of Astronomical Terms* (Garden City, New York: The Natural History Press, 1966).

CHAPTER 18

1. Fridtjof Nansen, *In Northern Mists* (New York: Frederick A. Stokes Company, 1911).

CHAPTER 21

1. James A. Mavor, Jr., of the Woods Hole Oceanographic Institution on Cape Cod, Massachusetts, in the November 1966 issue of the Woods Hole magazine *Oceanus*. Mavor visited Thera aboard the Woods Hole vessel *Chain*, with E. F. K. Zarudski as chief scientist.
2. The Greek scholar is Professor Angelos Galanopoulous.

CHAPTER 22

1. Dr. Maurice Burton in Part 2, 1973, of *Animal Life*.
2. This division of the coastal zone into 20 biotopes was made by the University of Texas along the Gulf of Mexico.
3. The research on noises fish make has been done largely by Mrs. Marie Poland Fish and William H. Mowbray, an electronics engineer, both of the Narragansett Marine Laboratory of the University of Rhode Island.
4. Jim Fish, a bio-acoustician at the Naval Undersea Research and Development Center, San Diego, California.
5. The parrot-fish and damselfish noises were reported by Texas A & M University's John D. Sartori, Thomas J. Bright, and Thomas E. Burke.
6. Johannes Schmidt, a Danish oceanographer, located the breeding place of the eels, on expeditions aboard the ships *Thor* and *Dana*.
7. The fish was caught on a summer night in 1964 from the University of Miami's research vessel *John Elliott Pillsbury*. The chief scientist on the trip was Donald P. de Sylva of Miami.
8. The quotation about Aristotle is from the late Robert Cushman Murphy, Lamont Curator of Birds at the American Museum of Natural History, New York City.

CHAPTER 23

1. A. R. Burn, *Alexander the Great and the Hellenistic Empire* (New York: The Macmillan Company, 1948).
2. *La Vrai Histoire d'Alexandre*: I once saw an original manuscript at the Yale University Library. It has been quoted by the General Dynamics Corporation's Electric Boat Division, which builds nuclear submarines, and built the first one for the United States, the *Nautilus*.
3. James Dugan, *Man Under the Sea* (New York: Harper & Row, 1956; paperback, New York: Collier Books, 1965).

CHAPTER 24

1. Vilhjalmur Stefansson, *Great Adventures and Explorations* (New York: The Dial Press, 1947, 1952, 1962).
2. Sir Clements Markham, "Pytheas, the Discoverer of Britain," in *Geographical Journal*, June 1898.
3. The authority that Bronze Age Norwegian ships could have sailed the open sea is Dr. A. W. Brögger, who spoke in 1936 after considering rock-carving pictures of ships from the Bronze Age. Dr. Brögger is quoted by Vilhjalmur Stefansson in *Ultima Thule* (New York: The Macmillan Company, 1940).
4. H. O'Neill Mencken, quoted in Vilhjalmur Stefansson, *Ultima Thule, op. cit.*
5. Vilhjalmur Stefansson, *ibid.*
6. Frank Debenham, once director of the Scott Polar Research Institute at the University of Cambridge, England. See his *Discovery and Exploration* (New York: Doubleday & Company, 1960).
7. Fridtjof Nansen, *In Northern Mists* (New York: Frederick A. Stokes Company, 1911). This book is the story of Arctic exploration.

CHAPTER 27

1. An English research scientist, Dr. David H. Jones, in *Smithsonian* magazine, December 1971.
2. The invention of the astrolabe is described in *Bulletin of the U.S. Naval Oceanographic Office*, 21 December 1971.

CHAPTER 29

1. J. B. Buel, *Heroes of Unknown Seas and Savage Lands* (Philadelphia: World Publishing Co., 1851). Buel reports that a Portuguese historian, Antonio Galvano, tells of the Roman trip across the top of Russia.

2. "All the stars he [Hipparchus] described," wrote Harvard University astronomer Cecilia Payne-Gaposchkin, "with the same brightness and practically at the same place, are in the skies of today." This shows the slowness of change in the skies, as well as the accurate observation of Hipparchus.

CHAPTER 30

1. David E. H. Jones in *Smithsonian* magazine of December 1971 discusses the astronomical calculator.

CHAPTER 31

1. John E. Warme, assistant professor of geology at Rice University, Houston, in *Rice University Review*, Fall 1971.
2. Dr. Albert E. J. Engel, professor of geology at the Scripps Institution of Oceanography, La Jolla, California, discovered the 3½-billion-year-old fossils.
3. Dr. J. William Schopf of the University of California at Los Angeles discovered the 3.1-billion-year-old fossils.
4. E. H. Bunbury, *A History of Ancient Geography* (London: John Murray, 1879).

CHAPTER 32

1. Douglas Phillips-Birt, *A History of Seamanship* (New York: Doubleday & Company, Inc., 1971).

CHAPTER 34

1. Fridtjof Nansen, *In Northern Mists* (New York: Frederick A. Stokes Company, 1911).

CHAPTER 35

1. E. H. Bunbury, *A History of Ancient Geography* (London: John Murray, 1879).

CHAPTER 36

1. Geoffrey Parsons, *The Stream of History* (New York: Charles Scribner's Sons, 1929).

Bibliography

IN ADDITION to the books listed in the Notes, others consulted for the preparation of this book are:

ANDERSON, JOHN R. L. *Vinland Voyage.* New York: Funk & Wagnalls. First published in London in 1967.

ANVILLE, MONSIEUR D'. *Compendium of Ancient Geography.* London: Printer for R. Faulder, 1791.

ARISTOTLE. *The Works of Aristotle. Historia Animalium.* Edited by Sir David Ross. Oxford University Press, 1910. Reprinted 1967.

ARMSTRONG, RICHARD. *The Early Mariners.* New York: Frederick A. Praeger, 1968.

ARNOV, BORIS, JR. *Oceans of the World.* Indianapolis and New York: The Bobbs-Merrill Company, Inc., 1962.

Assyrian and Babylonian Literature. Introduction by Robert Francis Harper. New York: D. Appleton and Company, 1904.

ATKINSON, WILLIAM C., transl. *"The Lusiads" by Luis Vaz de*

Camoens. Hammondsworth, Middlesex, England: Penguin Books. 1951. A translation in English prose of the Portuguese poem about Portuguese ocean explorers, mainly Vasco da Gama.

AUSTRALIAN MUSEUM, SYDNEY. *Australian Natural History*, December 1969. An issue about Captain Cook.

BARR, STRINGFELLOW. *The Mask of Jove.* Philadelphia and New York: J. B. Lippincott Company, 1966. A history of the Roman Empire.

———. *The Will of Zeus.* Philadelphia and New York: J. B. Lippincott Company, 1961. History of Greece through Alexander of Macedon.

BARROW, JOHN. *Cook's Voyages of Discovery.* Edinburgh, Scotland: Adam and Charles Black, 1860, 1874. Cook's early exploration of the Pacific.

BATES, MARSTON, AND HUMPHREY, PHILIP S., eds. *The Darwin Reader.* New York: Charles Scribner's Sons, 1956.

BEAGLEHOLE, J. C. *The Exploration of the Pacific.* Stanford: Stanford University Press, 1966.

———. *The Life of Captain James Cook.* Stanford: Stanford University Press, 1974.

BEAZLEY, CHARLES RAYMOND. *Prince Henry the Navigator.* New York: G. P. Putnam's Sons, 1895.

BERRILL, N. J. *Journey into Wonder. Exploration of the Natural World and Voyages of Discovery.* New York: Dodd, Mead & Company, 1951. Paperback edition: Collier Books, 1951.

BOWEN, FRANK CHARLES. *The Sea.* 4 vols. McBride, 1924–26. He also wrote *The Golden Age of Sail,* 1925.

BUNBURY, E. H. *A History of Ancient Geography.* London: John Murray, 1879. Maps of Ulysses' wanderings, Alexander's campaigns, and Eratosthenes' world.

BURN, A. R. *Alexander the Great and the Hellenistic Empire.* New York: The Macmillan Company, 1948.

CARPENTER, RHYS. *Beyond the Pillars of Hercules.* New York: Delacorte Press, 1966. Travels of Hanno, Pytheas, and Alexander the Great, among others.

CARY, M., AND WARMINGTON, E. H. *The Ancient Explorers.* London: Methuen, 1929.

CASSIDY, VINCENT H. *The Sea Around Them.* Baton Rouge: The Louisiana State University Press, 1968. The Atlantic Ocean, 1250 A.D.

COOMBS, CHARLES. *Deep-Sea World.* New York: William Morrow and Company, 1966. The story of oceanography.

CUMBERLAND, RIGHT REVEREND R., D.D., Bishop of Peterborough. *Sanchoniatos of Byblus, Phoenician History.* Translated by Dr. Cumberland. London: W.B. for R. Wilkin, 1720. Sanchoniatos was a historian in Beirut about 1250 B.C. At the New York Society Library.

DEBENHAM, FRANK. *Antarctica.* New York: The Macmillan Company, 1961.

DUGAN, JAMES. *Man Under the Sea.* New York: Harper & Row, 1956. Man's efforts under the sea.

R. FARBROTHER, ed. *Ships.* London: Paul Hamlyn, 1963. Much on ancient ships.

GREEN, PETER. *Alexander the Great.* New York and Washington: Praeger Publishers, Inc., 1970.

HAMILTON, H. C., AND FALCONER, W., transls. *The Geography of Strabo.* London: George Bell & Sons, 1903. At the New York Society Library. Another edition, London: Henry G. Bohn. 1854. At the Mercantile Library, New York City.

HARVEY, SIR PAUL. *Oxford Companion to Classical Literature.* Oxford, England: Oxford University Press, 1937, 1940.

HEATH, SIR THOMAS. *Aristarchus of Samos.* Oxford at the Clarendon Press, 1913. At the New York Society Library. A history of early Greek astronomy.

IDYLL, CLARENCE, P., ed. *Exploring the Ocean World.* New York:

Thomas Y. Crowell Company, 1969. A history of oceanography.

JONES, T. E. *Aristotle's Researches in Natural Science.* London, 1912.

LAMB, HAROLD. *Alexander of Macedon. The Journey to World's End.* Garden City, New York: Doubleday & Company, Inc., 1946.

LIVERMORE, H. V. *A New History of Portugal.* Cambridge University Press, 1967.

MCKEON, RICHARD. *Introduction to Aristotle.* New York: Random House, Inc., 1947.

MARWICH, HUGH. *Orkney.* London: Robert Hale, Ltd., 1951.

MOORE, HILARY B. "Ships at Sea: Maritime Facts of Life." In *U.S. Naval Institute Proceedings,* April 1971, p. 35. Prehistory—trade routes Africa-America.

NATIONAL MARITIME MUSEUM (Great Britain). *Three Major Ancient Boat Finds in Britain.* London, 1972. Includes the Brigg boat and discoveries in North Farriby, Sutton Hoo, and Guernsey.

RAWLINSON, GEORGE. *Herodotus.* London: John Murray, 1875. At the Mercantile Library, New York City.

RAWLINSON, GEORGE. *The Story of Phoenicia.* New York: G. P. Putnam's Sons. London: T. Fisher Unwin, 1889. At the New York Society Library.

ROSENBERG, NORMAN D. "Odysseys to the Isles." In *Oceans* magazine, No. 1, 1972. About the Orkney Islands.

Sanchoniato or Sanchoniatos. *See* Cumberland, Right Reverend R.

"Were Ancient Alabamians Sailors?" In *Science Digest,* June 1972, p. 87. The skull-mound people of Alabama, who may have sailed around the world.

Seneca's Tragedies. Edited by Frank Justice Miller. New York: G. P. Putnam's Sons, 1916–17.

SERRANO-CAMPILLO, DR. EDUARDO. *The Origin and Evolution of Biological Thought.* Mexico, 1966. History of zoology and related sciences.

THOMAS, PHILLIP BRENNON. "Nights in Pliny's Garden." In *Natural History*, March 1972.

U. S. Army, Topographic Command, Geographic Names Division. *Undersea Features.* Gazetteer No. 111. Official standard names. Approved by the United States Board on Geographical Names. Washington, D.C.: June 1969. Names of undersea features are listed alphabetically and by quadrangles or blocks covering the oceans.

WALLENQUIST, ÅKE. *Dictionary of Astronomical Terms.* Translated and edited by Sune Engelbrektson. Garden City, New York: The Natural History Press, 1966.

WARMINGTON, E. H., ed. *Greek Geography*, 1934. Reprint, New York: AMS Press.

WELLS, EVELYN. *Hatshepsut.* Garden City, New York: Doubleday & Company, Inc., 1969.

Index

A.D., B.C. introduced, 221
Aeneid (Vergil), 182
Aetna, Mount, volcano, 186
Africa: Menelaus, 72; Necho, 87 ff.;
Persians, 90; Sataspes, 98; Hanno,
98 ff.; Carthaginians, 169; Eudoxus, 170; Strabo, 187; Europeans explore, 1400s A.D., 187, 224–
225
Agricola, Julius, 207
Agriculture: 18 ff.; olive, 38; Peru cotton, 45; potato, 46; Phoenician,
36–37
Aids to navigation: astrolabe, 167; bottom samples, 105, 106; compass,
180, 224; pole, depth, 56; gnomon, 92, 115, 149; lighthouse,
161; line overboard, 105, 106; sailing directions, 102; mathematics,
166; *Stadiasmus*, 216; timepieces,
58, 66; wind directions, 170
Alabama, University of, 47
Alexander, Greek captain, 200
Alexander of Macedon, 131 ff.; lowered in diving chamber, 135
Alexandria, 136, 165, 173 ff., 193;
Pharos, lighthouse, 161, 184

Algae, oldest fossils, 186
Alphabet, 68 ff.; 76
Amber, 85, 86, 148
America, 80, 82, 153, 181, 197, 225 ff.
Amphora, 23, 193
Anchors, 102, 134
Angli, mentioned by Tacitus, 208
Animals (*see also* Biology; Zoo): 165;
domesticated, 19; scarab, 20; hon-
eybees, cattle, horses, camels, 20;
oldest life, 186; prehistoric, 5, 12,
186; Red Sea and Nile, 55; sheep,
goats, pigs, dogs, 19; unknown in
sea, 128, 201, 228
Antony and Cleopatra, 182
Arabia Felix, 55
Arabian Sea, 220
Archimedes, 166, 171, 234
Arctic, 85, 176, 188, 199–200; Pytheas
reaches, 147, 154, 157 ff.
Argo, 73–74, 186, 197
Aristotle, 117 ff.; 136, 137, 139, 156,
173
Astrolabe, 167
Astrology, 9–10
Astronomy, *see* North Star; Sun
Aswan, Egypt, 171

Atlantic, 11, 67, 88, 97–98, 101, 102,
    107, 181, 216
Atlantis, 112 ff.
Atoms, 110–111
Augustus Caesar, 162; sends fleet to
    Germany, 192; his roads, 184
Australia, men on logs in today, 6
Azores, 82, 109

B.C., A.D. introduced, 221
Babel, on map, 85; Tower of, 132, 161
Babylonia, 27, 30, 44, 68, 85, 86, 94
Bacteria, oldest fossils, 186
Ballast stones, 37, 39
Bass, George F., 72, 77
Bay of Biscay, 101; Pytheas in, 150
Beaker people, reach Orkneys, 40, 41
Beer, Pytheas encounters, 151
Benguela Current, West Africa, 89
Bering Strait, 176, 200
Berlitz, Charles, 68
Biology: Alcmaeon, 96; Alexander of
    Macedon, 131; Aristotle, 118 ff.;
    great depths, 228, 231; Hanno,
    99; Phoenicians, 79 ff.; Pliny, 201;
    Ross, 227; Strabo, 186; tame ocean
    animals, 232
Birds, as guide to mariners, 186
Bireme, two banks of oars, 95, 150
Black people, of Africa, 98
Black Sea, 51, 73, 92, 209
Botanical gardens, Alexandria, 165
Bottles overboard, 156
Bottom samples, 106
Bottom of sea, 233
Bow, early mechanical device, 71
Bradwood, Bruce W., 19
Brazil, 90–91, 103
Brigg boat (hollow log), 15, 22
Bristlecone pine, 43
British Isles, 101, 150, 195, 208, 216,
    217
British Museum, London, 23, 95
British Museum (Natural History),
    London, 19
Brochs, 97
Bronze, found on Phoenician ship, 72
Bunbury, E. H., 186
Byblos, 36, 69

Cabins, ship, 22, 23
Cables, use of, 57
Cabo de Roca, Portugal, 188
Cabot, John, 214
Caius Dullius, 176
Calendar, 33, 221
California, University of, 234
Cambridge, University of, 137
Canals, 27, 41, 54
Canary Current, 89
Canary Islands: Hanno, 99; Homer,
    78; Juba, 182; Phoenicians?, 88,
    90; Portuguese, 45; trade winds,
    90
Cano, Sebastian del, 225
Canoe (hollow log), 15, 46
Cape Agulhas, 88
Cape of Good Hope, 88
Cape Guardafui, 43, 158
Cape Horn, 13
Cape St. Vincent, Portugal, 150,
    188
Cape Verde Islands, 88, 99
Carausius, 217–218
Caravels, 103
Carnarvon, Lord, 70
Carracks (skin boats), see Curraghs
Cart, 27, 30
Carter, Howard, 70
Carthage, 80, 100–101; 103–104;
    109 ff.; 148–149; 176, 220
Case Western Reserve University, 2
Caspian Sea, 107, 172, 213
Ceylon: Greeks, Romans, reach, 187;
    Megastehenes on, 157; described
    in Periplus, 206; Phoenicians, 91;
    Ptolemy on, 212
Chain (ship), 240
Challenger (1872–6), a ship, 228
Challenger Deep, Pacific, 231
Chicago, University of, 19
Chickens, 56
Chimpanzees, 99
China: 205, 207; Egyptians, 23;
    Greeks, 196; Romans, 176, 205;
    Ptolemy, 213; Roman ambassador
    reaches, 215
Chinese: Eratosthenes mentions, 172;
    junks, 23; cable-drill for oil, 176

Christ, Strabo a contemporary, 184;
    acrostic *Ichthus*, 216
Chronometers, 58
Cinnamon, Land of, 158
Claudius, circumnavigates Britain, 195
Claudius Ptolemaius, *see* Ptolemy, as-
    tronomer and geographer
Clipper ships, 227
Coasting voyages: Egypt to China?, 23;
    Jason and *Argo*, 73; Mediterra-
    nean, 29; perils of, 50
Cockles, 39, 124
Coconuts, 46
Cod, 11, 44, 48, 106
Coliseum, 207
Colossus of Rhodes, 161
Columba, St., 221
Columbia University, 233
Columbus, 26, 46, 58, 101, 103, 137,
    147, 172, 178, 182, 191, 214, 225,
    232
Comoro Islands, Indian Ocean, 88
Compass, 9, 76, 170, 180, 224; points
    of, 9, 170, 180, 224
Connecticut, University of, 234
Continents, Strabo on unknown, 189
Cook, James, 177–178; 226–227
Copepods, 123, 124
Copernicus, Nicholas, 165, 211
Copper, 16, 72, 230
Coracles, *see* Curraghs
Cormac, Ireland, 221
Cotton in Peru, 3000 B.C., 45
Courage, of sailors, Horace on, 182–
    183
Cousteau, Jacques-Yves, 233
Crabs, 122, 124
Cranes, 129, 186
Crap-shooting, ancient, 72
Crater Lake, Oregon, 114
Crawfish, Aristotle on, 122
Crete, 29, 31, 57 ff., 113–114
Crete-Egypt trade route, 38, 39
Crocodiles, 99, 132
Cromlechs, 153
Crustaceans, 12, 122 ff.
Curraghs: 44; Britons to Iceland?, 152,
    153, 200; described by Himilco,
    102; Pytheas probably sees, 150;

Curraghs (*cont.*)
    St. Brendan, 233; Saxons' boats,
    159, 217
Current of water, man uses, 1
Currents: around Africa, 89 ff.; 117;
    156; Gulf Stream, 216
Cyprus, 26

Dangers, imagined, of sea, 50 ff., 75 ff.
Dark Sea, 181
Dart, Raymond A., Professor, 4
Darwin, Charles, 186
Days of week, Babylonians name, 86
Deep-diving submarine, 231
Deir el-Bahari, expedition, 53 ff.
Del Cano, Sebastiano, 225
Demiachus, Strabo criticizes, 188
Democritus, 110
Demetrios Phalareos, librarian, 136
Denmark, 17, 43
Depth of ocean: 200 B.C., 179; 79 A.D.,
    Fabian and Pliny, 200; 1818,
    Ross, 227; 1840s, Maury, 228; late
    1800s, *Challenger* and *Tuscarora*,
    228; today, 231, 233
Dhows, Arab ships, 47
Diatoms, 123
Diaz, Bartolemeu, 170, 225
Dicaearchia, a port for Rome, 190
Dicaearchus, 154
Dionysius Exiguus, 221
Dionysius Periegetes, 207
Directions, north, south, east, west, 9
Divers: Alexander, 135; Assyria, 79;
    Byzantium, 216; first, 27; Greek,
    95, 111; hose and helmet, 118;
    oysters, 77; pearls, 135; salvage,
    194; snorkel, 219; in deep-diving
    vehicles, 231
Dog, 5, 19
Dover, England, 181
Drake, Francis, 225
Drugs from the sea, 230
Dublin, Ireland, 211

Ear, Eustachian tube of, 96
Earth, air, fire, water, 85, 94, 95; flat, 9,
    76, 92, 93; oldest living things,
    186; round, 9, 92, 93, 94, 110,

Earth, air, fire, water (*cont.*)
117, 156, 165, 171, 177–178, 185,
199, 225; size of, 117, 171 ff.,
213–214; zones of, 94, 118
Ectabana, Persia, 132
Ecuador, Valdivia pottery of, 45
Eels, 126, 187, 231
Egypt: Alexandria, 130 ff.; amphora,
23; boats on Nile, 22; calendar
365¼ days long, 33; Corinth
trades with, 83; figurehead, 23;
first drawings of sails, 31; fleets for
long trips, 42, 43, 54; harpooning,
71; Hatshepsut, 53; lighthouses,
160 ff.; Medinet Habu, 71; model
boat, 22–23, 42; Nile floods, 9; out
of sight of land, 42; petroleum
embalms dead, 132; picture language, 24, 68; rafts, 47; Rameses
III, 71; sails, 22; shipbuilding, 42;
ships strengthened by cable, 57;
spontaneous generation of insects,
124 ff.; telling time, 33, 57; Tut-
ankhamen, 71; voyages to China?,
23
Elbe River, 159
Electricity, 85
Electron, 85
Elements, 94, 96, 110
Elephants, 132, 158, 201
Empedocles of Acragas, 94
Energy 1, 4, 6, 7, 15, 22–25, 198, 228
Engineering, *see* Seven Wonders of the
World
Engineering, ocean, 109
Engineers, Alexander of Macedon's,
132
Engines and motors, man's first steps
toward, 166
Eratosthenes, 171 ff., 213
Eroli, 221
Etruscans, 100, 194
Euclid, 165, 167
Eudoxus of Cyzicus, 169–170
Eudoxus of Snidos, 115, 149
Europa, Phoenician princess, 69
Euthymenes of Massilia, 98
Euxine Sea, *see* Black Sea
Ezon-Geber, port, 90

Fabian, 200
Faeroe Islands, 43, 151
Fathom, definition of, 196
Fayum Sands, 22–25
Fibers, 20, 89
Fire, 4, 7; hollows log, 15
First anchor chains, 134
First anchors, 102
First Arctic explorer, Pytheas, 147, 154
First depth over a mile found, 179
First fleets for long trips, 42, 43, 54
First globe to represent earth, 177
First known aid to navigation, 56
First known Roman geography, 195
"First known map of the inhabited
world," 92
First Mediterranean sailors to enter
Black Sea, 73–74
First mention of plankton (?), 152
First names given to ships, 182
"First natural history," 118
"First northern voyage," 100
First ocean explorer, 74
First out of sight of land, 32; signif-
icance, 34
"First research establishment," 165
First road signs, 37
First sailors on South Atlantic, 163
First sailors whose names we know,
53 ff.
First ship around the world, 225
First ship's passenger whose name we
know, 163
First shipwrecked sailor, 51
First sounding of deep sea reported,
179
First timepiece known, 57
First tourists, 164
"First voyage of discovery with scien-
tific importance," 154
First wind vane, 181
Fish, Aristotle on, 119 ff.
Fish, Christian acrostic, 216
Fish, diseases of, 128, 231
Fish farming, 70, 884, 229–230
Fish tagging, today, 156
Fish *Kasidoron edom*, newly found, 128
Fishing off Grand Banks, Canada, 226
Fishing-boats, old and modern, 103

Fishhooks, earliest, 11, 14, 44, 48
Fixed stars, 176, 177
Flat fish, Aristotle on, 120
Flavius Vegetius Renatus, 219
Flying fish, whizzing sound of, 121
Fleets, first long trips of, 42, 43, 54
Flemming, Nicholas C., 57
Flounder, 120
Folsom man, prehistoric, 12
Food, 24–25, 31
Fortunate Isles, 33, 78, 81, 82, 89, 97,
    112
Fossils, 107, 185, 186
Four winds, 76
Framework, of ships, 57
Frankincense, 55, 158
Franks, pillage Romans, 216–217
Freight, 17, 24, 26, 31, 38, 39, 43, 55,
    74, 83, 157, 164, 190, 192, 221
Fresh water from sea, 230
Frisians, 208

Gades or Tartessus, near present-day
    Cadiz, 36, 80
Gaiseric, 220
Galilee, 163, 193
Galileo, 211
Ganges River, 137
Garden of Eden, Iraq, 27; Lebanon, 36
Gath-hepher, 163
Gelidonya, Cape, 77
Geography, 67, 92, 95, 103, 107, 150,
    172–173, 184, 186, 189 ff., 191,
    195, 210, 211 ff.
Geometry, Euclid and, 165
Germany: first mention of Germans,
    159; Pytheas reaches?, 151; Ro-
    mans reach, 192
Gibraltar, Strait of, 67, 73, 80, 83, 88,
    98 ff., 107, 150, 172
Globe, first, 177
Gnomon, 92, 115, 149
Gold, 26, 74
Golden Chersonese, Malaysia, 212
Golden fleece, 73–74
Golden plover, long flights of, 46
Goldfish, 70
Gorillas, 99, 100
Grand Banks, 226

Great Bear, 76, 189
Great Rift Valley, Africa, 3
Great Sea, Mediterranean, 38
Greek ships, 29, 95, 108–109
Greek temples, landmarks, 29
Greenland, 151, 224, 227
Green Sea of Darkness, 181
Gruntfish, 121
Guide to restaurants, 188–189
Guinea, Hanno establishes settlements
    in, 99
Guinea Current, 89
Gulf Stream, 216

Hadrian, Roman emperor, 209
Halley, Edmund, 167
Halley's comet, 167
Hamilcar, of Carthage, 98
Hammurabi, 41
Hanno, of Carthage, to Africa, 98 ff.
Harpooning, in Egypt, 71
Harvard University, 19
Hatshepsut, Queen, 53 ff., 92
Hawaii, James Cook reaches, 227
Hawaii, University of, 233
Hearth, 750,000 years old, 4
Hebrides Islands, 40, 97, 200
Hecateus, 95
Henry, Prince, of Portugal, 224
Heraclides of Pontus, 156, 157
Heraclitus of Ephesus, 96
Herculaneum, 203
Hercules, 35, 36
Hermit crab, 122, 124
Hero, 198
Herodotus, 89, 105, 106, 107, 161, 179
Herring, 11, 120, 122, 123
Hesiod, Greek writer, 81
Heyerdahl, Thor, 47
Hiero II, 164
Hiero of Soli, sailor, 136
Himilco, of Carthage, sails north, 98,
    100 ff.
Hippalus or Hippalos, monsoon wind,
    196, 206
Hipparchus, 176, 177
Hippocrates, 111, 117
Hippopotamus, Hanno sees, 99
Hiram of Tyre, 74

Homer, 75 ff., 82, 85, 94, 131, 173
Homo habilis, prehistoric man, 3
Horace, 81–82, 182–183
Horus, a god, 69
Howe, Dr. Bruce, 19
Humboldt, Alexander von, 90
Hunger, ships reduce, 18 ff., 24
Hunters, 1, 5, 18 ff.
Hurricanes, 232
Hydrography, 133, 134
Hydrostatics, 166

Ice, 152, 207
Ice floes, 73
Iceland, 152, 200, 221, 223, 224
Ichthus, 216
Iliad (Homer), 75; Alexander's copy
    of, 173
India: Arabs reach?, 47; chickens, pea-
    cocks, 56; Columbus sails for, 225;
    Greeks, Romans, 196; Hiram, 74;
    Menelaus, 73; Phoenician figure-
    head, 170; Phoenicians reach?, 91;
    Pliny, 200; sailors trade with, 56
Indiana University, 48
Indonesia, 91, 196
Indus River: Alexander follows to sea,
    133; changes sea's color, 201;
    seven mouths of, 206
Insects in amber, 86, 148
International Astronomical Union, 171
International Union of Geodesy and
    Geophysics, 171
Iraq: dog, prehistoric, 19; canals, 27;
    claims Garden of Eden, 27
Ireland: Cormac sails from, 221; Dub-
    lin, 211; Hilco may reach, 470
    B.C.; St. Brendan, 223; Solinus
    says free of snakes, 216; Strabo
    knows of, 187; Tacitus, 207
Isle of Man discovered, 220
Isles of the Blessed, *see* Fortunate Isles
Isopod, *Bathynomus giganteus,* 14
    inches long, 6 across, 124
Itineraries, Roman road maps, 219

Jason in *Argo,* first ocean explorer,
    73–74, 186, 197
Jellyfish, eat copepods, 123

Johanson, Dr. Carl, 2
Joined-legs animals, 122, 123
Jonah, first ship's passenger, 163
Juba, King, 182
Julius Caesar, 181
Justinian, 221
Jutland, 151

Kart-hadshat (Carthage), 80
Kasidoron edom, a new fish, 128
Kattegat, 195
Keel, 83; Saxon ship's, 159
Kenya, Africa, 3; Mount Kenya, 212
Kepler, Johannes, 165, 167, 211
Khyber Pass, 131
Kilimanjaro, Mount, Africa, 212
Killer whale, *Orca,* 151
Kon-tiki, Thor Heyerdahl's raft, 47
Krakatau or Krakatoa, blows up, 114

Laboratories at Alexandria, 165
Lake Nemi, Italy, 194
Lake Rudolf, Africa, 3, 5
Lamont-Doherty Geological Observa-
    tory, Columbia University, 233
Land and sea change places, 96, 105–6,
    107, 172, 185, 232
Land's End, Britain, 187, 208, 211
Larva(e), immature or early forms,
    124–125
Lead, 148
Leakey, Louis Seymour Bazett, 3
Leakey, Mary D., 3, 4
Leakey, Meave, 3
Leakey, Richard E., 3
Lebanon, claims Garden of Eden and
    Noah's tomb, 36; alphabet stone,
    69
Lesbos, island, 118
Lever, 30, 166
Libraries, Aristotle's, 173
Lichens, 44, 103
Lifeboat, 196
Lighthouse at Alexandria, 161–162,
    184, 192
Limpets, 124
Line overboard, 56; Herodotus, 105–6;
    modern, 106; Pytheas, 150; to
    6,000-foot depth, 179; Romans,

Line overboard (*cont.*)
193; St. Paul, 195; the word
"fathom," 196; John Ross, 227;
Challenger, Tuscarora find depths
almost 5 miles, 228
Ling, a fish, 44, 48
Literature, beginning, 75 ff.
Little Bear, Phoenicians use, 41
Livy, describes salvage, 194
Lizard, The, headland in southwest
Britain, 211
Lobster, Aristotle on, 122
Lobster, spiny (crawfish), 122, 125
Loch Ness monster, 221
Log and log boat: 1, 5 ff., 11, 14, 27,
182
London, or Londinium, 195, 211
Longest-living things, 43, 44
Louisiana State University, 234
Lyell, Sir Charles, geologist, 186

Machines: bow-and-arrow, 71; calcula-
tor, 180; Hero's steam, 198;
screw, pulley, lever, Archimedes',
166; ships', 228; steamships, 228,
229
Mackerel, 123
Madeira, Carthaginians reach?, 159;
Carthage's Hanno reaches?, 99;
Phoenicians reach?, 88
Maes Howe, temple, 40
Magellan, Ferdinand, around world,
225
Mail, motto for, 107
Mainland, largest of the Orkney
Islands, 40
Malabar Coast, India, 74, 106, 200
Malagasy Republic, 88
Malay Peninsula, 46, 196
Malta, 43, 195
Manganese nodules on sea bottom, 230
Maps: 600 B.C., Babylonia, 85; 611–547
B.C., Anaximander, 92; 500 B.C.,
Hecataeus, 95; Strabo, 184–191;
Marinus of Tyre, 210; Ptolemy,
211; Roman road maps, 188, 219;
today's maps of sea bottom, 233
Map-making: Pytheas applies astron-
omy, 149; Eratosthenes makes

Map-making (*cont.*)
world map, 172–173; Hipparchus'
projections, 176; Crates, globe,
177; Strabo's, 188; Romans sketch
mappa on linen, 188; Agathodae-
mon of Alexandria, 213
Marcus Aurelius, emperor, 209, 215
Mare Tenebrosum, Dark Sea, 181
Marianas Trench, Challenger Deep,
231
Marinus of Tyre, geographer, 210
Markham, Sir Clement, 149
Marseilles, France (Massilia), Greek
colony, 98; home port for Pyth-
eas, 148–149
Mathematics: 30; astronomy, 86; ge-
ometry, 165; proof, 166; trigo-
nometry, 176; aids navigation,
166
Maury, Matthew Fontaine, 228
Mausolus, King, tomb of, 161
Measurements, 177, 190
Medea, 73
Medicine: Alexandria, 136; dissections,
165; Hippocrates, 111
Medinet Habu, Egypt, temple, 71
Mediterranean, *Ho Pontos*, 51
Megasthenes, traveler, 157, 188
Mercury, Heraclides on, 157
Mermaids, 75, 100, 134
Mesopotamia, 26–27; divers, 27; canals,
30; Ur of the Chaldees, 30
Metal (copper age), 26; today, metals
from sea, 230
Metropolis, 114
Metropolitan Museum of Art, 53
Metuhotep I, sends fleet to Punt, 54
Mexico, 11, 50
Miami, University of, 234
Microbe, super, 232
Midnight sun, 152
Millipedes, 122
Minerals from sea, today, 230
Minoans, out of sight of land, 38–39;
ships of, 31
Minos, King of Crete, 114
Minucius Felix, Roman lawyer, 216
Mizzen mast added, 194
Molecules, 110

Mollusks, 80 ff.
Monkey, on cable aboard ship, 57
Monsoon, 88, 169, 196, 200, 206
Monster, sea: first picture of, 39; Himilco mentions, 101
Monsters, 82, 136, 157, 188, 207, 221; Scylla, 75
Moon: phases of, 9; course of, 34; men on, 34; and alphabet, 68; Paremides, 94; Pytheas, 151; Hipparchus, 177; Seleucus, 176; Posidonius, 178; life on, 207
Mosquitoes, 123; larvae of, 125
Mountains of the moon, 212
Mozambique Current, 89
Mu'allium, pilot in Arabian Sea, 220
Murexes, in Tyrian purple, 80, 122, 129
Myos-hormos, 157, 187, 205
Myra, in today's Turkey, 218
Myrrh, 55, 158
Mytilene, on island of Lesbos, 118

Nabu-ri-mannu, 94
Nansen, Fridtjof, 154
Naples, 193, 202
National Geographic Society, 3, 113
Nature, energy in, 4, 6, 19–20, 25
Nautiluses, 39
Navy, 83, 118, 176, 317
Nearchos, 133 ff., 157, 164, 172, 189
Nebuchadnezzar, King, 160
Necho, pharaoh, 87 ff., 133, 170
Needles, sewing, in compass, 224
Nemi, Lake, Italy, 194
Nero, Roman emperor, 195, 203
Nevada, 43
New Amsterdam, 218
New York, 218
Nihisi, Egyptian sailor, 53 ff.
Nile River, 53, 54, 71, 82, 105, 124, 203
Noah: ark, tomb of, 36; son, Ham, 36
Norsemen, 40, 48, 97, 153, 181, 200, 208, 215, 216, 217, 220, 221, 223, 224
Northern Ocean, 208
North Star, 9, 34, 41, 76, 167
Northwest Passage, 214

Norway, 70, 151, 152, 172, 176
Nydam, 208

Oars: 17, 30, 32, 56, 70, 71, 73, 77, 82, 83, 89, 95, 99, 108, 150, 163, 176, 208
Oceanus, 82, 103
Octopuses, 39, 125
Odysseus, 75 ff.
Oestrumnides, tin and lead islands, 101
Oil, see Petroleum
Oldest life on globe, 186
Oldest living thing, 43
Olduvai Gorge, Africa, 3, 4
Olive, 38, 72, 190
Olympias, Queen of Macedon, 131, 132
Olympic Games, 131
Ophir, 74
Oporto, 150
Orca, killer whale, 151
Oregon, Crater Lake in, 114
Oregon State University, 233
Orkney Islands, 39, 43, 97, 151, 159, 195, 200, 207
Orosius, 220
Ostfold, 48
Ostia, port for Rome, 192
Out of sight of land, 32 ff., 44 ff., 50, 76, 97, 107, 179, 185, 197
Ox-hide line measures depth, 105
Oxford, University of, 137
Oysters, 77, 124

Pacific: men cross in 3000 B.C.?, 45–46; explore today, 52
Paddles: Brigg boat, 16; man's first, 6; replaced by oars, 30
Panama, sea-snake swarm, 127
Pantelleria, island, 67
Papyrus: 23; sails, 23; rafts, 37, 47; manuscripts, 173; lines, 175
Parahyba, Brazil, 90
Parmenides, 94, 98, 118
Parrotfish, 122
Patagonia, 12
Paul, St., shipwrecked on Malta, 195
Peacocks, 74, 91, 157

Pearl fisheries: Indian Ocean, 206; Mesopotamia, 27
Pennsylvania, University of, 48
"Peoples of the Sea," naval battle, 71
Pericles, Greek statesman, 110
Periplus: Black Sea, 209; Indian Ocean (Erythrean Sea), 201, 205, 210; of Hecataeus, 96; of Scylax, 96, 102, 103; of Pytheas, 154; Stiasmus of Great Sea, 216
Persia: Battle of Salamis, 108; messenger service before mail, 107; petroleum in, 132
Peru: Hiram reached?, 74; cotton of, 45
Petrie, Flinders, Professor, 41
Petroleum: Alexander's men see in Persia, 132; Chinese cable-drill for, 176; lights lighthouse, 162; in steamships, 228; today, from offshore, 230; used to bond bricks, embalm, caulk ships, 132
Pharos, 161–162; a landmark, 192; Strabo describes lighthouse, 184
Phidias, sculptor, 110, 160
Philistines, 71
Philo Herennius, Phoenician historian, 36
Philolaus of Taretum, 110
Phocaean Greeks, to Tartessus, 83
Phoenicians: 29, 35 ff., (sail out of sight of land); home, land, 36–7; Seneferu, 42; alphabet, 57 ff., 67, 69, 74; Homer, 75; purple dye, 78 ff.; colonies, 80; Necho, 87 ff., 90, 93, 101, 103; describe Atlantic, 101; Battle of Salamis, 109, 137, 158, 170
Phoenician ships, 23 ff.; framework, 57; ballast, 71; shock absorber, 77; caulked with petroleum, 132
Piccard, Jacques, 231
Picts, 97
Pilots, 201
Pindar, 73, 80–82
Pine bristlecone, oldest plant, 43
Pepfish hibernates, 121
Planets, 115; orbit in ellipse, 167
Plankton, 123, 152

Plants, long-lived, 43, 44, 186
Plato, 112 ff., 117, 234
Pliny the Elder, 161, 199 ff., 234
Pliny the Younger, 203
Plover, golden, flights over sea, 46
Plumbing 500,000 years old, 4
Plutarch, 207
Plymouth Rock, 226
Polaris, 41
Pole, measures depth, 56
Pollock, 44, 48
Pompeii, 203
Pomponius Mela, 195
Porpoise, 120, 127, 128, 232
Ports, portholes, 94
Portugal, 12, 224, 225
Poseidon, sea-god, 133; temple of, 99, 110
Posidonius, 178, 179, 213
Post office, New York, 107
Potato, sweet, crosses Pacific, 46
Prehistoric man, 1–19; studies sea, 13
Pritchard, Dr. James B., 69
Protists, among oldest fossils, 186
Ptolemais Epitheris, elephant port, 158
Ptolemy, astronomer and geographer, 210–214; 235
Ptolemy I starts lighthouse, 162
Ptolemy II finishes lighthouse, 162; sends Eudoxus on trip, 169
Ptolemy III and Eratosthenes, 171
Ptolemy IV (Philopator), 175
Ptolemy V, luxury ship of, 176
Puebla, Mexico, 12
Punt, unknown country, 43, 54, 67, 82, 158
Pygmies, 77, 82
Pyramids of Giza, 161, 164
Pyrrha, Aristotle's lagoon, 119
Pythagoras, 93, 94
Pytheas, to Arctic, 147 ff., 172, 188

Quadriremes, 175

Raft, early, 17; Egyptian, 47; Phoenician papyrus, 37
Rainbow trout, 229
Rameses III, pharaoh, 71, 173
Reade, Harold E., 236

Red Sea, 53, 87, 187
Regular meals, new for men, 24–25, 31
Rhode Island, University of, 233
Rhineland people, 40
Rhine River, 151, 159
Rhodes, island of, 194
Ribs, of boats, 22
Rice University, Houston, 111
Risk, need to take, 2
Road signs, first, 37
Rock shell, a mollusk, 80
Rome, 176, 192 ff., 207, 209, 216–217,
    221–222
Ross, John, 227
Row—longest?, 89
Rudder, oars as, 71, 76
Rudolf, Lake, Africa, 3, 5
Russia, 73; Siberia 12, 13

Sacred Promontory, Cape St. Vincent,
    187
Sahara Desert, Romans cross, 210
Sahure, pharaoh, 43, 54
Sailing directions, see Periplus
Sailors, first, iii, 1, 6
St. Brendan, 223
St. Nicholas, comes from sea, 218
Salamis, Battle of, 109
Salt, 37; on fish, 119, 164; in sea, 96,
    117
Salvage, 194
Sand glasses, 58
Santa Barbara, California, 13
Santa Claus, 218
Santa Maria, 150
Santa Rosa island, California, 13
Sardinia, Sea of, 179
Sarepta, Phoenicia, 35, 69
Sargasso Sea, 101, 103, 126, 128
Sataspes, 98
Saxons, 159, 217, 220
Scallops, 121, 129
Scarab, 20, 69, 72
Scandinavia, or Scatinavia, 200
Scilly Isles, source of tin, 101, 187
Scotland, 97, 151, 207
Scripps Institution of Oceanography,
    233

Scuba diving, early, 79
Scurvy, sailor's disease, 51
Scylax, Perplus of, 102
Scylla and Charybdis, 75
Sea anemone, flower-like animal, 129
Sea-grant Universities, 233–234
Sea lions, domesticated, 232
Sea robin, 121
Sea serpents, 30, 136, 201, 206
Sea shells, fossils, 107
Sea snails, 79 ff., 129
Sea snakes, 126, 127, 136, 201, 206
Seahorse, 121, 122
Seals, domesticated, 232
Seaweed, 101–2, 188, 240
Seleucus of Seleucia, 176
Seneca, predicts discovery of America,
    197
Seneferu, pharaoh, fleet of, 42
Senegal, 98, 99
Sennemut, Egyptian sailor, 53 ff.
Sesotris, pharaoh: built canal, 54
Seven Wonders of the World, 160 ff.
Sharks, 51, 76, 121, 123
Sheba, Queen of, 74
Shellfish people, 10,000 B.C., 47
Sheshonk I, pharaoh, 74
Shetland Islands, 40, 97, 151, 176, 195,
    200, 207, 212
Shipwrecked sailor, first, 51
Siberia, 12, 13
Sicily, 43, 80, 98, 111
Sidon, Phoenicia, 35, 87, 90
Sierra Leone, 99
Simon Peter, 193
Singapore, 46
Sirens, see Mermaids; Homer
Sirius (dog star), 9, 86
Skylax of Caryanda, 132
Smithsonian Institution, 45
Snorkel, 219
Snow, Mediterranean man learns of,
    107
Solar system conceived, 110, 164–165
Sole, 120
Solinus, says Ireland free of snakes, 2,
    216
Solomon, 74
Sostratus of Cnidus, architect, 162

Soundings, 56, 105, 179
Southern California, University of, 234
Spices, 157, 206
Sponges, 95, 125, 135
Spontaneous generation, Aristotle on, 124 ff.
Squid, 125–126, 187
Stanford University, 234
Stars: constellation, 86; first used, 82; fixed, 176, 177; Homer, 76; navigation, 8–10; Nile flood, 86; Strabo, 189; zodiac, 86
Statue of Liberty, 161
Stavanger, Norway, 44, 48
Steam power, 198, 228, 229
Stefansson, Vilhjalmur, 39, 149, 152
Stone Age man, 9, 12 ff., 16, 17, 18, 22, 26 ff., 33, 34, 43, 44, 48
Stonehenge, England, 34, 43
Storms, 75, 81, 90, 217, 232
Stormy petrels, 123
Strabo, 34–35, 179, 184–191, 197, 223, 234
Sturgeon, a fish, 107
Submersible, deep-diving vehicle, 241
Sun: Anaxagoras believes earth moves around, 95; Anaximander on, 93; Apollonius invents astrolabe, 167; Aristarchus says sun center of solar system, 164–165; course of, 34; eclipse predicted, 34, 84; Heraclides says Venus and Mercury orbit, 157; Hipparchus says earth orbits, 177; Homer on, 76; Maes Howe, 40; midnight sun, 152; motion suggests round earth, 93; navigation by, 8–10; Phoenicians see on right hand, 87, 90; planets orbit in ellipse, 167
Sun-dial: Anaximander, 92; Pytheas uses gnomon, 149; Eudoxus, 115
Sunfish, 121
Sunken cities, 50–100; known, 112; Strabo, 221
Sweden, 208
Swimming, 6, 13, 27, 79, 181, 203
Switzerland, Stone Age wheat in, 19
Swordfish: sword of, through hull, 186
Syracuse, 83, 217

Taautus, Cosmogony of, 36; alphabet, 37
Tacitus, 207, 208
Tagus River, 12, 14, 27
Tarshish, Phoenician colony, see Tartessus
Tartessus, 36, 80, 83–84, 103, 113, 169, 190
Temple of Moon, Sun, Orkneys, 40
Temple of the Winds, Athens, 180
Texas, University of, 234
Texas A and M University, 234
Thalamagus, 176
Thales, 84, 85, 129, 166, 167
Themistocles, 109
Theophrastus, marked seaweed, 156
Thera, 214
Thinae (China), 205, 207
Thothmes III, pharaoh, 56
Thucydides, 83, 84, 111
Thule, Ultima, 151 ff., 172, 195, 197, 207, 212, 221
Thuty, sailor, 53 ff.
Tides, 133, 151, 172, 176, 178, 181
Tierra del Fuego, South America, 12
Tilapias, a fish, 70
Time, measure, 30, 57, 58, 94–95, 115–116
Timosthenes, 170
Tin islands: Cassiterides, 148; Oestrumnides, 101
Tin oxide, 72
Titus, mock sea battles of, 207
Toadfish honks, toots, growls, 121
Tobias, D. V., 4
Tortoises, Aldabra, 201
Tourists, first, 164, 193
Tower to the Winds, 180
Trade winds, 90
Treadwell, Captain T. K. (Tex), USN, 229
Triremes, 82, 84, 108, 150
Triton, 180, 181
Tropics, Sataspes sails toward, 98
Tuna, 42, 102, 106, 119, 120, 123, 187, 188, 231
Turdetania, 190
Turkey, Cape Gelidonya, 71
Turkey, Stone Age wheat in, 19

Turtles, Aristotle on, 129
Tuscarora, American ship, 228
Tyre, city, 35, 80, 87 ff., 134 ff., 210
Tyrian dye, 35, 39, 79 ff., 103, 129, 131

Ultima Thule, *see* Thule
Ulysses, 75 ff.
Undersea archaeology, 29, 71
U.S. Coast Guard Academy, 234
U.S. Naval Academy, 234
U.S. Navy, bathyscaphe of, 231
Universe, 9, 93, 110, 165, 167
Unknown animals of sea, 128, 228
Ur of the Chaldees, 30
Utopia, man seeks, 33, 78, 97, 112, 159

Valdivia pottery, 45
Vandals, 220
Vega, 41
Vehicle, man's first 6; others, 7, 15, 22 ff., 27, 223, 231
Venus, a goddess, temple on ship, 164
Venus, planet, 94, 157
Vergil, *Aeneid*, 182
Vesuvius, Mount, 200 ff.
Victoria, 225
Vikings, *see* Norsemen
Viking ship, remains of, 208
Virginia, 226

Walsh, Lieutenant Don, USN, 231
Washington, University of, 233
West, men sail, 172, 178, 188, 190, 191
Whale, killer, 2, 151
Whale, pilot, 232
Whale shark, 227
Whales, 101, 120, 134, 163, 187, 227, 228, 232
Wheat, Stone Age crop, 18
Wheel, 27, 30, 132, 188, 219
Wilkes, Admiral Charles, USN, 227
Wind rose, 170, 180, 237; Homer mentions four winds, 76
Wind vane, first, 181
Wisconsin, University of, 233
Woods Hole Oceanographic Institution, 233

Xenophanes of Colophon, 96

Yale University, 234
Year, length of, 94–96, 115, 177
Yemen, southern Arabia, 74

Zanzibar, 74
Zeus, statue of, at Olympia, 160
Zinjanthropus, prehistoric man, 3
Zodiac, 86
Zones, earth divided into, 94, 104, 118, 147
Zoo, at Alexandria, Egypt, 165